An idea can come from anywhere: families, colleagues, friends, or a sign on the side of the road. Entrepreneurs live for that breakthrough moment where you find the missing piece that elevates an idea from "good" to "great." Scott's book breaks down what it means to not just find but create the opportunities to catapult your success.

—Jeffrey Hayzlett, Primetime TV & Radio Host, Speaker, Author, and Part-Time Cowboy

This book isn't just about getting started. It's about building the foundation for a great company and living the life of your dreams.

—Brian Smith, Founder of Ugg

Real life principles that actually work.

—Frank Shankwitz, Creator and Cofounder of the Make-A-Wish Foundation

Scott Duffy demonstrates that it doesn't matter how big your dream. If you apply the lessons in *Breakthrough*, you can go from underdog to leader of the pack.

—Rudy Ruettiger, Notre Dame Football Player & Inspiration for the Movie *Rudy*

I'm an avid reader of business books and am so thrilled that someone finally wrote this book, which covers business and the (more important) personal side of entrepreneurship. Learning from a seasoned entrepreneur (rather than a professor) makes all the difference. Scott's been in the trenches, and that makes this book a must-read for all entrepreneurs!

—Kalika Yap, President of Entrepreneur Organization Los Angeles and CEO of Citrus Studios

D0012528

Breakthrough is a must-read for anyone who wants to achieve more in their life. It's a perfect roadmap for you both personally and professionally.

—Randy Garn, *The New York Times* Bestselling Author

The perfect solution for anyone who has ever asked, "How do I succeed in business?"

—Greg Reid, Bestselling Author, Speaker, and Filmmaker

Scott Duffy is a natural storyteller. His entertaining style of delivering a message ignites the "aha" moments needed to break through to the next level.

—Alan Taylor, TV and Radio Host at Entrepreneur Media

Scott's ability to connect with his audience is unparalleled. His passion for life and to help others is infectious. In *Breakthrough*, he shares how to harness your passion to create the life of your dreams.

—Jason Reid, Co-CEO of the National Services Group

In Breakthrough, Scott shares how to combine the right mindset, the right team, and the right resources to create the business of your dreams.

—Myles Kovacs, Cofounder of *DUB* Magazine

Scott Duffy's insights, hard-hitting stories, and power-packed strategies make Breakthrough worth every penny. If you feel like you're running in circles with your business and running out of ideas to propel you forward, buy this book!

—Kedma Ough, Innovation Director SBDC and Author of *Target Funding*

Scott is one of the most positive, dynamic, and creative people I have had the good fortune to know. No one is better at helping entrepreneurs achieve breakthroughs—both personally and professionally—than Scott Duffy!

—Doug Brignole, Mr. Universe and Mr. America Winner, Author, Speaker, and Entrepreneur

It's not just about starting strong; it's about finishing even stronger. Scott Duffy shares how to *Breakthrough* at every stage in your business and build winning companies!

—Jennifer Rulon, MS, Owner and USA Triathlon Level I Coach at jenrulon.com

Taking your business to the next level requires a whole new set of skills. If you have plateaued and you're ready to crush it, Scott Duffy's new book *Breakthrough* will show you exactly what you need to reach that level, scale any new venture, and keep climbing.

—Summer Felix-Mulder, Cofounder of The Draw Shop

breakthrough

HOW TO HARNESS
THE AHA! MOMENTS
THAT SPARK SUCCESS

SCOTT DUFFY

Entrepreneur
PRESS

Entrepreneur Press, Publisher
Cover Design: Andrew Welyczko
Production and Composition: Eliot House Productions

This publication is designed to provide accurate and authoritative information
in regard to the subject matter covered. It is sold with the understanding that
the publisher is not engaged in rendering legal, accounting or other professional
services. If legal advice or other expert assistance is required, the services of a
competent professional person should be sought.

Library of Congress Cataloging-in-Publication Data
Names: Duffy, Scott (Business consultant), author.
Title: Breakthrough: how to harness the aha! moments that spark success / by
    Scott Duffy.
Description: Irvine, California : Entrepreneur Media, Inc., [2018]
Identifiers: LCCN 2018007174| ISBN 978-159918-622-1 (alk. paper) |
    ISBN 1-59918-622-5 (alk. paper)
Subjects: LCSH: Success in business. | Inspiration. | Entrepreneurship.
Classification: LCC HF5386 .D83 2018 | DDC 658.4/09—dc23
LC record available at https://lccn.loc.gov/2018007174

Printed in the United States of America

22 21 20 19 18   10 9 8 7 6 5 4 3 2 1

To Lily and Lexi
I am so proud to be your dad.

contents

chapter two
what you need to know when getting started

chapter three
the most important decision you will ever make: who is your tribe?

breakthrough two
Assembling Your Resources

chapter four
business planning

chapter five
securing your crew 87

chapter six
unlocking creativity 115

chapter seven
raising capital 135

breakthrough three

Taking Your Idea to Market

chapter eight

getting in the game 159

chapter nine

speaking to your customers 177

breakthrough four

Growing and Scaling for the Long Term

chapter ten

the entrepreneur's road map for lifelong success. 193

foreword by
david meltzer

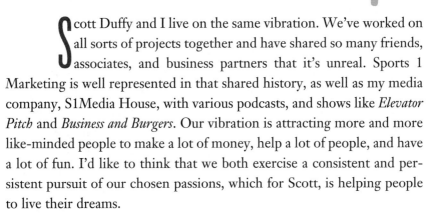

Scott Duffy and I live on the same vibration. We've worked on all sorts of projects together and have shared so many friends, associates, and business partners that it's unreal. Sports 1 Marketing is well represented in that shared history, as well as my media company, S1Media House, with various podcasts, and shows like *Elevator Pitch* and *Business and Burgers*. Our vibration is attracting more and more like-minded people to make a lot of money, help a lot of people, and have a lot of fun. I'd like to think that we both exercise a consistent and persistent pursuit of our chosen passions, which for Scott, is helping people to live their dreams.

Knowing Scott all these years has given me a unique insight into who he is. Scott has had the opportunity to work with big personal brands like Tony Robbins and Richard Branson, and he was there when early-stage companies like CBS Sportsline, NBC Internet, and FoxSports.com became big media brands. But I can tell you that beyond the resume, as a person and as a personality, Scott is the guy who loves a good moment. You know the kind of moment I mean? The kind that takes your breath away. That kind that opens doors to something amazing, something new. When Scott is rocking it as a keynote speaker, interviewing someone for a television or radio program, or working it on the red carpet to amp up a moment, he really makes it giant-sized and larger than life. He knows that this may very well be that person's one chance at being seen or heard and by elevating others, he elevates himself, because he knows that chance may not come again.

Scott is the Sherpa. He's the guy who helps people find their way in those moments. He helps them recognize the power they hold in their hands to get their message out into the universe. He helps them find their frequency, share their vibration, and attract and empower more people to be happy. In *Breakthrough*, Scott puts us in the room with entrepreneurs and business owners as they experience those moments (he calls them "aha" moments) and use them to forge new paths for their businesses.

You'll see as you read that these breakthroughs are the result of taking those "aha" experiences and instilling them into actionable plans. Scott is a born storyteller, so you'll see he's not only given you some really solid directives on how you, too, can achieve business breakthroughs, but he also takes you on a fun and exciting journey. He has done the work, experienced the highs and lows of starting and running a business, and now he shares that lived experience with you.

Something I talk a lot about (and you can read about in my blog) is the spirit of excellence. It's a mindset, a concept made popular by one of my mentors, the extraordinary Napoleon Hill. Hill utilizes what is called the QQMA formula in his everyday life that pushed him to go to the extra mile in an endeavor. The QQMA stands for The *Q*uality of service you render, the *Q*uantity of people you serve, plus the *M*ental *A*ttitude and enthusiasm you put behind the pursuit of your potential.

This spirit of excellence, the QQMA formula, applies to so much in each of our lives, and you'll see it in the people you read about in

Breakthrough. Personally, I strive for a consistent, persistent enjoyment of the pursuit of my potential, and I try to infuse the spirit of excellence into everything I do. Of course, I don't always achieve it, but I always strive for it. It's so important that you enjoy the journey in pursuing and instilling the spirit of excellence consistently every single day.

That's what I think about when I read Scott's words. Not only do we need to recognize the "aha" moments in life, but we also need to combine them with that spirit of excellence to truly reach a breakthrough. If we do that, our potential is endless.

—David Meltzer, CEO of Sports 1 Marketing, award-winning humanitarian, international public speaker, and bestselling author

"brace!"

I have a long bucket list of things I want to do before I "kick the bucket." At the top of that list is something I've wanted to do since I was 16 years old: make a landing on a U.S. Navy aircraft carrier. When I was in high school, the movie *Top Gun* came out and was a huge hit. In the first scene of the film, star Tom Cruise comes in to land on an aircraft carrier, and it looks like he's not going to make it. But against all odds, he nails the landing. Since seeing it, I've wanted to recapture that feeling by actually doing it myself.

Well, I finally got my chance. In 2015, I had the opportunity to spend a night on the USS *John C. Stennis* aircraft carrier, which was out in the Pacific practicing for war games. The purpose of being out there was to learn from the commander of the fleet and captain of the ship how he leads amazing teams so I could translate those lessons for the audiences to whom I speak each year. But I hadn't really thought about the fact that in order to get to the aircraft carrier, I had to land on it!

Here's the thing: I was the most nervous flier you could ever meet. So when I got to the naval base at Coronado the morning we were supposed to leave and met the pilot of my plane, who looked like he couldn't have been more than 16 years old, I was not filled with confidence. Trying to reassure myself, I asked him, "How many times have you done this? How many times have you landed on the aircraft carrier?" And he said, "Eighty-six times."

Feeling somewhat better, I said, "Well, good. That means this feels like nothing to you. You're not nervous. You're totally confident that we're going to nail it." And he looked me dead in the eye and said, "No. Every single time I land on the aircraft carrier I am absolutely terrified, but terror is a good thing because it keeps me focused."

The young pilot continued, "Maybe this is a good time for me to share with you the three scenarios." I thought, *Three scenarios? No one ever told me about scenarios!* But first, he explained how the landing would work.

"We fly out over the Pacific, and we get up against the ship," he said. "We'll be right alongside them, and I'll get clearance to land. We'll turn the aircraft, and I have 14 seconds to line up for landing. When you think of a landing, this isn't like landing on a Southwest Airlines plane. This isn't going to be smooth, and here's why: The ship is propelling forward. It's bobbing up and down, and it's rocking left to right, so I have to match that exact movement in order to land correctly on the deck. So ten seconds before we land, we're going to yell 'Brace!' Your job is to put your hands across your body and prepare for a crash, because what we're going to execute today is what we pilots call a 'controlled crash.' When we come down to land, there is a hook that will drop from the back of the aircraft and a wire across the deck of the ship. And my job is to hook that wire. That wire is going to stop us from going 160 miles an hour to zero miles an hour in 2.5 seconds flat.

"So scenario number one is this. When we come down, to give ourselves the best shot at catching the wire, we are going to smash the plane against the deck, and if we do this right, you're going to hear metal scraping across metal. If we execute this perfectly, we'll hook the wire, and the plane will stop."

I liked scenario number one, although it was still a bit scary. Then he explained scenario number two: "We come around and yell, 'Brace!' and I come down for our controlled crash. Bam! We hit the deck, but we miss the wire. But here's the trick. I have less than two and a half seconds, because of our speed, to identify that we missed the wire and pull the plane back up for takeoff. If I don't manage this in time, we go off the end of the ship, which leads to scenario number three."

For some reason I didn't feel good about number three, but I listened anyway. "Scenario number three is what we call a water landing, and they'll tell you more about that when they get you strapped up."

I was freaking out about what was behind door number three. They were going to explain it once I was strapped in, when it was too late to back out? I got the sense that scenario three might not end well. But I was in it to win it, so we got in the plane and took off.

We headed out to sea and circled back until the pilot could see the ship. We started to turn, and at the ten-second mark he yelled, "Brace!" Hands across our shoulders, we got ready to land. We slammed against the deck, and we missed! Now deep in scenario number two, we went back up and circled around. I was terrified—and worried that we would face scenario three, which was a water landing. We came back around—"Brace!"—slammed against the deck, missed, and pulled back up. I was even more terrified, but told myself third time was a charm. We came around again. "Brace!" We missed and went back up. The fourth time, we slammed against the deck, and we nailed it. Nailed. It. I had never felt so relieved in my life.

I don't want to scare any aspiring entrepreneurs, but that's a little like the feeling you have every single day as an entrepreneur. You may have the perfect plan, you may have a perfect team, you may execute flawlessly, but somehow, for some reason, you miss. And you may miss and miss and miss again and again until eventually, you nail it. Trying and failing can be a scary process, and, like my *Top Gun* moment, it can often make you feel like you're headed right off the edge of the ship. But you know what? It also makes you feel alive. And isn't that why you're an entrepreneur? To live your life to the fullest? To take a risk, to step out on the edge just a bit, and break through your obstacles to reach your goals? My goal with this book is to help you nail that landing the first time out. And if you don't, at least you'll know how to pull up, circle back around, and do it all over again.

Post *Launch!*

I wrote this book because of the feedback I received after I released my bestselling book *Launch!: The Critical 90 Days From Idea to Market* (2014). In *Launch!*, I taught people how to take their idea to market. I have a lot of experience launching businesses. I started my career working for bestselling author and speaker Tony Robbins. In my mid-20s, I shifted from training to tech and was on the ground floor of several small businesses that became big brands, like SportsLine.com (now owned by CBSSports.com), Xoom.com (which became NBCi/NBC Internet), and FoxSports.com. My last company was like Expedia for private jets and was acquired by Virgin. I was fortunate enough to stay on and run that company for a couple of years and had the opportunity to learn from one of my entrepreneurial heroes, Richard Branson. What I learned from these experiences was how to take ideas to market and grow them quickly and efficiently, using far less capital than most people could imagine. These are the lessons I shared in *Launch!* As a result, people came back to me after reading the book and applying the lessons, and they'd say things to me like, "Scott, you know, I read the book, watched you speak, took your courses, and I've applied what I've learned. And I've launched, and now things are going really well. I've gone all in. But what do I do next?"

At that point, I realized I had never really had to think about what you do next: Most of my business experience was launching companies and then exiting them relatively quickly. So for the past two years, I went on a mission: to find the most effective ways of growing and scaling a business in today's economy. I interviewed many of the top entrepreneurs and innovators of our time. This included people like

Daymond John, David Meltzer, Nicole Arbor, Shaun White, Gary Vaynerchuk, Roland Frasier, and so many others. As a result, I was able to identify a path for not only taking your idea to market but also growing that idea exponentially. The result of that two years' worth of work is the book you hold in your hands.

I've tried to make this book as practical as possible. Think of it as a playbook, rather than a textbook. I always hated textbooks. In fact, I don't think I've ever made it through one—they are too long, too boring, and packed with too much irrelevant information. I find that people learn more through storytelling, so I've taken big concepts and broken them down into smaller, more digestible, true-life examples. These stories are directly tied to my hands-on experience, which ranges from being a solopreneur to working on bootstrapped startups and launching companies as an executive inside some of the world's largest global brands. These stories provide lessons that can be applied immediately, as we move quickly from the personal side of entrepreneurship into the strategies and tactics necessary to break through to the next level and bring your vision to life.

Since this book goes beyond your company's launch, I will also talk about scaling and growing your business. We'll cover staying nimble, making quick but smart decisions, listening to advisors, bringing in the right people, maintaining a positive culture, learning from mistakes, and other key areas of concern that will be part of your business all its life. In fact, maintaining your balance on the roller coaster that is running a business will be an ongoing challenge. Therefore, you may want to periodically go back and reread some of the stories for motivation and to remind yourself of their relevant lessons. Keep this playbook handy.

We're going to move fast, but before we dive in, I want to make sure you have the right mindset for getting started in business. First, let's get rid of a few myths and misconceptions. For example, take "I have a great idea, but it's not the right time. I have to wait for everything to line up perfectly." Too many people use this as an excuse, whether they are launching, growing, or scaling a business. They focus on perfection, not progress. As a result, they never get out of their own way and fail to pursue their dream. The key to success as an entrepreneur is finding an opportunity, and when you find it, executing like crazy.

You may also hear people telling you that you're too old, or even too young, to start a business or to jump to the next level of growth. The truth is that you can start a business at any age, and you can change how you do business at any time. Consider Nick d'Aloisio, the British inventor who sold his mobile news aggregation application, called Summly, to Yahoo! for what was reportedly almost $30 million in 2013. He was only 17 at the time (he founded the company when he was 15). The average entrepreneur doesn't even get started until age 41. Many don't make their first million until they're over 50. In fact, Bernie Marcus was 50 when he cofounded Home Depot, and Charles Ranlett Flint didn't launch IBM until he was 61. So age doesn't matter.

There's also the idea that you need to be an expert or guru in your industry to start a business. That's not necessarily the case at all. Reed Hastings had virtually no video experience when he founded Netflix. Janus Friis and Niklas Zennström founded Skype despite very little background in online video and phone (though they had general telecom experience). What did Richard Branson know about airlines or mobile phones? Nothing. Larry Ellison, Mark Zuckerberg, Mark Cuban, Jeff Bezos, Larry Page, Sergey Brin all perfected something about which they initially began as less than experts—and became billionaires in the process.

People will also tell you, "It's been done before." So? You do not have to be the first in the industry to become the best. Entrepreneurs do not operate in a vacuum, but rather in a diverse ecosystem. One innovator creates opportunities for the next generation of go-getters. If you see a way to improve on a product or service that people already use, you should be encouraged by someone else already playing in that space—that proves there is real demand for it.

One final misconception is that you've tried to grow a business before, but things went sideways instead of up. You're not alone. Most entrepreneurs don't make it on their very first try. If you've taken a shot at entrepreneurship in the past, you'll recognize elements in this book that you missed the first time you started a business. Maybe you entered an oversaturated market, lost sight of your customers' needs or wants, or were unprepared to face changes in the global workplace. Life happens when you're starting and running a business. The key to overcoming your challenges and trying again is knowing how to pivot. Now it's time to re-engage and circle back to nail that landing.

Make it a habit to learn from your experience, and always ask why things happened the way they did. Turn failure into a springboard that drives you forward, rather than an excuse to hold you back.

"Aha" Moments: Five-Year-Old Fridays and the Power of Asking Why

One of the people I talked to while writing this book was Jeff Hoffman, a good friend and one of the top innovators of our time. He is the cofounder of Priceline.com, which is valued at more than $88 billion, and several other successful businesses. Jeff and I both have young daughters, and one day when we were talking about them, he told me a story that really hit home.

Jeff explained that he had recently taken his 5-year-old daughter with him to work. Now, anyone who's been around a 5-year-old knows that at that age they are in their "why" phase: They ask "why" about everything. They want to know why things happen and how they work.

So once Jeff got his daughter buckled up in the car, she started asking questions immediately. Pointing to the black piece of plastic that separates the front window from the back window of every car, she asked, "Dad, what is that thing called?"

Glancing at the plastic divider, which Jeff had never noticed before, he said, "I don't know."

She asked, "Why?"

"I don't know."

She then asked, "Why don't you know?"

She asked again and again and again, until he eventually replied, "Well, honey, I don't think there is a name for that piece of plastic."

At which point, his daughter said, "But, Dad, if it doesn't have a name, how do they know what to call it if they have to order more?"

Jeff started to laugh, and a couple of minutes later she asked, "Dad, how do they make carpet?" And Jeff said, "I don't know."

She asked, "Why not?"

And on and on it went, with more questions all the way to the office.

As they walked through the lobby, they passed two large machines. Once they reached Jeff's office, his daughter asked, "Dad, what are those two big machines in the lobby?"

Jeff, shaking his head, said, "I don't know."

And again she asked, "Why not?"

"Well, I never thought about them," he replied. But he started wondering, "Why *don't* I know what those things are?"

So he called the office manager. "I have a question," he said. "What are those two big things in the lobby?" There was a pause, and the office manager responded, "I don't know."

Now it was Jeff's turn to ask, "Why?" And the office manager acknowledged that as long as he had worked there, he had walked past the machines without really noticing them. "They just look so big and important, I figured that somebody was using them, but I never asked why they were there," he said. Now curious, he told Jeff he'd figure it out.

About an hour later, the office manager came into Jeff's office. Jeff was doing a little work while his daughter was carefully working on a coloring book. He said, "I've got good news and bad news. I asked everybody on the floor about those machines, but nobody had an answer, so I sent an email out to everyone in the company to find out. The good news is we can have those machines picked up today. The bad news is, they're paper collators that nobody in the office uses. In fact, nobody even knew what they were, and we've been paying for them for years!"

It was then that Jeff had one of those "aha" moments—you know, those moments when the lightbulb flares on and you get the spark that leads to an idea. He said, "We need to start asking 'why' more often in our business." So the following day, which was a Friday, he introduced Five-Year-Old Fridays, in which everyone comes to work, gets together in their teams, and, like 5-year-olds, starts asking, "Why?" They question every little thing they do to run their business.

That first Five-Year-Old Friday led to all kinds of big discoveries. For example, they found out one of the divisions was creating, printing, and paying to ship a report to its customers. They realized that not only were they needlessly shipping this printed report out in the age of email, but also, after doing some homework, that the customers didn't even realize they were receiving them, let alone read them. So by cutting out that paper and postage alone, they saved hundreds of thousands of dollars in an eco-friendly manner.

What I learned from Jeff (and his daughter) that day is the importance of constantly, maybe even obsessively, asking "why" in your business. I learned that when you start to question things, you wind up creating these "aha" moments, which combine a sense of wonder with the knowledge of how to get something done.

To me, "aha" moments are like puzzle pieces. At first, they may not make sense in the big picture, but over time, as you continue to ask "why" and test your assumptions, the puzzle pieces start to fit together, and the picture becomes clearer. Eventually, everything fits together perfectly, leading to the breakthroughs necessary to drive your life and business forward.

After talking with Jeff, I started to craft a process for creating breakthroughs in my own business, and the results were amazing. In thinking about this second book, I asked myself: Wouldn't it be amazing if I could teach others how to leverage their own "aha" moments in a way that leads to a never-ending stream of breakthroughs?

That's what this book is all about: sharing the "aha" moments I've had in my life and my business to stimulate your thinking and constructing a process that enables you to take these puzzle pieces and put them together in a way that helps you create your own breakthroughs.

The lessons in this book are not academic. They are based on my personal experiences. I started my career working in the business and personal training industry before falling in love with technology. I moved to Silicon Valley and spent the next 20 years launching and growing companies from a very early stage. Some have been big successes while others have been equally big failures. No matter the outcome, the lessons have been invaluable, and I'll share them all with you in this book.

But many people were involved in my success and the success of each one of these businesses. In this fast-paced world, there will be others involved in your entrepreneurial success as well.

My First "Aha" Moment: Ink vs. the Mac

As you navigate the process of recognizing and applying those "aha" moments, you must learn to adapt and roll with the changes. That's a breakthrough lesson I learned early in life.

I've been called a "serial entrepreneur." Whatever the intent, I love the name. It speaks to my history as well as my passion.

At a very early age, my family exposed me to business. For 50 years, three generations on my father's side—my father, grandfather, and great-grandfather—ran a printing and engraving shop. One of the things I remember most about my childhood was my father, like all good tradesmen, coming home with the distinctive smell of a hard day's work—in this case, the ink on his hands and clothes.

Back then, printing and engraving was a hands-on business. Skilled craftsmen spent years as apprentices, learning their trade. Photographers, engravers, and dot etchers pooled their skills, working with advertising agencies to create artwork that they molded into advertisements, billboards, and all sorts of printed materials. Their industry played a vital role in marketing and held a well-recognized place in society. My family made money, the skilled employees were paid well, and everybody took pride in their work. Then computers turned the business on its head. I saw it happen.

I have always straddled the digital divide. The year after I finished grade school, typing class became mandatory. The year after I graduated from high school, computers became a fixture in the classroom. As a freshman in college, I bought an electronic typewriter, and I really thought it rocked. But in my sophomore year, my roommate arrived carrying a fancy computer of his own. He called it a "Mac." That desktop machine may have been primitive by today's standards, but he was light-years ahead of me. Being able to use a word processor to do your homework? *Wow!*

When the first Apple Macintosh arrived at my father's printing business, the process of producing an advertisement changed forever. Tradesmen on both sides of the table—the ad agencies and the printers—were deeply invested in the old way of doing things, including the skills they had developed over a lifetime. They didn't change the way they did business overnight. But that single computer created a weird energy in the shop, almost as if everyone had suddenly seen the future. To complicate matters, it was literally in the middle of the office. You couldn't avoid it. Some of the workers in the shop embraced it. Others tried to pretend it wasn't there.

The guys on the floor may have had some sense that soon the job of the craftsman, working with paper, rulers, and glue, would become obsolete. It almost felt like they were walking around on tiptoes, hoping they could keep the giant asleep for another week or even a day.

It didn't work, of course. With the Mac, processes that took three men three days by the old methods could be completed by one man in three hours. Prep jobs could be done for a fraction of what they had cost a year or two earlier. The cost of making corrections or changes to a printed piece dropped significantly. As customers learned of these efficiencies, the savvy ones insisted that those savings be passed on to them. The smell of ink in the room began to fade.

The Mac initiated the change, but the internet accelerated it. Soon nobody needed to drive around delivering printing proofs to their customers; instead they were emailed. Knocking on doors and pursuing sales leads the old-fashioned way also ended. Despite decades of stability, new technology disrupted the industry rapidly. Many businesses vanished, along with the three-martini lunch.

This was a big lesson for me at an early age. The good men I grew up with had a lot to lose by not adapting. Many were afraid to change. They were afraid of the unknown. But the ones who embraced change learned to use the Macs (or other new technologies) and thrived. Some even opened new shops where they did the same work, only better, faster, and cheaper. They found new pride in their work. Those who refused to change? Well, some of them became unemployable.

The experience made one thing crystal clear: You have to envision the focal point of your life through the windshield, not the rearview mirror. This is a perfect example of an "aha" moment. It didn't center on some innovative method of printing created by my father. Instead, it was all about adapting to the new technology on the market.

How I Turned the Worst Day Into the Best Day of My Life

The next challenge to my ability to adapt came while I was attending the University of San Diego. I was starting a business, playing sports, and living on the beach. I was having the time of my life. Then, after midterms in the fall of 1989, a group of friends and I packed up our cars and headed out on a ten-hour drive south to the beaches of San Felipe, Mexico. I thought I was bound for fun in the sun and a great time with friends.

And then, in a heartbeat, everything changed.

We were several miles south of the border, traveling on a two-lane highway. There was nothing but desert on both sides of the road as far as one could see.

Suddenly, a truck pulled out right in front of us. There was no time to stop, and we hit it squarely at about 75 miles per hour. Sitting in the passenger seat, I was tossed about like a beanbag. My head went through the windshield and my arm went through the door. All four of us in the car were injured. The guys in the truck just drove off and left us there, alone in the desert, bleeding and in pain.

It was the *worst* day of my life.

How many times in your life have you been going down a road, doing everything right? Your timing was perfect. You had a solid plan and team in place. You've executed flawlessly. Then, out of nowhere, something knocked you off course. Think about those moments when the ground just moved under your feet, when everything you had done up to that point had to be thrown out. You had to start over, right?

That's exactly what happened to me.

The accident was bad. The hospitals, tests, and recuperation were no better. I ended up at the Scripps Clinic in La Jolla with significant head injuries, two brain hemorrhages, and a long road to recovery. I couldn't read without headaches or nausea, and I couldn't even bear to watch TV. Studying was out of the question, so I was forced to drop out of school.

Despite having lost so much in that accident, I developed a habit in the weeks and months afterward that changed my life forever. I started listening to motivational books on tape. The first program I listened to was from Tony Robbins, and throughout my recovery, I got my hands on others, including audiobooks from Jim Rohn, Brian Tracy, and Zig Ziglar. I listened to these audiobooks all day, every day. I was inspired by the idea that if you had the desire, and were willing to make a commitment to follow through and take action, you could achieve virtually anything you wanted in life. All the resources you needed to get started were within you now or within your reach.

Sometimes my head hurt so much that I had to keep the volume so low that I could barely hear the tape, but I still absorbed everything they had to teach me. I also learned that many of these trainers were based in San Diego. I decided that when I got better, I would go back to school and apply for an internship with one of them. My first target was Tony Robbins.

Due to the early success of his infomercials, Tony was on his way to becoming a household name. So I knew I'd have to do something to stand out and get his attention. I thought it through and finally came up with an idea. Tony is a big guy, at 6 feet, 7 inches tall. So I got a very tall cardboard box, filled it with packing material, and enclosed my resume and samples of all his biggest accomplishments (a copy of his book, one of his tapes, a flier to a live event, and a picture of him and his wife I found in a magazine). I also enclosed a flier that asked,

"How can Robbins Research benefit with Scott Duffy as a member of its team?" In answer, I listed my traits and all he would gain by hiring me as an intern. I figured the box was so big that he would engage with it, curious to see what was inside. If I was lucky, he'd remember me. I didn't want to blend in (in a competitive business, neither should you). Then I waited, hoping something good would happen.

Well, it did. My package got the reaction I'd hoped for, and I got a call from Mike "Hutch" Hutchison, who was leading Tony's team. He invited me to come in for an interview. Two more interviews followed. During the third, Hutch asked me to stand at the front of the room as if I were facing a big audience and rapidly fired questions at me. After about 20 minutes, he left the room, leaving me alone. The minutes ticked by. I waited patiently, thinking how awesome it would be to work with them. Finally, after an hour, a manager came in and said they had forgotten I was still in the office . . . but I was hired! Not as an intern, but as a full-time employee.

My work for Tony in the coming months took me on the road, often traveling from city to city, promoting his live events, especially "The Power to Influence," one of his first business programs. Up to five times a day, I would go into offices and deliver part of the program to a group of employees, selling them on going to see Robbins live. I was immersed in the Robbins way of thinking; I must have seen him teach ten courses over the next year. Traveling the country, I soaked up his wisdom and shared it with others. Working with his team helped me recover and propelled my life in a whole new direction.

When I started working for Robbins Research, I was 21 years old. I spoke to more than 200 companies, from FedEx to Mary Kay Cosmetics. I learned to look at the world differently, not only through Tony's teachings, but also through the teachings of others in the industry and the people I came to know along the way. I met people who have remained among my best friends to this day. I had incredible experiences, and, more important, I was exposed every day to people who overcame huge obstacles and looked at them as growth opportunities.

This shifted my mindset. It taught me the power of controlling my focus both personally and professionally. It showed me that no matter how bad a situation may seem, we can learn from it and assign a new meaning to it that moves us closer to our goals. It made me realize that mastering this skill could have a tremendous impact on my life and my business and opened my mind to a sense of what is truly possible.

I remember having lunch in Seattle with Tony and our team. I talked to him about how terrible the accident in Mexico had been. I told him I felt like I had to throw everything away and start over. But so much good had come out of it: new experiences, a more powerful way of thinking, a sense of unlimited possibility, a solid foundation for business going forward, and great new friends. Though it was a horrible experience, it was ultimately a personal and professional breakthrough for me.

His response really put the experience in perspective: "You have good days and bad days," he said. "But you don't know which is which until someday way down the line because you don't know what you will make of that experience."

Over the years, I've found this to be one of the most important lessons I have learned, both in life and in business. What has happened to you in the past matters much less than what you learned from it and how you apply that lesson going forward. What really matters is how you break through.

As an entrepreneur, you too can overcome your wreckage. Everyone has experienced similar setbacks. Maybe your business failed or you were laid off; maybe you were hurt financially, filed for bankruptcy, or lost a house. Perhaps you suffered an accident or an illness or had your heart broken. Just remember it's not the experience that matters—it's what you *do* with the experience. Nothing in life has any meaning other than the meaning you give it.

One of the keys to success is taking every experience life brings you and repackaging it in a way that empowers you and helps you move forward. Think about your own personal wreckage, whether it's in business, in your private life, or on a highway: You can either stay trapped in it or move forward. My friend Myles Kovacs, founder

BUSINESS AND BURGERS

Last year an old friend, Alan Taylor, and I started a new show called *Business and Burgers* (www.businessandburgers.com). The show is a search for the best burger in America with a side of tasty business advice. We travel around the United States, going to a new city each month. While we're there, we go to the top restaurants, brewhouses, and pubs and invite the area's top entrepreneurs to come share with us the lessons they have learned in business over amazing burgers and sides.

We have interviewed everyone from Daymond John of Shark Tank fame to Myles Kovacs, the founder of *DUB* magazine. A frequent question I'm asked is, "What is the most common trait you find with these top performers?" I've thought about it, and the answer is simple. They all share an unbelievable, obsessive passion for learning.

You see, change used to be slow and linear. But today it's exponential.

Let's take a look at jobs. I just read a report saying that the top ten jobs graduating students were applying for in 2017 didn't exist ten years ago.

In fact, that one thing you did five years ago that made you you? That one superhero power you had, that magic bullet you always went back to in business? That's your baggage today.

And the top performers know this, so they make learning a practice. They create company cultures based around constant and never-ending growth. This even carries over to their personal life. For example, one of the number-one things top performers do is provide gift books to their friends.

** BUSINESS AND BURGERS**, CONTINUED

You can launch your company with tremendous passion for the business. You can execute your vision flawlessly. But if you don't have a plan for learning, you won't be able to keep up with a constantly adjusting market, and you can become irrelevant very quickly.

---

of *DUB* magazine, the leading magazine for custom car enthusiasts, talks about having two choices: You can get bitter or get better. When you recognize that you have this choice—since there is always an opportunity out there—you can have a breakthrough moment!

With a Little Help From My Friends

This book isn't just about my own "aha" moments and breakthroughs. In the past 25 years, I've also benefited from working with some of the greatest entrepreneurs and innovators of our time, including people like Branson and Robbins. In the following pages, I'll share stories about how they, and others, have dealt with their own breakthroughs.

You may ask: *What could I possibly have in common with these people?*
The answer is: *everything.*

They started with a vision, just like you. They backed it up with passion and perseverance. They have all been through the ups and downs that come with being an entrepreneur or launching a new initiative inside a big organization. They combined working hard with hard-earned lessons to create successful ventures with lasting impact—just as you will do. They provide insight, motivation, and practical knowledge that has helped me and can benefit you.

I am absolutely committed to doing whatever I can to help you achieve your dreams and contribute to others in a positive way. I have set up a website with free tools and video-based lessons to provide you with additional inspiration and support. I encourage you to visit

---

IT'S WHAT I LOOK FOR

My youngest daughter is named Lexi. She is eight years old and she is a money magnet. She seems to find it everywhere.

I'll never forget last summer when Lexi and I were at Disneyland. When we walked through the gate, she looked on the ground and found $20 bucks. A couple hours later, we were walking down Main Street and—bam!—she found another $5 on the ground. Later that evening, we went on our favorite ride together, "Big Thunder Mountain." As soon as Lexi sat down, she put her hand in the pocket where you throw your things to secure them for the ride. Guess what? She pulled out another fiver. So, I asked her, "Lexi, how is it that you are so good at making money?" And she said, "Dad, it is simple. It's what I look for."

The question I have for you is this: What do YOU look for? What are the areas you are looking to break through in your business?

---

www.scottduffy.com/breakthroughbook. In addition, I've included an appendix checklist that will help your own breakthroughs. In return, I ask just one thing: While you work through this book, suspend any doubts about your ability to recognize those "aha" moments and create your own breakthroughs. Believe that you can be more, do more, and have more than you ever thought possible. If you follow the lessons in this book, we'll begin to make your dream come true. Life doesn't wait!

Let's get started!

breakthrough one

UNLOCKING YOUR IDEA

so what's your big idea?

Every business starts with an idea. It's the thing that keeps you up late at night and gets you up early in the morning. Sometimes it's never been done before. Other times it's been done, but it can still be improved upon. We'll be discussing the keys to turning your idea into a thriving business in the upcoming chapters. But this is not just a question of practical steps. It's about the intangibles that don't necessarily come from business how-to classes, textbooks, podcasts, or seminars. Thinking big, recognizing that business ideas and breakthroughs may be right under your feet, and taking risks are all part of turning dreaming into doing. That's what will take you from sitting on the sidelines to launching a business and making your dreams come true.

Consider what characteristics make up the entrepreneurial spirit. You need to have passion to make your idea a reality. You have to be willing to let go of whatever is holding you back. You must be ready to take risks and have unbridled enthusiasm coupled with the knowledge that nothing is a sure thing. It's also important to recognize upfront that you will rarely see anyone who made it entirely on their own. Sure, there are world-renowned entrepreneurs who are household names, but even they have a team who helped them get where they are: advisors, partners, and even family.

In this breakthrough section, I want you to look for those "aha" moments, those pieces of the puzzle that have the power to create breakthroughs in your life and business. I want you to absorb the messages within each story, heed the practical advice, and apply what you read to your own entrepreneurial journey, whether you are just starting out or have some miles under your feet. I want you to keep your eyes and ears open for the breakouts and "aha" moments that may be right within reach in your own life. Remember, my family went very quickly from years of ink to a newfangled solution with a Mac—that was a breakthrough in the industry (and an "aha" moment for me). Breakthroughs can come in different sizes; they can affect a company, disrupt an industry, or become a global phenomenon. One of the keys to harnessing the power of a breakthrough is believing that anything is possible.

The Secret to Turning Your Dreams into Reality

I hate mosquitoes. I hate everything about them. But a few years ago I found myself on my way to a place named . . . *Moskito Island!*

When you spend time with highly successful people like Richard Branson, you can't help but notice that they think big. They have big ideas and make big plans. This isn't simply because they have the money to do so—it's largely how they made their money in the first place. Now, you may be wondering how I got from mosquitoes to big ideas. Bear with me. A few years ago in 2008, I was in the Caribbean with the Virgin Group's global leadership team and about 40 Virgin CEOs from around the world for "The Gathering," as Richard Branson called it, to share information and grow from one another's experiences. With night falling, we all climbed into small boats and shoved off from Necker Island, which had been Richard's private retreat for about 20 years, heading toward the nearby island he had just purchased.

Unlike Necker Island, Moskito was no resort. It was completely deserted—there was literally nothing on this lump of land—and by the time we got there, the sky was pitch black. We were about as far east in the Caribbean as we could be. As we approached the island, no lights greeted us until we circled around to the opposite side, where we saw torches flickering on the lone strip of beach.

We went ashore and grabbed dinner at a small buffet. Looking for a place to sit and eat, I came across Richard and a group of Virgin executives eating and talking passionately about something Richard apparently wanted to buy.

I sat down on the beach next to him and chimed in, asking what he was interested in buying.

"The rain forest," he said.

"Which one?" I asked.

"The Amazon," he replied. (I guess if you're going to buy a rain forest, it might as well be the biggest one!)

I was shocked. How can you buy the Amazon? Knowing Richard, I can't say I was totally surprised he would think that big, but still, my mind marveled at the thought. I mean, who even *owns* the Amazon? Who would you buy it from?

Then I said what I suspected everyone else was thinking: "That's impossible."

Richard got a look in his eyes that I'd never seen there before. Looking back, I remember seeing the same look in the eyes of Tony Robbins and other global leaders. It said: *How can you get in the way of possibility?*

I've come to understand that this way of thinking is absolutely invaluable for any entrepreneur who wants to build a successful business. Not one of the successful people I know started with everything they needed, but they understood the difference between having resources and being resourceful. They learned how to identify what they needed and acquire what was required every step of the way. They understood—as Richard did, as Tony Robbins does—that if you have the right mindset, people, and resources, you can achieve virtually anything.

Look at it this way. You have an idea. No matter how big or small, the idea lives inside you. It drives you, it keeps you up late at night, and it gets you up early in the morning. Some people may say it's impossible, but that's just because they've never seen it done before. Or maybe you believe it's possible, but you're not convinced you're the one to do it. Maybe it requires capital and people and other things you just don't have. But in the world according to Branson, those are just obstacles to be overcome. Back at the beach on Moskito Island, Branson responded to my telling him his idea was impossible by saying, "If you want to learn how to buy a rain forest, I'll teach you how to do it."

Always start with your "why." Why are you doing this? Because building a successful business is hard work. And if you're not strongly rooted in why you're doing it, when times are tough, it is too easy to quit.

All of us on the island knew Richard's "why." He wanted to stop the slashing and burning that was destroying the rain forest and protect the indigenous animals. The talk swirled around the positive impact you could have if you controlled the rain forest. Richard pointed out that you could stop the slashing and burning of vegetation, save the animals that were being killed or taken out of their environment and sold, and help slow global climate change. These are issues that Richard has been passionately dedicated to for years. He's donated millions of dollars to environmental causes and has even teamed up with alternative medicine researcher Chris "Medicine Hunter" Kilham to tour the Amazon rain forest in search of indigenous pharmaceutical plants, which may be cultivated someday in the jungles (by the people who are now destroying them) and sold through the Virgin Group. On Necker Island, Branson has also done his part to protect rain forest animals, creating a sanctuary for endangered Madagascar lemurs.

So if we think like Branson, now that we know our "why," the next question is: "How" are we going to do it?

"First of all," Branson said back on Moskito Island, "*Imagine* you wanted to buy the rain forest. How would you do it?" Then he started peppering us with questions:

✻ "To accomplish this goal, do you have to buy the rain forest, or could you just lease it?" That was a huge shift in mindset for me!

✻ "Second, if you got me in the room with a willing seller, do you think I could negotiate a good deal?" I said, "Yes! I would bet on you."

✻ "Third, how many people do we know with significant wealth who could contribute to leasing the rain forest and, more important, get behind our cause? Think of how many people in this world would do whatever they could to contribute, even a small amount, to such a noble cause. What if it didn't matter if you gave a dollar or a dime?" He was effectively talking about crowdsourcing the rain forest! He continued to probe with a series of questions. Each answer inspired greater confidence that it could actually be done.

Here's my point: In less than five minutes, Richard Branson made buying the rain forest sound easier than eating a bowl of soup. That's part of the difference between business rock stars like Richard and everyone else. They have developed the skill of suspending all disbelief. They have opened themselves up to true possibility. Richard helped me understand that if we have the right mindset, the right people, and the right resources, with enough time there's nothing that he—or, when I thought about it, any of us—can't achieve.

That evening on Moskito Island left me deeply impressed by the intensity of Richard's conviction because he made the seemingly impossible sound easy. He took a big problem, one that seemed almost larger than life, and chunked it down into smaller, more manageable pieces. Because he was so open to possibility, he asked better questions, eliciting more productive responses and solutions from the group.

But Richard Branson is far from alone in setting lofty goals and doing something to accomplish them. There are dozens of examples of entrepreneurs who have succeeded with revolutionary ideas that at first seemed so big as to be impossible for mere mortals. They saw openings, they came up with solutions, and they applied them. Sometimes the solutions seemed crazy, but the entrepreneurs didn't let that stop them. They paid attention to those "aha" moments.

Indeed, if you look at the history of capitalism, you'll see that while there are myriad ways to make a fortune, the real mega-fortunes are held by the entrepreneurs and innovators. These folks don't just think outside the box; they don't even recognize there was a box.

Many of the most successful entrepreneurs of our age achieved their success because they were the first to grasp the potential applications of new technology. Bill Gates became Bill Gates because the Mother's Club at his school bought an early computer with the proceeds from a rummage sale. In the eighth grade, young Bill started writing code when virtually no one else his age even knew what a computer was. He saw this as an opportunity: If only he could make it easier for the average person to use one of these machines, they could be very useful. MS-DOS was born.

Steve Jobs saw that people loved personal computers and avidly used Gates' operating system—but he found the machines and the Microsoft software clunky. So he created his own hardware and software with Apple Computer. Thirty years later, he applied the same principles to his game-changing iPhone.

In the late 19th century, John D. Rockefeller saw that crude oil was being discovered all over the place, but realized the guys with the oil had no way to efficiently get it to market. He built a pipeline network, and Standard Oil (the predecessor of ExxonMobil, Chevron, and several other major oil companies) was born.

If you think about it, all the great dotcom fortunes were created in the same way, but instead of being inspired to move oil in a new way, these guys figured out how to move data over fiber-optic cables. Jeff Bezos thought it would be pretty cool to be able to buy stuff over the internet, so Amazon.com was born. Mark Cuban started Broadcast. com because he wanted a way to stream college basketball games over the internet. He sold it to Yahoo! for $5.7 billion in stock. Mark Zuckerberg knew students at Harvard wanted a way to connect with each other over the internet. Facebook was the result. Larry Page and Sergei Brin were frustrated by how hard it was to find what you were looking for online. Enter Google.

All these entrepreneurs had breakthroughs that began as either "crazy ideas" or as improvements on what someone else had tried. They did it first, or they did it better. In fact, many of these business legends simply came up with a better way to do what was already being done. For example, Bill Gates, Steve Jobs, Jeff Bezos, Larry Page, and Sergey Brin didn't create the computer or the internet. Instead, they leveraged existing technology and built new solutions on top of it to create thriving businesses. Rockefeller was not the first to lay an oil pipeline, and Henry Ford did not invent the car. But they created new ways to deliver their goods better, faster, and cheaper. Unlike the Wright Brothers, who were among the first to build and fly an airplane

 WHAT'S YOUR WHY?

As I mentioned in Richard Branson's story about wanting to buy a rain forest, the most important part of getting started is understanding "why." Why are you doing this thing? This step is crucial because building anything great is going to be tough, and if you're not firmly rooted in why you're doing this thing, when times get tough, it will be too easy to quit. If you have a strong enough "why," you can always figure out "how" to succeed. Your answer to "Why?" is what creates the fire inside. It is that special quality that gives you the "stickability" to overcome whatever life, and business, throws at you.

successfully, these business legends used existing technologies in new ways to benefit millions of people.

So the next time someone throws out a wacky idea—like, say, printing books on a press, using electricity to light a house, broadcasting radio waves, watching moving pictures on a TV, surfing the internet, developing commercial spaceflight, or buying a rain forest—know that there is someone out there who thinks with no limitations, is assembling the right resources, and is intent upon making his or her dream come true. *That person might even be you.*

Passion

I recently had an opportunity to sit down with Andy Walshe, the director of high performance for Red Bull. I think that sounds like the coolest job on the planet!

Andy's job is to work with extraordinary individuals, at the top of their game in sports, business, music, arts, culture, and so on. He wants to understand how they perform and get the best out of themselves so we can support them as they work to achieve their dreams.

So I asked him, "What's the most common trait or traits you find in high performers?"

"First and foremost is passion," explained Andy. "Top performers bring a love of what they do, and that's so important because no matter what you're doing, at a certain point in time, year in, year out, it sucks. It's terrible, and it's boring, and it's hard to get up out of bed. Without that passion, it is impossible to make it through those times. You see, successful people all have this long history of work, dedication, and perseverance that has allowed them to develop the skills to get where they are.

"Second, they tend to thrive when things are going terribly wrong. While that's not always the case, that capacity to bring the best version of yourself forward when it's not the ideal scenario really is a skill that we've worked hard to understand and also train. It's that stick-to-it-ness."

I've found this to be true. I was talking with Tony Hawk, maybe the most popular skateboarder in the world, and he told me it took him more than *ten years* to create some of the killer tricks we see him perform.

Let's not forget Diana Nyad, the ultra-endurance swimmer, who in 2013 became the first person to swim from Havana, Cuba, all the way to Florida without a shark cage. She chased this dream for 35 years! Diana first stood on the shore in Havana in 1978 at the age of 28. She was young. She looked across the water and said, "Nothing is going to get in my way!" But she was humbled. She tried to make the swim five times. During those attempts she was surrounded by some of the deadliest creatures in the sea, and she swam with no cage! She was even stung on one attempt by the sugar cube-sized box jellyfish, which has the most potent and deadliest venom on earth. She should have died that night, but lived to fight another day. By the time she made it she was 64. How do they stay with it? One word—passion.

Sometimes There's Oil Right Under Your Feet

All the passion in the world, essential as it may be, isn't the silver bullet of success. But if you marry passion and self-awareness, you're primed for a breakthrough. Sometimes that self-awareness can be as simple as realizing that you don't have to look far and wide for a great opportunity.

Between the time I spent in the training business and breaking into technology, I got stuck in a transition. I worked at a bar and lived near the beach in Santa Monica. I was in my early 20s and really struggling to find my way, wondering what path I should take next.

I had so much passion, energy, and hustle. I knew if I got a break, any break, I would do an amazing job. But I just couldn't find one.

How many times have you been ready to make a move, but couldn't seem to catch a break? I kept asking myself, how was I going to make an impact? How could I put all my ambition to work? I looked and looked for the right place to plug in, but nothing seemed to fit.

Then a friend gave me a book that helped set me on my entrepreneurial path. Called *Losing My Virginity: How I Survived, Had Fun, and Made a Fortune Doing Business My Way* (Currency, 2011), it was the autobiography of a British guy named Richard Branson. Yep—the same guy who wanted to buy the rain forest.

The book inspired me in many ways and helped me think about my future with a whole new perspective. It was a real "aha" moment for me. *Losing My Virginity* got me to try new ideas, take a few chances, and put myself in a better position to discover my Big Idea. It inspired me to become an entrepreneur. But where should I start?

The first conclusion I reached was that the future was in China. I read a lot of business books, and everybody back then (this was more than 25 years ago) seemed to be talking about business in the Far East. I decided to enroll in a class to learn the language and look for businesses working with China. Looking back, I think maybe I got hooked on the idea of China because I couldn't seem to find any opportunities near me. California was in a deep economic recession at the time, so I figured why not go thousands of miles away—literally to the other side of the globe—to find a place where I could make money?

It was a pretty smart idea, I thought, but I soon discovered the truth of that old saying that sometimes being lucky is better than being smart. In a piece of accidental good timing, I was introduced to a gentleman named Al Checchi, who was then co-chairman of Northwest Airlines, just one week before I was scheduled to take my first Chinese language class. He had worked on a business deal with my mother, and she shared with him how I was trying to find my way. He offered to help. That meeting changed the course of my life once more.

Let me paint the picture for you, because Al's journey is all about breakthroughs. Al started off working for Bill Marriott, helping to build the Marriott hotel empire. In the 1980s, he moved on to work as a dealmaker for the billionaire Bass brothers of Fort Worth, Texas. The Basses made their money in oil and then diversified in all sorts of directions. One of their biggest holdings was a 25 percent stake in the Walt Disney Company, a deal that Checchi personally oversaw. At the time, Checchi reported to legendary money man Richard Rainwater, who eventually became a billionaire in his own right.

When I met Al, he had recently taken Northwest Airlines public. He asked me what I was going to do with the rest of my life. I told him my future certainly wasn't in California. Instead, I explained, I was going to go to China because that's where all the opportunities were.

Al listened, looked hard at me, and then started talking. He told me that, years before, just like me, he struggled to figure out his path, imagining himself running all over the world in pursuit of different projects. But his boss at the time told him a simple story about a man who had bought land in Texas.

The guy spent all his life and his entire fortune searching for diamonds. Eventually, he ended up in Texas. Since there's a lot of very old rock in central Texas, he felt confident of a big score. The prospector hunted and hunted and dug and dug on the land he'd purchased. After weeks in the Texas sun, the back of the man's neck was tanned as dark as saddle leather and his aching back would never be the same . . . but still no diamonds. Finally, he gave up and left town. He was so disappointed that, in a moment of anger, he sold the land for a dollar.

The buyer, Al told me, was an oil wildcatter. This guy had a different hunch about what was to be found in that earth. He proved himself right when, drilling the very first well, he struck oil.

I'm not sure he needed to, but Al gave me the moral of the story anyway. "Everything you're looking for is right here," he told me. *"It's right under your feet."*

There's nothing like having a great mentor point this out to you, someone who has already been down the road you are traveling, who is not as close to the situation and therefore has some perspective. Like the diamond prospector, our focus can be so fixed that we can't look at the bigger picture in a new way. Sometimes we're just not open-minded enough to recognize the opportunities around us, but they are there, every single day, in every direction you look: globally, locally, everywhere.

Your job is to look again. You don't have to go to the Great Wall because the answer may be closer than you think. For me, it turned

NOT SURE WHERE TO START?

Last year I had DirecTV installed at my house. The technician asked me to walk him around and show him where all the TVs were. While I was showing him around, I asked how long he had been doing his job. He said almost 20 years. I asked how he liked it. He said, "I hate my job. I struggle to get out of bed each day."

I then asked what he'd like to do. He said he'd like to be an entrepreneur, own his own business, and control his own destiny, but the problem was he didn't know what business to start or what he should do.

When he was ready to leave, I said, "I'd like to give you an exercise. I'd like you to go home tonight and call the five people you spend the most time with. Ask those five friends, if someone called you and said, 'I need someone to do x,' what would they prefer you to do?" I then asked him to text me their answers.

That night I didn't get a text—I got a call. The technician was fired up! He'd had his own "aha" moment and was poised for a breakthrough. He said all five friends said the same thing: If they needed a home theater system installed, he would be the first person they'd call, and if he offered the service they would refer others. In fact, one of the five friends said he would pay the technician to come over that weekend and install a system at his house!

Then the technician said something interesting. He said, "But I can't charge him." I asked why. He said, "Because I love doing this work, and setting up these systems is so easy. It's just common sense."

And what I told him was this: "What is common sense to you is not common sense to everyone else. Otherwise, everyone would do it. That is your business right there."

※ **NOT SURE WHERE TO START?**, CONTINUED

One year later, I got another call from the same technician. After he installed his friend's home theater system, other people who saw it asked him to do the same thing for them. He started getting referral business and then advertised. Business soared. He was able to quit his job and in his first year made $75,000 doing what he loved to do.

There was oil right under his feet.

---

out Silicon Valley was just up the road—right under my feet, so to speak.

Are You Sitting on Top of a Billion-Dollar Idea?

In the previous section, we talked about recognizing what you already have at your fingertips. Sometimes we can't see what's right in front of us, and often, solutions to everyday problems turn out to be our ticket to a breakthrough. Consider the story of Sara Blakely. She bought a new pair of cream-colored slacks, planning to wear them to a party. But when Sara put them on and looked in the mirror, she didn't like how her butt looked. The panty lines ruined the whole effect, and she needed to find some way to smooth them over, fast. So she cut the feet off a pair of pantyhose, put the slacks back on, and headed out to the party.

Little did she realize at the time that she was about to tap into her tremendous entrepreneurial spirit, but this was an "aha" moment. Even though her first experiment didn't provide the perfect solution—the hose kept rolling up her legs that evening—it kicked off the process. Plus, she really, *really* wanted her invention to work. Her moment of inspiration, born out of a combination of necessity and vanity, became her Big Idea.

Sara, you see, was a born entrepreneur. As a youngster, she created haunted houses and charged neighborhood kids admission. As a teenager, she set up an unlicensed, unapproved babysitting business at a nearby Hilton hotel, watching kids for $8 an hour. She was a cheerleader and a debate champion with an especially strong desire to succeed on her own terms. She listened to tapes her dad had lying around, including Dr. Wayne Dyer's *How to Be a No-Limit Person* (Nightingale-Conant, 2014). She played them so many times she practically memorized them.

For a time, not everything in her life fell into place as she hoped. After trying and failing to get into law school, Sara auditioned for jobs at Walt Disney World. Too short for the Goofy costume, she eventually buckled visitors into rides. She later found jobs selling office supplies, even hustling fax machines door-to-door. Then she learned how to cold-call, and realized she was a natural salesperson with an ego impervious to rejection. At 25, she became her company's national sales director. Her life was starting to get on track—and then those cream-colored slacks came along and changed everything.

Sara was convinced there was a way to make it work, and she did. With $5,000 saved up, at the age of 26, she invested in her vision for the future of underwear. By day, she worked full time selling office supplies; at night, she researched patents and studied fabrics. She also got turned away by numerous undergarment manufacturers who weren't about to take the time to help her make a prototype.

When she finally figured out how to keep the abbreviated hose from riding up her legs, she saved money and wrote her own patent. She found a factory operator with daughters who liked Sara's idea so much they forced their dad to make it. She came up with a name, too: *Spanx.*

She designed her own flashy packaging and set about selling her new product. Her wares went on sale at upscale department stores like Neiman Marcus, Bloomingdale's, and Saks. When she didn't think Spanx were getting prominent enough placement at Neiman's, she bought her own display rack, smuggled it in, and set it up by the cash register.

Armed with all her chutzpah and desire, born entrepreneur Sara Blakely got a break even she couldn't dream of when, in 2000, Oprah Winfrey touted Spanx as her favorite product of the year. The orders came rolling in, and Sara finally quit her day job.

Sara harnessed the power of her "aha" moment to crack the code of entrepreneurship and made it work for her: She took a perceived need and, with her business instincts, made it a business breakthrough. Her story has some lessons for all of us. Consider these:

❋ *Think big.* Remember how Richard Branson wanted to buy a rain forest and had a plan to do it? Sara's vision was a bit more practical. She wanted to sell to *millions* of women. Remember that the size of your vision will help determine the size of your success. Keep in mind that almost every franchise, big brand, and major product began in the mind of a single entrepreneur.

❋ *Embrace failure.* From an early age, Sara put herself out there—cold-calling, selling door-to-door, and learning how not to take rejection personally. Failure is an integral part of being an entrepreneur, as you will see in other stories throughout the book. Accept it and use it to your advantage.

❋ *Leverage technology.* When Sara started Spanx in 2000, she had to use the Yellow Pages to find someone willing to make her prototypes. Today, you can research everything on the internet. Technology can help in other ways, too; the advent of 3-D printing, for example, has made it easy to produce prototypes of many consumer goods.

❋ *Be inspired.* Spanx made $4 million in its first year; today the company has sales of $250 million a year. Sara still owns 100 percent of her business, and in 2012, at age 41, *Forbes* named her the youngest self-made woman billionaire in the world. To do this, she didn't need to reinvent the wheel. And you, whether you're an entrepreneur or intrapreneur who innovates from within an existing company, don't necessarily have to either. Sometimes a key improvement or iteration can change everything.

Think about the return on Sara's investment: from $5,000 in savings to $1 billion. Today, she is the youngest self-made female billionaire in America. She had been looking for an opportunity, working hard to find it, and all the time she'd been sitting on her big idea.

How to Harness the Power of the Entrepreneur Economy

The story of Spanx proves you don't need to be the biggest player in town to succeed. Sometimes an idea born of necessity in your bathroom can be the "aha" moment you need to get in the game.

Truly there has never been a better time than today to be an entrepreneur. There are more businesses, products, and services being launched than at any other time in our history. Increased competition and faster-moving product and business cycles are all contributing factors.

This scares the hell out of big business.

Ten years ago, the barriers to launching and building a successful company were often too high for small entrepreneurs. As a result, a big company's competition was primarily limited to other big companies. They could literally look outside their window and see their competition. They knew each other well; they could size each other up and compete effectively with one another. But those days are over.

In this new era, the low barrier to entry for new businesses has created fierce competition on every front. The modern entrepreneur, who is either using his existing business to bring new products to market or launching a new venture from the ground up, moves more quickly than a big business and can often position himself to meet customer needs better, faster, and cheaper. To make things even more difficult for big businesses, there are literally millions of entrepreneurs armed with laptops, smartphones, and free business tools from the internet nibbling at their heels. Competition now comes from anywhere and everywhere.

Today's rising entrepreneurs run leaner, stronger, more efficient, and more profitable companies. Some have lost their savings or jobs, so they've had to reinvent themselves in ways they never imagined. Now they are hungrier and driven by real determination. They move fast because they have to; they move with purpose because they are forced to.

Most large companies have bloated cultures that move too slowly to compete against this new breed of entrepreneurs. While 90 days is enough time for an entrepreneur to launch a new business, product, or service, it takes most big businesses 90 days to decide whether to even get in the game. Once they reach a decision, it might take them another *900* days to actually do it.

On the other hand, many entrepreneurs, despite their potential for speed and agility, still rely on a combination of passion (which can only take you so far) and strategies that are out of step with the best practices of the new economy. Entrepreneurs like Richard Branson, Bill Gates, or even John D. Rockefeller seemed to take gigantic risks, putting everything they had both personally and professionally on the line. Not everyone is comfortable in that role, nor is it responsible for them to take on that much risk.

But today, being an entrepreneur isn't about building the next Virgin or Google or Facebook. It's about transforming what you are good at and passionate about into a moneymaking venture that benefits others in the process.

Today, even a small entrepreneur can think big and learn how to take on any size competitor. We're living a modern-day version of David and Goliath, where a small, agile entrepreneur is defeating a big corporate giant every day. This is your opportunity. Seize it.

Small Is the New Big: Why Crushing Big Companies Has Never Been Easier

So how do you make the entrepreneurial economy work for you? Well, in big business, change used to be linear. A company could plan ahead several years down the road, and the cost of launching a business to compete with entrenched players was beyond the reach of many would-be entrepreneurs. As a result, the lack of innovation and competition meant big companies moved at a snail's pace.

Today, change occurs at an exponential rate, and the pace of innovation is unparalleled. The cost for an entrepreneur to jump into a market has dropped dramatically and is no longer a barrier to entry. The internet, mobile technologies, and a virtual workforce have eliminated many of the advantages once held by those with deep pockets.

This shift represents a big problem for big business. The deep-rooted cultures at most large companies make it difficult for them to keep up. If they remain inflexible and unwilling to change the way they approach today's competitive world, they will die from the inside out.

But the change is good news for flexible entrepreneurs like you, who can move faster, get closer to customers, respond more quickly to changes in the marketplace, and run your businesses for a fraction of the cost. You don't resist the pace of change. You embrace it. In the new world order, small is the new big.

Here's how fast a small company can move in and disrupt an entire business:

Under the previous paradigm, a company created a product or service. It was a hit, and, over time, the company got bigger. They continued to add new features and started raising their prices. The company could do this because the demand was there, but they had little competition. Then one day a customer looks at his credit card bill and says, "I don't want to pay all that money anymore." He also realizes he needs only one thing, the original thing he signed up for. "I don't need all this other stuff," he says. "And I certainly don't want to pay for what I don't need."

So the customer decides to start his own company. He plans to strip out all the fancy features he doesn't want to pay for and offer just one thing, the very same thing he currently likes about the big company's product. He finds a free legal service online and incorporates; then he sets up an account with Google to get free email, contacts, calendar, office applications, and document storage. He gets free voice and video calling through Skype and free wifi at the corner coffee bar, and he syncs everything between his laptop and mobile phone.

The business is established—in an elapsed time of, say, *90 minutes.*

Next, our entrepreneur goes online to do some research. A few internet searches produce market data and access to free reports. By poking around social media platforms like Facebook and Twitter, he can quickly find out if others think the idea has legs. Our founder logs onto LinkedIn to share the news of his new venture and seek some help. A developer who likes the idea and hates big companies volunteers to do a little coding. The new team collaborates on a business plan, using free software to write it.

To sum up, a customer of a big business identified a problem and established a company to solve that need in one afternoon. He has access to much of the same market information as the competition. Social media conversations led to the drafting of a business plan and the assistance of a developer, who has already started building the product. These people are executing—remember, it's still the first day—and they've spent zero dollars so far.

This new little company builds something basic, a minimum viable product with one feature and one benefit. What they release is pretty crude but—check this out—they give it away for free. Other people who had the same problem with the big company's product flock to the new business. The big company is slow to recognize what is happening, so they fail to respond with an alternative solution. They bleed market share to the startup. And a new entrepreneur is launched, with a product and a team and a market—the building blocks of a multimillion-dollar business.

Our theoretical business happens to be a technology company, but the process is the same across the board. It starts with one unhappy customer with a laptop, mobile phone, internet connection, and social media account—one customer who decides to take matters into their own hands and find a better solution to a problem.

When big, entrenched industry leaders see this happening from their spacious headquarters, it's terrifying because it's proof that the scales have tipped. Even their best ideas may not work because they will take too long to execute.

That's an opportunity for entrepreneurs, but it's also the reason I consult with businesses, large and small, all over the world, teaching them how to create a more entrepreneurial culture. Does your business culture allow for the kind of fast action required to compete in the entrepreneur economy? If not, you're in deep trouble. In business, nimble creatures adapt, while the dinosaurs die off.

It reminds me of a conversation I had on Necker Island with Richard Branson while attending that conference at his Caribbean home. I told him that my whole life had been lived in launch mode, opening new markets where we had to educate customers about their needs while we were selling to them. I pointed out he had often taken the opposite approach. "You go into the biggest markets with the most entrenched customers and go head to head," I said.

As usual, his response taught me a lesson. He said, "I go into big markets where people have already proved they want the product and will pay for it. Their wallets are already open. Then I just look for one person that has a problem. Find that one person and one problem, and if the market is big enough, that represents a big business opportunity. And that's what I do."

Now it's your turn. Use the advantages entrepreneurs have over big businesses. Create innovative products and services that have a positive and lasting impact. Make your dream a reality by bringing your idea to life.

Five Steps to Bring Your Idea to Light

From opening a restaurant to writing a book to launching a brand-new product, people have innovative ideas every day. Most people, unfortunately, do not follow up on those ideas for a simple reason: They don't know what to do first, next, and finally. Richard Branson had a plan; so did Sara Blakely. Here are five basic steps to creating a manageable plan of action so you can harness the power of your big idea:

1. *Be clear about what you want.* What is your big idea? What is keeping you up at night? What would you pursue if you knew you could not fail? Write it down if you want to make sure you can see it every day.

2. *Break your big idea into small pieces.* No matter how big the vision, you will always improve your chances of success by breaking the job down into smaller, bite-size pieces and attacking them one at a time.

3. *Be resourceful.* Nobody starts out with everything they need to succeed. The best entrepreneurs are resourceful enough to pick up the pieces they need at each step of the process.

4. *Surround yourself with great people.* There are two ways to learn: trial and error and modeling. Trial and error costs valuable time and money. Instead, surround yourself with great role models who have already accomplished what you want to achieve. Find out how they did it: Learn their belief systems, strategies, and the order in which they do things. Do the same things to produce the same results. With modeling, you can reduce your risk of failure and speed up your success.

5. *Execute like crazy.* Outwork, outthink, and outsmart the competition.

Once you have your plan in place, you can start to think more deeply about how to execute it and reach the next level of your business. But before you do that, you need to unburden yourself from whatever is holding you back from making that next breakthrough.

Learn to Let Go

We all have our reasons for not getting started. Unlike Sara Blakely, who was ready to jump right into entrepreneurship, some of us may be more resistant to taking the leap. As a result, we put up roadblocks for ourselves. Do any of these rationales sound familiar?

✴ It's too late.
✴ I'm too tired and/or hungry.
✴ I have to feed my kids.
✴ My boss would never let me do it.
✴ I need to walk the dog.
✴ I can't afford it.

✸ The project's too big.

✸ People will think I'm crazy.

✸ I can't do that and do the job I have.

✸ I don't know the right people.

✸ I didn't go to the right school.

✸ The company would never get behind this.

✸ How will I get paid for it?

✸ I'll just start tomorrow.

✸ And the biggest one of all: I'm afraid.

Unfortunately, our fears, combined with the stories we tell ourselves about why we can't succeed, keep us from getting started. To bring your big idea to life, the first thing I want you to do after you have your plan of action in place is to let go of all your excuses. Simply step away from them and get on with it.

Let me tell you about spider monkeys. The spider monkey may be the most elusive animal in the rain forest. They're so quick that you can't sneak up on one of these wily little forest creatures with a net. They're way too fast for that. But bestselling author and speaker Greg Reid tells a useful story (similar to the one you may have read in *Zen and the Art of Motorcycle Maintenance*) about how to successfully trap the spider monkey by playing to its weakness. The spider monkey possesses the human tendency to grab on to things he thinks he can't live without. Then he refuses to let go.

Greg describes the hunter's strategy. He finds a log in the rain forest, drills a hole about 18 inches deep, and drops a couple of peanuts down the hole.

In time, a spider monkey will happen along and smell the delicious peanuts. He'll reach his arm down the hole and grab them. But the hole is sized such that, when the monkey closes his hand around the peanuts, his clenched fist gets stuck in the hole. He could open his hand, drop the peanuts, and pull his hand out of the hole. But he can't both get the peanuts and get free.

Long ago, native hunters discovered that they could drop the bait in the hole and then just wander off for an hour or two. When they came back, all they had to do was drop a net over the stubborn monkey, who was so obsessed with those peanuts that he would hold on tight even as the hunter closed in.

My advice to you is, *Let go of that nut!* Don't be a spider monkey. Let go of those fears, excuses, and stories you've come up with about why you can't succeed. Let go of those things that hold you back.

Maybe you're holding on to a fear of failure or some regret from the past. Maybe it's a fear of the unknown. Maybe it's a dead-end job you can't bring yourself to walk away from, or a bad relationship, or destructive habits, or the wrong kind of friends. Got anything you want to add to the list? Like that monkey, we believe what we're holding on to is more important than survival—but it just may be what is holding us back the most.

So quit holding yourself back. Put the past where it belongs—in the past. Take bold steps to walk away from something you know isn't bringing you anything but anxiety, frustration, or sadness. People have overcome a lot, including physical disabilities that would have stopped many of us from creating our own success. Beethoven went deaf, but his late-in-life works are some of the greatest music man has ever heard. Milton was blind, but he wrote literature that will be read until the end of time. Stephen Hawking was diagnosed with ALS at the

---

 THE BEGINNER'S MIND

Famed NBA coach Phil Jackson was once asked what makes players like Kobe Bryant and Michael Jordan better than anyone else. He said they approach each day like it was the first time they ever played the game. In Zen Buddhism, we call this concept *shoshin*, which means "beginner's mind." In today's world, we need that combination of open-mindedness and adaptability to break through.

How do you create a breakthrough? Open-mindedness, adaptability, and hard work.

---

age of 21, but he went on to become one of the world's most notable physicists.

Whatever your excuse is, it isn't good enough.

Think about what would happen if you decided to let go of the peanut. How would your life change if you really decided to go for it? What would happen if you made your biggest dreams come true?

Would you spend more time with your family? Would you take up a hobby? Would you buy a new home? Would you travel around the world? Would you found a charitable organization that gives back to others?

I learned many years ago that the only thing keeping you from achieving everything you want is the crazy story you've made up about why you can't have it. Now is the time to seize your opportunity and create the life you deserve.

So drop the peanut. Just let it go. Then try climbing a tree to see what opportunities lie on the other side.

what you
need to know when
getting started

M uch of what we do in life is trial and error. In business, I'd like to think that there are two ways to learn. The first is by trial and error which takes up valuable time and money. And the second is through modeling. Modeling is when you find a company that's doing things the way you envision doing them in your own business and learn from them. In this chapter you'll read stories that will provide guidelines that can help you reach a breakthrough more quickly. Yes, there will always be some trial and error, but the more you can minimize it, the better. Always be prepared for failures along the way to success and remember, no matter how great an opportunity appears, nothing in business is a certainty.

The Sure Thing

Have you ever had a "sure thing"? An idea for a business or product that was just so good you knew it could not fail? When you shared the idea with others, their jaws dropped. As you got started, everything fell into place: your timing, your team, and your execution were all flawless. You *knew* you could not lose. So you doubled down, maybe put everything you had on the line.

And you failed.

I've been there.

In 2005, I was closing in on a deal to run a new internet business when I got a call from my buddy Jason Port. He heard I was in the market for a new business opportunity and encouraged me to take a look at private aviation.

After 9/11, he told me, private aviation's growth had skyrocketed. Passengers on commercial flights had grown frustrated with increased travel times, long lines at security, having to remove their shoes, and the rest of it. Private jet charter suddenly emerged as a terrific option for business travelers. Jason also told me that, despite its growth, private aviation remained highly inefficient, so there might be a good opportunity for skilled internet entrepreneurs to help the industry operate more efficiently.

I looked at the charter business. The numbers showed growth in users and revenue like I hadn't seen since the dotcom boom, but the business was highly fragmented. In commercial aviation, there were a handful of operators, like American, Continental, United, Delta, and Southwest, that controlled virtually all the passenger seats and owned hundreds of aircraft. Private aviation was completely different: There were approximately 2,500 operators in the United States alone, typically controlling only three planes each.

When it came to selling seats for commercial flights, companies like Expedia, Travelocity, and Orbitz could easily connect travelers to commercial flight schedules, making it simple to search for, find, and purchase a trip online. In contrast, just as my friend had told me, the private aviation industry was incredibly inefficient. Nobody had yet aggregated the supply and demand in one place to make it easy to purchase a trip on a private jet. To book one, you would have to find a local operator through word-of-mouth, old-fashioned phone books, or by calling the local airport. Once you got a charter operator on the phone, he would then have to create a custom quote for your trip, often initiating a back-and-forth wave of faxes. The process was made tougher still because the guy answering the phone was sometimes the guy flying the plane!

After doing my research, I decided to tackle this problem. I started Smart Charter in 2006 as an online marketplace and booking tool for private aviation. Think of it as Expedia for private jets. My goal was to match up supply and demand, simplifying the process of buying and selling trips on private jets.

I opened an office in Los Angeles and hired a great team (from companies like Google, Expedia, Yahoo!, Travelocity, and JPL) to build the business. In September 2006, we began to raise money, and I was introduced to Richard Branson's Virgin Group. Richard was my longtime hero as an entrepreneur, and his company was among the most respected aviation brands in the world. In April 2007, Virgin bought a controlling interest in my company. We were rebranded as Virgin Charter, and it was my job to run the business.

All this reinforced my belief that we had a "sure thing." We were in a growing market solving a big problem. Our timing, our team, and our execution had been great. Now, with Virgin as an investor, how could I lose?

So I doubled down. Went all in. I was in the right place at the right time . . . *or so I thought.*

We launched as Virgin Charter in March 2008. The first quarter of 2008 was incredible for private aviation. There were more private aircraft sales, more fractional sales, and more charter hours flown than just about any other time in history. The day we launched, Richard and I were on CNBC to make the announcement. But two other news stories caught my attention that day: concerns about an economic recession and a spike in oil prices. That's when I began to fear that things might begin to change, and not for the better.

The business started to go sideways quickly. In the first half of 2008, oil prices soared. Typically, airlines pass along fuel costs to their customers, but prices were rising so fast that they couldn't recoup their costs fast enough. Many airlines' business models were destroyed almost overnight. While that was bad news for the big commercial airlines, they had an advantage we did not: many more passengers among whom to divvy up the increased fuel costs. Charter operators couldn't just add on a small fuel surcharge for each customer. In March 2008, the average charter on a private jet from Los Angeles to New York sold for approximately $30,000. A few months later, fuel costs had pushed that up to almost $45,000.

A predictable chain reaction followed. People who would previously charter big planes instead went with small ones. People who used to take long trips on chartered planes opted for short ones. Many stopped chartering altogether.

Our business was burning more capital than we planned, meaning we needed cash to survive. We decided to raise money to provide operating capital for the business. I was on the road for weeks and managed to secure partner meetings with three prominent venture capital firms. But my highest hopes rested with a meeting with Menlo Ventures, located in Silicon Valley, in September 2008.

The day before the meeting, I flew from Los Angeles to the Bay Area with Brian Pope, our COO. We locked ourselves in a hotel room and prepared to give a great presentation. Upon arriving at Menlo Ventures, we were taken to an office and asked to wait until we were called into the meeting. We were so focused on preparing our pitch that neither of us had looked at the headlines that day.

When we were finally asked to join the group, there were almost 50 people in the room. They were all in the prayer position: heads down, thumbs furiously working the keyboards on their Blackberry phones. There was a steady flow of assistants bringing yellow sticky notes about phone calls that needed to be returned immediately.

Everything seemed strangely tense, so I asked what was going on. One of the partners looked up and told me that Lehman Brothers had just declared bankruptcy and the market was down 500 points!

You won't be shocked to learn the meeting didn't go well. The world was about to change. Those were the days when the stock market would fall 300 points in a day and then 300 more the next. We were headed into the deepest recession since the Great Depression.

We didn't get the cash we needed, and our "sure thing" wasn't about building something anymore—it was just about saving whatever we could.

We'd started with a great idea, with timing that seemed perfect, a great team, and a solid plan. We got the Virgin Group behind us and received Richard Branson's stamp of approval. I'd gone all in, putting all my chips on the table. Sure, there were many things I could have done better. But in the end, I just lost the hand.

Here's the problem with sure things: There's nothing really *sure* about them. There can't be—there are just too many moving parts in any business. Too many things that need to go right. Too many things you can't control. What appeared to be the best opportunity in my life turned into a financial disaster. And what I learned from this experience, the "aha" moment, was this: The most important job for every entrepreneur has nothing to do with business. The most important job is learning how to protect yourself. So if things take longer than planned, cost more than expected, or go sideways, you can bounce right back.

In entrepreneurship, everyone has ups and downs, highs and lows, wins and losses. There are no sure things. In fact, every idea begins as just that, an idea—it's not good or bad until you see where it goes. The most important part of your job is to mitigate your risk, so if things go sideways, you don't lose everything and you can bounce back.

The Fastest Way to Lose Your First Million (or Keep It)

Start by asking yourself this: How much are you willing to risk? How much would you be willing to put on the line to make your dream come true?

There's an old joke: How do you walk away from a Vegas craps table with $1 million? The answer: Start with $2 million. There is a long-standing correlation between risk and reward: the more you risk, the greater the potential reward—or disaster. The less risk you take, the less you will win or lose. In any business endeavor, there will be risk because there is no such thing as a sure thing, as we've seen. As so many of us have learned the hard way, you have to find your comfort level—how much can you *realistically* afford to risk and still be able to sleep at night? Knowing the answer to that question will help you break through to the next level of your entrepreneurial journey.

Many entrepreneurs have a fear of getting started. They are afraid of what could happen to them financially if things don't work out. Many of them have heard stories about people who put everything on the line, all the money and assets they had, and then lost it. Managers in big companies have heard similar stories about peers taking risks and their projects going upside-down. Those tales typically end with people losing their jobs.

But the very best entrepreneurs understand that when launching a new business or product, risk should be calculated, well-planned, and well-conceived. The risk should be baked into the formula so you, your family, and your job are all protected if things don't work out.

Based on years of experience training and coaching, I know the number-one mistake entrepreneurs make is mismanaging their money (and thus, their risk) from the start.

The causes are clear. Most are overly optimistic about how fast they will generate cash flow. They also underestimate startup costs and the length of time it will take to get traction. Over time, their businesses demand more cash. They start pulling out more and more of their own money to get their businesses underway. They get caught up in the momentum of the process, trying to balance the demands of the business against all their other personal responsibilities, and they lose track of how much cash they have on hand and how much has been committed to go out the door.

Similarly, optimism about cash flow and underestimating costs also happen inside big companies. Brand managers get overconfident thanks to a previous success and make a big bet on a new project, or they try to fudge the numbers on how quickly the project will be profitable to get management to move forward.

The result for entrepreneurs? One day they get a shocking bank statement in the mail saying their account is empty. The startup money is spent—worse yet, so is next month's mortgage. Inside a corporation, there is a different dynamic, but the same sense of denial is often in place.

When the horrified entrepreneur looks back, wondering how this all came to pass, part of the explanation is obvious. I know this sounds basic, but you'd be amazed how many entrepreneurs don't go through the trouble of separating their business accounts from personal accounts. The result can lead to a significant amount of stress for any new business owner or even personal catastrophe.

This doesn't have to happen to you. There are some basic strategies you can apply today to make sure of it.

Create a Solid Financial Model for Your Business

Determine where your company's cash will come from and what expenses will soak it up. Money in, money out. Then estimate how much time the business will need to create enough profit and free cash flow to be self-supporting. For a business, free cash flow is like oxygen—without it, the business cannot survive. Once the business generates enough cash to operate on its own, you can reduce your personal exposure.

Once you've estimated how much money you will need, cut your revenue projections in half. Then cut them in half again. Then do it one more time, to balance out your natural optimism.

Now take the amount of time you think it will take to get started and double it. Building sales and free cash flow always takes longer than most entrepreneurs expect.

These numbers may be hard to digest, but this approach will give you a reasonable sense of what you will need and how long it will take to get to a place where you no longer have to contribute outside capital to make ends meet. If you're launching a business that involves personal financial risk, here are a few more things you need to do today.

Determine How Much Money You Are Willing to Risk

Now that you have a reference point, figure out your risk tolerance: *How much are you willing to lose?* Your business has to be funded somehow, and the odds are that much of the funding will come from you. Unless you have a track record in business or some very deep-pocketed friends, raising money from investors could be difficult. Will the money on the line be your family's entire nest egg or just half? Are you going to bootstrap or borrow? Keep a photo of your family nearby when you start writing checks as a reminder that you may be risking their future as well as your own.

If you're launching inside a big company, how much are you willing to ask management to risk on this project? How much of your current budget are you willing to put on the line?

Talk Everything Through with Your Spouse or Significant Other

You *must* do this before jumping in. It's essential that the two of you agree on how much to put on the line. If you don't, that will create problems down the road—possibly very large ones—that will distract you from your business (and potentially ruin the relationship). You would do better to risk less and be on the same page than risk more and have your spouse be worried and resentful day after day. To be an entrepreneur you need to make firm decisions, and the first one should be not to invest what you need to support your family. You should never go so far on the edge or put yourself at so much risk that if things don't work out it becomes very hard to bounce back. That's why this book talks about taking small steps. This way you will be building each step of the way and evaluating the results before taking the next step forward. Remember, I talked about thinking big but taking small steps to reach that big idea and break through.

For intrapreneurs, launching a new project may mean taking on much more work with no additional compensation. As a result, it's important to get on the same page with your spouse about how much time will be required to do your job.

Open a Separate Checking Account for Your Business

Do it now. Every day I have my bookkeeper email me a summary of accounts and the prior day's transactions. When I wake up, it's one of the first things I see. It keeps me grounded so I know where I am financially in my business. When things are hard, sometimes entrepreneurs just don't want to know what is really going on. So I use this daily summary as an easy way for me to review and categorize my finances and make notes as needed. That way I don't get caught someday trying to track down a month's or year's worth of individual transactions. And because there is so little incremental work for your bookkeeper, the added cost should be far less than having to go back to a big pile of receipts and spend hours trying to piece everything together.

Once you have a sense of the capital needed to move forward, transfer the funds you are willing to lose into that account immediately. If your risk capital is tied up in securities or other investments, sell them and put the proceeds in the business account.

This is your seed money. Once you see it moved from your savings account to an account tied to risk, it becomes real. It focuses your attention. You see what's at stake. You'll thus have a clear financial framework to help you make better decisions and will act more strategically and less impulsively.

Corporate managers need to work just as hard not to commingle funds from their new project with other projects they may be working on. Doing so can lead to the same problems experienced by entrepreneurs.

What if that business account gets low or runs out? You can increase your risk threshold and put more money in, you can find an investor or partner, or you can sell or close the business. In these early stages, however, what's most important is that by separating your business finances, you will have created a mechanism whereby you will be forced to face the facts. You won't accidentally run through your personal finances and allow your spending to spiral out of control.

Keep Your Credit Cards Separate

Have one credit card for business expenses and another for personal use. This makes it possible to track and leverage every possible expense for tax purposes. Every expense related to your business should be funded from this account. Don't commingle anything.

Hire a Bookkeeper Your First Day in Business

Too often entrepreneurs wait to do this or put it off altogether, but you need someone to track income, expenses, assets, and liabilities. Having the correct financial data on hand is important for you, investors, and tax preparers. If you don't set up a system early and review it frequently, you will spend a tremendous amount of time and energy trying to reconstruct the details behind every transaction that affects your business.

The expense of paying a pro will be well worth the investment. Setup may take an hour, followed by monthly, weekly, or daily updates depending on how much activity there is in your accounts. As I mentioned earlier, my bookkeeper logs into my computer each day for a few minutes and updates the day's transactions. That means I have a report waiting every morning telling me exactly how all my business and personal accounts are performing. Because I set this up correctly from the start, it works out to a monthly cost of $100—money well spent.

Bringing a professional aboard will have a range of other benefits. Paying attention to your books at this early stage will establish good habits at your company and instill a sense of financial responsibility throughout the organization that may also spill over into your personal accounts.

Have an Attorney Set Your Business Up by the Book

We live in a very litigious society, so you need to protect yourself from liability. Set aside money to create a proper legal entity and get business insurance. Remember, your concern isn't only about the short term; there are larger, long-term issues that you need to consider. Keep in mind, too, that even if this is your venture, it's not just about you.

Entrepreneurs get caught up in thinking since the business is theirs, they may be the only ones at risk. But when you bring in investors and other team members, their future is also in your hands.

Learn How to Manage and Grow Your Personal Fortune

Even if business is good, some entrepreneurs and intrapreneurs whose companies are headed toward a big financial event (an IPO, sale, merger, etc.) spend so much time focused on making money for their business that they have no plan for what to do when they finally reap the benefits of all their hard work.

It is important to keep expanding your understanding of how money works so that as your business grows, you can invest your profits in a meaningful way to grow your personal fortune. Part of this process involves creating a great team of advisors, including bankers, brokers, accountants, and financial planners. Instead of trying to assemble this team all by yourself, find mentors who have already made their own personal fortunes and ask them for referrals. Their advice could be worth millions, literally.

Only Launch One Business or Product at a Time

Many entrepreneurs, to hedge their financial bets, try to get three or four plates spinning at once. Don't. We will talk later about the importance of focusing on one thing. I promise you, the best route to success is not to focus on ten things hoping one will work. Give the one thing your best effort.

Don't Stop

Once your business is past the startup phase and in the growth and scale phase, that doesn't mean it's time to stop doing all the above steps. Just as you can pour too much money into the business in the early stages, some business owners start to see profits and not only decide to put them back into the business—which is often how a company grows— but also decide it's time to play double or nothing and keep throwing more money at the business since growth is so addictive.

We've all seen gamblers win some money and decide they're on a roll, which leads to them throwing down not only their winnings but also a lot more until—oops—it all disappears. Business owners who see growth may decide it's time to expand, when it really isn't, or it's time to hire more people than they need, as the tech companies did during the dotcom bubble of 1998–2000. They brought in a ton of people they could not afford to pay, and most of them crashed and burned. Remember, even growth can hit the wall at some point, and attempting to grow too fast can be dangerous, especially if you're footing the bill.

As you grow and scale, your personal and business savings should remain separate, as should your credit cards. You should also keep your advisors close and listen to them. You need to maintain good habits across the board, which includes your body and your personal life as well as your finances and your advisors. After all, you are the glue that holds your business together—so keep your physical and emotional self in top shape for the long run, starting with your relationships at home.

All for One and One for All: Entrepreneurs and Relationships

I'm a huge fan of Starbucks. Like a lot of entrepreneurs, I'm addicted to their product, but from time to time, Starbucks has also served as my office. A few years ago, I had the opportunity to meet the billionaire entrepreneur and chief executive behind Starbucks, Howard Schultz, when he spoke to an entrepreneurs' group in Southern California. I was so excited to meet him and learn from his experience.

But when his speech was done, I was at first disappointed. You see, Schultz was touring in support of his book, *Onward: How Starbucks Fought for Its Life Without Losing Its Soul*. He gave a prepared talk, describing how in the late 2000s he steered Starbucks out of its crisis of overexpansion and loss of identity. He talked about reclaiming his CEO role, closing hundreds of stores and revamping hundreds of others, and how one day he shut down all 7,100 U.S. locations for three hours so baristas could get a refresher course on how to make the perfect espresso. Instead of being hell-bent for growth, Starbucks went back to being a nice place to go relax and get a good cup of joe.

It was a great story, but it sounded like a press release—it lacked candor. It didn't connect with entrepreneurs in the trenches. I wanted to hear his advice on how to be a better entrepreneur, and I knew I wasn't the only one.

After the talk, Schultz did a Q&A session. The last question finally proved to be the right one to get Schultz to open up. A good friend of mine stood up and said, more or less, "Mr. Schultz, I really admire you. I am a huge fan. You have an amazing story and a great product that I buy every day. But when you just spoke about the struggle when Starbucks fell on tough times, I couldn't relate. After all, you had $1 billion in your pocket while the rest of the entrepreneurs in this room are struggling. We are trying to figure out how to make payroll and *feed our families* at the same time. So, Mr. Schultz, I can't relate to you." And then he said thank you, turned, and sat down.

The room was silent.

What happened next made me Howard Schultz's biggest fan. He stood up, walked across the stage, and said to my friend, "I am exactly like you. Let me share a story."

The billionaire CEO then became the Schultz of 30 years ago, a bootstrapping entrepreneur like the rest of us. The story he told will stay with me for the rest of my life. In 1981, Schultz was just another Brooklyn kid looking for a break, working for Hammarplast, a Swedish coffee machine maker. When he first arrived in Seattle, he made a sales call on Starbucks at its first—and in those days, only—location at Pike Place Market. In Schultz's recollection, the day was magical, the sky blue, the city looking as dazzling as Oz. He decided then and there he wanted to work for Starbucks.

He eventually persuaded the founders to take him on as a marketing guy, but, after the owners declined his idea of including an espresso bar in Starbucks, he moved to Europe. There he acquired the rights to a coffee brand called Il Giornale. He returned to Seattle, looking to raise money to open his first Il Giornale coffeehouse. He was working for no pay, and his wife Sheri was pregnant with their first child.

His father-in-law flew into town and asked him to go out for a walk. He said to Schultz, "My daughter is seven months pregnant and her husband doesn't have a job, just a hobby. I want to ask you in a heartfelt way, with real respect, to get a job."

Schultz flushed with embarrassment. He went home to his wife and, later that night, told her about the conversation. He had thought over what his father-in-law had said and figured he probably should sell his interest in Il Giornale and get a real job, but he asked Sheri what she thought he should do.

Sheri set him straight. She gave him her "Rocky" speech (the one Adrian gave Rocky when he had doubts before the big fight with Apollo Creed). She told Schultz that they were in this thing together, that she believed in him, and that she was sure he would be able to raise the money for the coffee shop. And that he should not quit—he should go for it.

That was all he needed to hear. It was an enormous, almost irresponsible risk, but it paid off. He got the financing, and a few years later he acquired Starbucks.

What I realized at that moment (it was a big "aha" moment for me) was this: Because I had the business idea or the fancy title, I thought I was the most important person in each company I started. But I learned the most important person in the company was the person I came home to every day.

And this person has the worst job in the business!

In fact, I've given this person their own title. They are not the CEO, or Chief Executive Officer; they are the CVO: Chief Venting Officer. Being an entrepreneur can be a very lonely job. Often it feels like you have nobody to talk to. So what do you do? You come home and "vent" to your partner.

In an ideal world, all entrepreneurs would have people like Sheri to support their new ventures. But that's a lot to ask. The job of being a spouse, family member, or best friend of an entrepreneur is not easy. These people go through the wins and losses right alongside us. Sometimes they are as much at risk financially as we are. And too often, we take them for granted.

When Schultz was ready to give up on his dream and take a job because he needed to support his wife and new child, it was his wife who provided the "aha" moment, telling him she believed in his idea and he should pursue it. Sometimes the "aha" moment is right there in your own home, with your own family—it's the moment that changes everything. It did for Schultz, and the rest is coffee history.

Like Schultz, I've learned that successful ventures start at home. The first and most important job of any entrepreneur is to get on the same page as their spouse or significant other. If you're not in agreement, there are only two possible outcomes when things get tough: Either the business or the relationship will suffer.

Below are the things you need to ask to ensure you and your partner are on the same page:

❋ *How much financial risk are you willing to take?* If you are launching a new business, you are probably bootstrapping—that is, using your own money. You and your spouse need to agree on how much you're willing to put aside and how much you will risk in pursuit of your dream.

❋ *How much time will you allow me to commit?* To launch and build a successful business, there are times you will have to commit to your business first and your family, along with everything else, second. You will have too much on the line. There will be too many moving parts for you to tend to anything other than your business. That doesn't mean your family is less important to you. It means that for a period of time, both of you agree that this is something in which you need to immerse yourself in the interest of your shared future.

❋ *How much do you want to know about/be involved in the business?* Being an entrepreneur can be a lonely job. At times, it's difficult to find others to talk to about the challenges you face at the office. For example, there are certain things you may not want to share with your investors and some issues that need to be kept away from employees. You usually don't want to spend your time with friends talking about problems at work. So you go home and vent. But there's probably a limit to how much your spouse and family want to hear about it; know where that red line is.

The CVO, like Sheri, will share the entrepreneurial roller-coaster ride. He or she is expected to support you and hold your hand through it all, provide the "Rocky" speech when you get discouraged, or be the voice of reason if you lose sight of your goal or spend more than you agreed you could afford to risk. Success rarely happens overnight, and when you're in a relationship, it is never a one-person effort.

Some CVOs really want to be involved. They want to know everything and thrive on a blow-by-blow accounting of the day. Others can only take the ups and downs in smaller doses. You need to be sensitive to how much your significant other or family members can take.

One of the best pieces of advice I can give you is to calibrate your communication strategy to suit your life partner. Do you talk about business once a day or once a week? If things are tough, do you come home and share everything before bed or wait until the end of the week to get it all out? Come to an understanding that works for both of you and respect it. How you handle the pressures of your business can either kill or strengthen a relationship. Both sides need to work together. And take breaks: Put all talk of business aside so you can enjoy your relationship and share other aspects of your life. Remember, your significant other deserves some time off as CVO.

Keep in mind that some people come from families where stability was the rule, with nine-to-five employment and a weekly paycheck for life. For people brought up in such circumstances, the seesaw of entrepreneurship may be hard to handle. I was lucky that my wife at the time, Rachel, grew up in a family filled with entrepreneurs. She lived through good and bad times, so she doesn't get rattled easily. Even so, she doesn't want a daily blow-by-blow accounting of what happens in my businesses.

One of the biggest lessons I've learned is this: The way you spell love in a relationship with an entrepreneur is *t-i-m-e*. I got child care every Saturday and we would have lunch together. I am usually relaxed because I'm out of the office. Things that seemed urgent during the week don't matter. I got a chance to tell her what's going on and got her feedback. This exchange didn't take much time, but we needed to do it, and do it consistently.

You should put in place something similar once you've found a mutually workable strategy. No matter how understanding your life partner is, you still have to prepare him or her for the challenges you'll face in building your business. Most important, you need to be in alignment with regard to how much both of you are willing

---

BALANCING LIFE: IT'S A TEAM SPORT

What about balance? I believe to be great at anything, you need to be off-balance. Something will have to take a back seat while you put more time and attention into whatever it is you want to do well. My friend Sharon Lechter, world-renowned author and speaker, says that the only way to stay in balance is to stand perfectly still. Once you put one foot in front of the other, you are technically off-balance.

People are always asking me how I find a balance as an entrepreneur. The fact is, it's not always something you can do, at least not alone. Your partner needs to understand that. You have to be upfront with each other about your expectations and priorities while you pursue your business goals.

When I see entrepreneurs in great long-term relationships, they have one thing in common: date night. They always find one night a week to go out on a date and experience something together. It could be dinner, a movie, a show, whatever. But they commit to that personal connection at least one time a week to reconnect and stay aligned.

---

to risk, how much time you're both willing to commit, and what communication strategy works best for both of you.

How Do You Juggle All Your Priorities as an Entrepreneur?: Super Balls and Glass Balls

The entrepreneur must master the art of juggling. Your job, finances, spouse, family, and maybe your boss; your health, projects, and deadlines—they're all in the air, and you're always at risk of dropping one.

Some people juggle better than others and can manage to keep all those balls in the air indefinitely. Most of us, though, reach a point at which it just becomes too much, and one or two will crash to the ground. We might even drop everything.

It is therefore essential that you understand this rule of nature: *Super balls bounce and glass balls shatter.* You need to think about which balls are which in your life.

If you drop the super balls, they will keep bouncing on their own for a while, none the worse for wear. While you're working on launching your venture, you don't have to worry as much about the parts of your life you know are bouncy and resilient. Later, when you can turn your attention back to them, those rubber balls will take to the air again, no great harm done.

Glass balls are a different matter.

In fall 2008, the sky was falling. I was standing at the airport on Tortola Island with Steve Ridgway, the CEO of Virgin Atlantic Airways, waiting for a plane. Our businesses both faced big challenges, buffeted as we were by the harsh winds of the growing global economic crisis, which threatened the economic stability of almost every nation and institution.

My business was vulnerable. I felt vulnerable, too, as if I might blow off the jetway at any moment, but Steve looked calm.

So I asked, "Steve, with all the pressure on you, especially right now, what's the most important part of your job?" I expected to hear something like leadership, team building, or vision.

His answer was just one word: "Exercise."

Exercise? I was surprised and told him that. Steve said he was disappointed by my reaction.

Later that day, I sat next to David Cush, the CEO of Virgin America, on the flight home. I asked him the same question: "What's the most important part of your job?"

His answer? "Exercise."

Again, I was shocked. David hadn't been with us when Steve and I had spoken earlier. They hadn't had a chance to compare notes, but they both gave me the same answer. Two powerful guys, running big businesses at an extremely difficult time, and they both said the most important thing is *exercise*.

This was starting to feel like an "aha" moment for me. What were the chances of two guys giving me the same answer? The oddity of that coincidence made it stand out in my mind and pushed me to reflect on the question of how our physical well-being relates to our ability to navigate the often-rocky world of entrepreneurship.

Running your business will be stressful and arduous. You'll always feel like there isn't enough time for the ten thousand things you have to do, and if you could just squeeze a couple more hours of work into the day you'd really feel like you had something to show for it. But you can't keep going at a hundred miles per hour if you're out of gas.

We all have our own ways of dealing with stress. We keep going by fueling our tanks, and we can either choose good fuel, like healthy foods and exercise, or opt for a bad diet made up of things like alcohol and high-caffeine drinks, along with little to no exercise and probably not much sleep. But you know as well as I do that your physical health directly impacts your ability to perform at a high level and even influences your mental health. Exercise enables you to blow off steam and release stress, which ultimately helps keep you calm and thinking more clearly. It's an essential component for dealing with the challenges of entrepreneurship.

Your health is a glass ball. If you drop it hard enough, it won't just break. It will shatter, and you can't be sure you'll be able to put yourself back together again.

You may think you can't find the time, but you simply have to get out and get your body in motion every day. This doesn't mean you need to run a marathon or train as a triathlete. Thirty minutes a day will do it, even if it's just to walk around the neighborhood. What you need more than anything else is movement to get your heart pumping. You need some measurable physical activity to recharge your body and to release the stress that comes with your work. Remember, if you don't have a way to let off steam, *the stress will catch up to you.* You won't have the energy, strength, or endurance to do your job right. You and your business will be set up to fail.

If you have to schedule your day around exercise, do it. I asked Mark Moses, an über-entrepreneur you'll meet in Chapter 5, how somebody with a business schedule like his could fit the many hours of training it takes to be an Ironman triathlete into his day. He said, "I put my exercise on my calendar first and then schedule everything else around it. By getting in that time and training, I have more energy and a clearer head than all those people who spend their entire day letting stress build up behind a desk."

You'll be surprised by how getting your mind off your work will help you find solutions to the toughest problems your business faces. You know how sometimes you'll have an epiphany while standing in the shower? The same thing happens to me when I'm out for a walk. When you force yourself to exercise, you may feel guilty at first because you're taking a break from work—*while there's a deadline approaching!*—but, in reality, you're freeing up some bandwidth on your attention span. That will give your subconscious the extra processing power it needs to make breakthroughs.

So decide on an activity you enjoy and get some exercise every day. Pick a time of day that works best for you and plan your schedule around it. Try to get your workout away from home—there are too many distractions there and it can be difficult to really let go. If you can, do it alone, so you can let your mind wander and permit the stress to ease out of you. As an entrepreneur, you have to be flexible and ready for anything. Your business may or may not be around in ten years, but you want to be.

Distinguishing the glass balls from the super balls isn't hard—and it's all-important that you devise strategies to balance the pressures so you don't shatter what is most important in your life. When times get tough, you need to be the toughest person in the room. You can't be ready for that moment if you don't take care of yourself.

In the end, I thought about how all this culminated in a breakthrough, which was actually very simple. It was about prioritizing what's most important to you, and that starts with your health. If you don't take care of yourself, you can't be effective for your family, your business, or anything else. That means exercising and watching what you put in your body because health is the one ball you can't drop.

You will have to decide what your other glass balls are. For some people, it's spending a certain amount of time with their family; for others, it's a pastime that keeps them sane. People need to build their schedules around the things that are most important to them. Now let's think about another of those glass balls—your emotional health, and how asking better questions can set you up for success.

10,000 Reasons You Will Succeed

One of the biggest challenges entrepreneurs face is the emotional roller coaster they ride every day when launching, growing, and running a business.

You know exactly what I mean. You wake up in the morning, an investment comes through, and then you lose it. Suddenly, they change their mind again, and the money is back. The product is working as planned—then it goes down, now it's back up. The key employee you want to hire is a go but unexpectedly drops out. Later, he or she agrees to sign.

Taking a seat on this roller coaster can wreak havoc on your mind. The highs and lows can be exhausting. They can quickly drive you in and out of emotional states that won't help you run your business, will strain your relationships, and can have a negative impact on your health.

The single most important job of any entrepreneur is learning how to smooth out the ride and manage your emotions in a way that balances your energy, drives your business forward, and puts you in the best position to succeed, no matter what life throws at you.

You can do this by *controlling your focus.* The brain works a lot like Google. It gives you answers, but they're only as good as the questions you ask. When an investment falls through, the product goes down, or a new hire falls out, you start asking yourself questions to help understand what just happened and what it all means.

Most people don't understand that this dialogue is even taking place. They are conditioned to respond to circumstances in a very specific way, and they don't even know it. If that conditioning leads them to ask good, empowering questions, the business will go down one path. If it leads them to an endless loop of negative questions, their lives will go in a whole other direction.

Let's say that when you hit a bump in the road, your automatic response is to start asking questions like *Why do bad things always happen to my business?* and *Why can't I do anything right?* Then your Google-like brain will do a search and pull up 10,000 reasons why your business stinks. Your focus goes right to these answers, which will make you feel terrible. It's impossible to act in an effective way from that place.

Instead, you must teach yourself to ask a better set of questions, ones that empower you and your business, because having the right mindset immediately shifts your focus from a challenge to the opportunity it presents. These good questions prompt better answers, so rather than bemoaning your fate, you can hopefully set yourself on a more productive path that leads to a breakthrough.

Therefore, when things aren't going your way, what would happen if you started asking questions like *What is great about this experience? What can I learn from this experience?* or *How can I use this experience to help my business succeed?* Again, your brain will run a search. But this time, you'll get 10,000 reasons why you will succeed. That will put you in a much better position to drive your business forward.

If there is only one thing you take away from this book, it should be this: *Ask a better question*—and watch how your life changes forever.

That is the breakthrough I want you to focus on as you move through the stages of developing your business, for it is the backbone of how you harness the power of those little "aha" moments into bigger ideas and better breakthroughs. Always ask better questions.

If you want to develop a razor-like mindset, one that cuts through problems like a knife, here's how:

❋ *Recognize you are in complete control.* Nothing in life has any meaning other than the one you give it. You can choose how you evaluate any situation and where you place your focus.

❋ *Break your pattern.* The odds are that you have been running on autopilot most of your life, allowing your emotional state to dictate your inner dialogue. Next time you run into a problem or something threatens to knock you off course: *stop!* Pay attention to the questions you are asking to evaluate the situation, and if they are negative, interrupt your pattern with a new set of empowering questions. This will help you look at the situation in a whole new light. With enough practice, this powerful way of thinking will become automatic.

❋ *Develop new habits.* Developing the skill of focusing on what empowers you is like building a muscle. Your job is to exercise your mind every day. The best time to start is in the morning. Take control of your focus as soon as you wake up. Begin the day by asking questions that set you up to get the most out of the day, like: *What am I grateful for? Why will I succeed? How can I move this business forward today—and have an awesome time in the process?*

❋ *Never make a big decision at your lowest point.* Many times, it seems like we make our biggest decisions when we are in the worst possible position to think clearly. Next time: *wait!* Hold off until you can ask a better question. Wait until you have stepped away from whatever the situation is, physically moved to get the blood flowing, and released some tension. You will make a much better decision from a more balanced emotional state.

❋ *Pass this skill on to your team.* Imagine if everyone on your team operated from this place of razor-sharp focus, if they looked at everything that came their way as empowering tools that they could use to drive the business forward. Imagine if they were conditioned to find the opportunity to improve in every situation. Wouldn't they also make smarter decisions?

The decision is up to you. Are you ready to take control of your life? Are you ready to get off the roller coaster? If the answer is yes, then just do one thing—ask a better question—and focus squarely on the opportunity in everything life presents. Remember, you control your results more than you think you do. From the company you keep to your reactions to a crisis, you decide, either consciously or unconsciously, what your actions will be.

 THE OTHER HALF OF LIFE

Controlling your focus is only part of what determines how you will behave. Another way to control how you behave is to change the way you move.

If I asked you to describe a person who was down or had a hard day, it would be easy. Eyes looking down, shoulders slumped, and breath low and shallow. If I took that same person and simply had them change how they were holding their body—had them lift their gaze, bring their shoulders back, and breathe deeply—I could take them right out of that emotional state. That is because the way you use your body sends different signals to your brain.

Try it yourself. The fastest way to change the way you feel is to change the way you move. As Tony Robbins would say, "Motion creates emotion." So if you are down or having a tough day, get out and move. When you feel stuck in your business, get out of your chair and take a walk outside. Movement will instantly change the way you feel and put you in a better position to take on the day.

The Power of Visualization: What I Learned from the World's Greatest Snowboarder

The concept of applying habits of good self-care to your business as well as your personal life brings into sharp focus the fact that how you control your body often affects how you approach your business. Doing so can help you achieve that next breakthrough, and harnessing that power through visualization is one way to do it. Take the case of world-famous athlete Shaun White.

Shaun White is widely known for his amazing skateboarding and snowboarding skills. He has won three Olympic gold medals and more gold medals than anyone else in the X Games, not to mention ten ESPY Awards from ESPN. Shaun's mindset and approach to his sports don't just put him at the top of his game, but also provide some strong fundamental approaches for entrepreneurs at all levels. Let's take a look at some of them.

Modeling

Shaun uses modeling to create and build his tricks. "The tricks are built on something that's been done before in a way, unless it's something so outrageous that it's like you just had a crazy dream and decided to go for something. Otherwise, it's always built off of something else," explains Shaun, utilizing a key aspect of business: building on what is out there and making it many times better. "There's a stepping stone trick on your way to get to that place," adds Shaun. "When snowboarding, I was learning to spin, so obviously the first one would be a 180. Once I learned that, I built up to a 360 and then up to a 540 and 720 degrees of rotation. The last trick I did was a double flip 1440. It's gone pretty far from the first 180, but that's how I got there in that place. You always look around you for what people are doing and a way to make it your own."

Visualization

Visualization is huge when it comes to doing the types of tricks Shaun does. "Obviously, setting the goals is one thing, but actually attaining them and the steps you need to take is another," he says. "I really think about everything, honestly. I think about the music that's going to be playing, I think about what I'll be wearing, what the sky's going to look like. In fact, when going for the Olympic gold, I didn't just think about winning. I played the whole thing through."

For me, the real breakthrough here is harnessing the power of the way Shaun visualizes. Instead of seeing himself accomplishing his goal in the future, he visualized having already achieved it. He conditioned his mind to think he had already won because he had gone beyond the race and looked at it in so many ways. For example, Shaun's dream since he was a kid was to be on the cover of *Rolling Stone* magazine. So he visualized having won the gold medal and being on the cover as a result. He saw it, heard it, felt what it would be like to do the cover photo shoot. In fact, he even had his own custom clothes made for the shoot, including a pair of crazy pants! "I stepped into it and made it a reality," explains Shaun. The dream finally came true in 2006 (and again in 2010).

That was the first time I had heard that. Since that meeting, I've found this to be a very common practice among top performers. These visualization techniques can also help entrepreneurs see what they are looking to accomplish in advance. Don't just visualize reaching your goal, but keep going and visualize what comes next. Don't just visualize climbing Mt. Everest—visualize coming back down and how having done it impacts the rest of your life.

Chunk It Down

Have you ever set goals that were so big you intimidated yourself? Lofty goals like winning Olympic medals can certainly be reached, but sometimes setting some smaller goals can keep you more mentally and emotionally balanced. Plus you can make it more fun for yourself.

"I tend to set very high goals for myself and then some lower goals, something that's achievable that's more fun, more playful," explains Shaun. When he was a teenager, his goal was to win a big competitive series. But that goal seemed daunting at the time. Many of the individual events in the series gave away cars to the winners, so instead of focusing on the difficult task of winning the series, he focused on winning each individual event, which meant he would win a car.

"One year my goal was to see how many cars I could win," he says. "Honestly. I was around 16 years old, so I was stupid. Driving was on my mind. Man, I won about seven cars. It was ridiculous. I started donating some of them because I'm thinking, 'What am I going to do with them?' I'd rather just give this to somebody." Winning the series seemed overwhelming, so instead, Shaun focused on each individual event. As a result, he won so many individual events, he won the corresponding cars and, eventually, the whole series. "It was a way for me to downplay the magnitude of the situation and really make it into a more attainable goal. To be kind to yourself in that way I find helps me a lot," explains Shaun.

On Failure

As anyone in business should know, failure is part of the equation. Certainly this is very true in sports, where recovery time has to be quick. If you dwell on failure, you will lose the competition or the game. Shaun sees failure as something you need to experience to go on to bigger things. "If you're starting a business and you're failing, well, good," he says. "I'm glad you got it out of the way so that you can succeed later on. I fell on my run during practice right before the Olympics. It was my last practice run, and I fell.

"I was so happy that I fell. I was like, 'Thank God I got that out of the way.' I don't fall often, and that was a big one. There's a lot on the line, and I fell right before the event. I didn't let it freak me out. I just went, 'Thank goodness that happened to me so that I can now go out and do what I need to do.'" By keeping his focus on what mattered, he could go on and win the gold medal. My real "aha" moment in learning more about Shaun was the way he not only embraced failure, but was grateful for it. He repacked it in his mind, made a few adjustments, and used it as a tool to help him move forward. It's the same thing in business and in life. You learn through your mistakes.

"There have been so many occasions where I had a home-run T-shirt design or jacket or some apparel, something that I was going to put out. I was thinking 'This is going to crush it,' and then it didn't. You have to learn from that. Maybe it was the jacket—we were going summertime. Maybe it should have been a little lighter fabric. That's how you learn from your mistakes," explains Shaun.

Successful entrepreneurs, like athletes, learn from what they do wrong. Shaun always stresses the importance of going for the long run. "Don't go for these short-term wins. Know what you want to do and set forth that motion to get to that point. Don't let little things sway you. Be thankful for the mistakes because now you know in the future what to do," adds Shaun.

In the end, Shaun's messages work in any business venture. Visualizing puts the images in front of you so you can see the process and the results. Chunking down gives you smaller goals to help you stay focused on the steps it takes to achieve your larger goals while also minimizing the stress that often comes with reaching for the big payoff. And finally, failure is part of the journey; you should expect, embrace, and learn from it.

Dreaming Big: The True Story of Rudy, Football's Biggest (and Smallest) Underdog

As you think about how to bring all the advice in this chapter together, I want to leave you with a few thoughts on the power of dreaming big to overcome your obstacles as you reach the precipice of each breakthrough in the life of your business—and of your own life.

My buddy, football legend Rudy Ruettiger, is an amazing example of something both football players and entrepreneurs can relate to: overcoming the odds. (The 1993 movie *Rudy* was based on his life.) Rudy has traveled the world telling his amazing underdog story and has made it his mission in life to give people hope.

It's an American story—a story about someone with a dream who said they couldn't succeed. "I had everything going against me," Rudy says. "I really wanted to go to Notre Dame, but you had to have good grades. I didn't have the grades. I had dyslexia. I didn't know I had it until I went into the Navy. The dyslexia held me back from really getting help in school. I was held back, and I was focusing on my negative side instead of my positive side, so that's why I graduated third from the bottom in my class.

"My parents were blue collar, and my athletic skills were not on the top of the candidate list to go to Notre Dame," he says. But Rudy, the third of 14 children in his family, finally got into Notre Dame on his fourth try.

Rudy, however, had even bigger plans: he wanted to be part of the legendary football program at Notre Dame. "I'm not the tallest guy in the world, but I had a dream," he says. "I always looked at myself as someone 6-foot-5, not 5-foot-6. It's how you look at yourself that sets the stage for what you become."

What struck me is that Rudy never saw himself as having any sort of disadvantage. Instead, he found value in everything he brought to the table. In speaking with Rudy, the "aha" moment for me was seeing that until you learn to value yourself, no one else can place a higher value on you. As an entrepreneur just starting out, it is essential that you find the value in yourself and what you have to offer.

Having an Edge

As Rudy aptly points out, overcoming your worst habits (procrastination, perfectionism, you name it) may be the biggest challenge you must face to become the person you need to be, if you want to achieve your goals. Rudy refers to the mentality that is created through the process of overcoming these challenges as "an edge."

"Character comes out every single day in the entrepreneur," he says. "We all have highs and lows, and I think it's during those down times when we really see who a person is and what they're made of. You can see them stepping back from, or stepping up to, the challenge." He also notes the importance of learning from every setback. "You get the chance to go back and fix it."

Rudy's "edge" is another word for the perseverance an entrepreneur has to have. They will only find it deep down in the core of who they really are.

Making the Team

Most college football players, especially for the Division 1 schools, are recruited from high schools around the country by scouts looking for the best talent they can find. And yet Rudy defied the odds by walking on and trying out for the Notre Dame squad. His unlikely road to making the team built him a fan base, but it wasn't until the final game of the season that Rudy got to suit up for a game. "According to NCAA rules, only a certain number of players are able to put on a uniform for each game," he says. "I was never good enough to suit up. But right before that last game, they gave me a jersey with no name on the back. I was the last guy put on the roster that day. And then my teammates asked me to lead the team. Once you run out of that tunnel, and there are 60,000 people cheering, you think, 'Wow, am I glad I didn't quit.'"

As the game was winding down, the fans started chanting for him to get in, and his teammates were echoing the call. Finally, with 27 seconds left, Rudy was put in the game. "Now I'm on defense. Now you go into that zone. You don't hear the noise, you just completely focus. You've been practicing and preparing for this moment. Now you're ready," says Rudy. He was only in for three plays, but as the clock ran out, he sacked the Georgia Tech quarterback. "I got the tackle, and a group of guys that came out carried me off the field. I was embarrassed. I remember saying, 'What are you doing? Drop me, man!' One of Rudy's teammates kept saying, 'Oh man, you're the man!' I didn't understand that 'till later. You don't know the people that you touch through your hard work. That's why hard work's important. If you're doing the work, they'll follow you. That's the ripple effect," says Rudy, whose play was immortalized in the film.

"Here's the other thing for kids. I tell kids this all the time: You don't have to be the smartest kid in class to be somebody. Remember that. You don't have to be the best athlete to be somebody. Know that. Be a great contributor. Be a great teammate. You'll be the leader, you'll be hiring those guys," says Rudy.

As Rudy has proved, it's not the size of the dog in the fight, it's the size of the fight in the dog.

How big is *your* fight?

the most important decision you will ever make: who is your tribe?

You can have the right idea and the right plan. You can work harder than your competition. But if you don't have the right people around you, you won't succeed.

The people around you should inspire you, challenge you, motivate you, and be there for you when you really need them. You'll know when you find these people because you'll want to run ideas by them, brainstorm with them, and look forward to spending time with them. If, however, the people around you are pulling you down—whether in business or in your personal life—or impeding your progress, you need to seek out other people with whom to surround yourself. It's that simple.

Crabs in a Bucket: Maybe It's Time to Change the Circle of People Around You

Nothing is more important than the people you surround yourself with. This is not only true in business, but also in your personal life. You don't need me to tell you that the right friends and contacts can help in a thousand ways. So let's examine your personal ecosystem.

Odd as it may sound, I'd like you to start by thinking about crabs. Imagine you've got a bucketful of freshly caught crabs. If you look into the bucket, you'll see them squirming around, trying to figure out how to escape. Individually, they're each clawing and climbing over the others trying to get a grip on the lip of the bucket.

Should you put a lid on the bucket to prevent dinner from crawling away?

Don't worry about it. There's a funny thing about crabs—as soon as one looks like he's about to hoist himself over the edge of the bucket, the other crabs grab onto him and pull him back down. They can't understand that if they worked together and formed a chain, then all the crabs could easily climb out of the bucket and escape. But no—whenever one crab starts to show some leadership or initiative, it gets pulled all the way back down to the bottom. Eventually they just stop trying.

Have you ever felt like a crab in a bucket? Maybe your office mates criticize you for trying too hard and making them look bad. Your boss may not want you to move ahead because then he'd have to find someone else to do your busy work. Perhaps your friends think you're getting too big for your britches because you want something better for yourself and your family than what you grew up with.

Life is way too short to be a crab or hang around others who want to pull you down. The number-one determinant of who you are and, eventually, what you achieve in life and business is your environment. Think about all the places you spend time: at work, at home, in your neighborhood. Do these places bring you down or elevate you? Do you feel comfortable where you work? Is your home a sanctuary, or do you dread going there at the end of the day?

Do your friends look out for you, encourage you, and help you brainstorm? Or do they reinforce bad habits? Are they invested in your success, or do they secretly want you to fail so they can keep you in the bucket with them? How large and generous are their visions? Remember that people with small visions of themselves cannot have a larger view of you.

You owe it to yourself to separate from the "friends" who anchor you to a place you don't want to be. There will always be people trying to knock you down. You don't need them in your life. There will always be people who attack your big idea. Don't immediately dismiss what they have to say, but don't automatically buy into it either. Even if they seem to have the best intentions—they may really think they're trying to protect you—your job is to listen to their arguments, see if you can learn from anything they say, and apply it to your business or product to make it better. And if people say you're crazy and your big idea will never work, let their doubt drive you forward. Your attitude should be: *What do you know? You're just a crab in a bucket!*

Your Fab Five

How important are the people you spend your time with? The time you give to others is nothing less than precious—*and* an investment in your future.

My time with Tony Robbins taught me to look critically at the people around me. His circle included individuals who were either the very best at what they did or who aspired to become so: people like Quincy Jones, Peter Guber, and Pat Riley. Among these top business leaders, world-class athletes, and people committed to changing the world were many others who had overcome enormous obstacles. They found solutions that not only benefited themselves but also improved the lives of others along the way.

I'll never forget one member of Tony's circle who had gotten into a car accident on the way to his wedding. The accident left him paralyzed from the waist down, but instead of feeling sorry for himself, he went out and invented a line of aerodynamic racing wheelchairs. He didn't just empower himself—he helped others in the process.

Tony's people, including the team of trainers and sales reps I lived with on the road, helped instill in me a real sense of what was possible.

I learned to think in terms of networks as I assessed my own circle of friends. It taught me the value of the people you spend the most time with, and the need to recruit the right people into your life. At the end of the day, you are nothing more and nothing less than the average of the five people you spend the most time with. I call them your *Fab Five*.

The name "Fab Five" originally came from what many people consider the greatest recruiting class in sports history: the 1991 men's basketball team at the University of Michigan. In their freshman year, these players took their team to the NCAA championship, an unprecedented accomplishment. In the same way Michigan's coach recruited them, you need to recruit and build your own championship team around you. Let's begin by looking at your existing Fab Five and considering their impact on you today.

Make a list of the five people you spend the most time with outside of your family. If you're not sure who to include, just look at the numbers you call most often on your mobile phone. Now estimate what each of them earns, total the incomes, and divide by five. The result will usually be really close to what you earn. Crazy, right?

Even if money isn't important to you, try comparing your Fab Five's general health status and attitudes toward the people around them (this time, if you wish, add your family to the list). Chances are you fall somewhere in the middle of the pack. You are nothing less—and nothing more—than the average of the five people you spend the most time with.

Ask yourself how your Fab Five affect you. Are they pulling you up or pushing you down? If you told your five best friends, one at a time, over coffee or a beer that you were planning to start a business, what would their responses be? Would they be supportive or dismissive? Would they encourage you or try to shoot your idea down? Would they be keen to help you brainstorm? Or would they turn the conversation back to themselves?

Are your Fab Five a reflection of your higher aspirations? This is important because we tend to hang around people whose values are similar to our own. Rich people hang out with other rich people. Physically fit people hang out with other physically fit people. People in the arts hang out with other people in the arts, techies hang out with other techies, and slobs hang out with other slobs. If you want to know why you don't have more of the things you want in your life, the answer may be as close as those five numbers on your cell phone.

If you are reading this book because you want to break through and build a $1 million business, you need a Fab Five who can help you build that business. You need to spend your time with people who have *already* built $1 million businesses. Or $10 million businesses, since the people who have built $1 million businesses won't get you to the next level. Maybe you want to build a $1 billion business, but think you can't get access to billionaires. That's just an excuse. Pick up a book by Warren Buffett, follow Mark Cuban's blog, or attend live events with Tony Robbins. Want to be great at social media? Watch a video with Gary Vaynerchuk. You can also follow other very successful people on social media, such as Facebook, Instagram, and LinkedIn. Visit them, study them, listen to what they have to say on a regular basis to help drive you toward your goals. You can take advantage of the knowledge and support of these very successful people even though they aren't your actual "business team"; their wisdom can help you select the "hands-on" business team that will enable you to grow.

Immerse yourself in the way this core group of people sees the world. Learn how they program their minds. Let their learning and instincts wash over you. If you spend enough time reading and absorbing their material, you will start to pick up on how they act, think, and make decisions. Their state of mind will start to rub off on you and might provide you with some "aha" moments that lead up to your next breakthrough.

You may not want to hear it, but you might have to change your circle of friends. If the people you spend the most time with cannot help you get where you want to go, then you need to expand your network and make new friends. That doesn't mean you have to completely abandon your old friends, but the ecosystem of the entrepreneur needs a different balance. Finding success is a different pursuit from having fun, whether that's shopping for shoes or tailgating at the football game. The people you feel the most comfortable with—who perhaps

THE PEOPLE AROUND YOU

Are the people around you pulling you up or holding you down? Try some of these tips to find some answers:

- ☀ *Take inventory.* Write down the names of the five people you spend the most time with. Ask yourself: Do they support me? Do they want to see me succeed in my new venture? Or would they prefer to see me fail and keep me close? If it's the latter, cross them off your list and get them out of your life.

- ☀ *Find three mentors.* Answer this question: Who are your three mentors? If you don't know, you'd better get to work finding one . . . and another . . . and another. Important note: For someone to be a reliable mentor, they cannot have any stake in your business, or whatever area in which you need advice. They need to be completely independent and emotionally unattached so they have nothing to gain from their counsel. The reason for multiple mentors is because different people have different areas of expertise—for example, one may guide you in business strategy, another in marketing, and a third in how to make better business decisions. You also need mentors who know more than you do. Someone working their way up as you are can certainly be a friend and someone you can compare notes with, but mentors need to have answers from their knowledge and experiences that you do not yet have. And mentors aren't just for starting out in business—they should be there to guide you as you grow and scale.

- ☀ *Be selfish with your time.* Share your time with people you think can have a positive impact on you and your team. Don't share it with people who offer nothing in return.

are the ones who demand the least from you—aren't necessarily the ones who'll move you toward your goals.

When you incorporate new people into your circle, don't forget to give as well as receive—if you inspire them, they will in turn give more to you. Also, the people in your circle should not be "yes" men or women. People who are 100 percent behind you should still be able to give you some constructive criticism—not doubting you, but making suggestions that may help you.

Be careful to differentiate between good counsel and opinions. Opinions may come from well-meaning people, but counsel should come from experience—from people who have been there and done that.

Also, as my buddy Greg Reid says, use the "hand in the sand" method for taking in counsel or opinions. If you put your hand in the sand, close your fist, and pull it out, a lot of sand will run off the sides and fall to the ground. But a little will remain in the palm of your hand. The same thing applies to getting counsel—only hold on to what makes sense and let everything else go.

To move your life to a new level and break through to the next level in your business, you may have to blow away your old universe. The people and thinking that got you this far won't necessarily get you where you want to go. If they would, you'd be there already.

Personal Branding 101: What Do Those Note Cards Say About You?

As an entrepreneur, you need to create and manage your own personal brand. You must author your own story, paint your own portrait.

You may think you are selling a product, a service, a financial plan, etc., to your investors, division heads, partners, or employees. To be sure, those things are an essential part of your business. But it's really all about you because people invest in people. Every action you take helps others define you. Personal branding goes a long way toward cultivating your tribe as well as your customer base.

I run a personal branding exercise at one of my programs. Typically, there are about 20 people in the room. I encourage them to mingle while grabbing coffee and breakfast before the event. When it's time to get started, I invite the participants to sit in their assigned seats. On the table in front of each of them is a placard, and I ask them to print their names on them so everyone in the group can see. Each person then gets a stack of index cards. I ask them to look around the room, write one person's name on each of their index cards, and jot down the first five words that come to mind when thinking of that person. An assistant then collects all the cards, enters all the words the group used to describe each participant into a file, and prints them out so each participant sees only the words used to describe him or her.

Typically, people are shocked and horrified by the way others view them. For example, a person might think of himself as outgoing, but the index card shows the group thinks his behavior is obnoxious. Another person thinks she embodies success and confidence, but the group sees her as arrogant and standoffish. Often, the way others see them just doesn't sync with the story the person believes about themselves. It's little wonder they're not getting the results they want when they try to sell their ideas or raise capital in their businesses. Clearly, what they are projecting is not what they need to win people over.

What would that stack of note cards say about you? What is the impression you are leaving on others when you're trying to build your tribe? Is that personal brand serving you or stifling your growth? Is it taking you closer to or farther away from your goals?

Here are five steps to take control of your own personal brand:

1. *Identify your goal.* The first thing you need to do is get very clear about what you want to achieve. Do you want to take a consumer online business to market in 90 days? Do you want to release a new product that extends your company's footprint in the marketplace? Do you want to close financing for a big project? Do you want to create a rock-star team to help transform your local business into a global franchise? Who do you need to be to achieve that goal? What image do you need to project to bring others along with you?

2. *Understand where you are now.* Where are you today relative to where you need to be? What is the gap, and what changes do you need to make to fill that gap?

   To answer this question, go to the five people you spend the most time with (your Fab Five) and ask them to describe your brand. Then extend your pool to others with whom you have had fewer interactions; more distant acquaintances may offer even more valuable information because it is based on more immediate first impressions. By getting a handle on how others see you, you will learn what needs to be changed. If they say you're standoffish, when you think of yourself as shy, this is an area of your self-presentation you need to work on. Such knowledge alone can be curative.

3. *Recognize what your daily habits say about you.* Do your habits empower or disempower you? Daily habits can have a major impact on how people brand you. Your attire, manners, and degree of organization tell people about you—and the right presentation communicates that you are prepared and have pride in who you are and what you do. For example, when someone is physically fit and really takes care of herself, she presents as disciplined, committed, and apt to follow through. People can see and hear an energy in her physical presence immediately. Little things make a big difference, even if it's just the cut of your clothes or the warmth of your handshake—and you can take control of them.

   If you don't define who you want to be and manage your personal brand accordingly, people will do it for you. On the basis of the cues you give them, they will put you in a box. It's a box that best serves their needs and not yours, so make sure it's a box with which you want to be identified.

4. *Leverage technology to define and reinforce your brand.* Most people will first be introduced to you online, when they type your name in a Google search box or visit your LinkedIn, Facebook, and/or Twitter profile. They'll see the pictures and videos you distribute of yourself and what interests you. Use these tools

DON'T BE DEFINED BY YOUR ORIGINS

I'm a huge Los Angeles Lakers fan. One of my heroes growing up was Lakers owner Jerry Buss. He was a Depression-era kid who stood in food lines to eat, but he didn't let that experience define him. After he earned his doctorate in chemistry, he saved $83 from each $700 paycheck, and then got a few guys together and bought an apartment building. He built a real estate empire, enabling him to buy the Los Angeles Lakers. When he died in 2013, his net worth was estimated at $600 million, with the team being worth around $3.3 billion today. He wrote his own story and created his own brand. In the same way, you must decide what your story means. Don't leave it to others to decide for you.

to your advantage: Have a professional picture taken, include a link to your website, and make sure your copy is brief and to the point.

5. *Be yourself.* Don't pretend to be someone else. When developing a personal brand, authenticity is key. If you try to pass yourself off as someone you are not, people will find out, and that will undercut your credibility. Be original and be creative. Present a sincere, heightened, but accurate version of yourself. Don't try to be what you think other people want you to be. When investors and customers meet you, you want them to think, "This is a person I want to do business with."

If there are things in your career that you are afraid others will react negatively to, don't try to hide them. Address them upfront, and by doing so, take control of the conversation. For example, if you failed at an earlier business venture, don't try to conceal it. Illuminate it by sharing what you learned from the experience and how you are applying those lessons going forward. Most people would rather get behind someone who took a shot, even if he failed. People who have learned from their mistakes bring wisdom to the new venture. Knowing that and applying it to your brand can only help you build a more authentic tribe of both colleagues and customers.

breakthrough two

ASSEMBLING YOUR RESOURCES

business
planning

S pace has always fascinated me. I can sit in front of my computer, open YouTube, crank the volume all the way up, and watch the space shuttle take off again and again.

A few years ago, I had an opportunity to meet with a space shuttle commander, and I was totally psyched. When I finally got a chance to sit down and talk with him, I asked the one question I had always wanted to ask an astronaut. You see, when I watch the shuttle land on TV, there's a few minutes after it enters the atmosphere when the entire ship is surrounded by a ball of fire. So I had to ask, "When that happens, are you just totally freaking out?"

The commander laughed and said, "No. When we're surrounded by fire, my head is down and I'm busy and I'm working, trying to land the ship. But there's a moment that occurs just before that that's really a bit tricky. Picture this. We are traveling in the space shuttle over the earth going 20,000 miles an hour, upside down and backwards. In order to land the ship, I have to flip the shuttle all the way around, and I need to position the nose of the shuttle at the perfect angle of approach. If the tip of the nose of the space shuttle is not at the perfect angle of attack, the second we hit the atmosphere, the whole ship explodes."

I said, "That sounds risky."

He looked back at me and said: "Risk should never be risky. Risk should be well thought out and planned out in advance. Systems should be put in place. Alarm bells should go off. If things don't work out as planned, things take longer than planned, things go sideways, you can recover and bounce right back."

The same is true in your business. I talked a bit about risk in the last section. Remember: You want to reduce or eliminate as much risk as possible by planning ahead for everything from hiring and employee retention to balancing the entrepreneurial lifestyle with your personal commitments. Good planning goes a long way toward reducing risk and putting you in a better position to succeed, no matter the circumstance.

Even if you are a one-person show, and even if you surround yourself with a ton of technology, you'll need support and resources to help achieve your goals. Too many people think they can do it all themselves—until the computer breaks or the package has to be there yesterday. Knowing how to find and evaluate talent is part of being an entrepreneur, as is making sure you have the right people in place.

Running a business also means balancing your numerous work responsibilities with the rest of your life. All work and no play, or all play and no work, just won't cut it. Incorporate this balance into your business as well: develop a culture that makes people want to come to work every day.

Of course, the one resource that makes it a business rather than a hobby is having the cash flow necessary to start and keep the business moving forward. Entrepreneurs need funding, which can come from their own assets, family and friends, partners, VCs, angels, or all of the above. But before anyone will part with their cash, you need to be well-versed in presenting your business to the world.

Dealing with people, money, and balance can all be risky ventures. Learning how to mitigate that risk by planning ahead is the goal of this chapter. In coming chapters, we'll share how to build the right plan, hire and retain the right people, and put the resources and capital in place to grow and scale your business.

Goals and How to Achieve Them: Building Biceps and Businesses

Entrepreneurs are impatient people by nature. Once they have their big-picture objectives, many go straight from scribbling an idea on a bar napkin to execution. They rush out and start executing without a plan. But the first step to assembling your resources is to set goals and create a plan with a solid strategy behind it. Once you have a clear vision of where you are going, you can better identify the resources you need to get there.

While goals and objectives may give you a direction to go in, they don't tell you what specific things you need to do to succeed. Although the strategies you use to accomplish your goals will evolve as you do business, the clearer you are from the start about your tactics, the better shot you have at building a winner. My favorite example of the power of combining clear goals with a well-thought-out plan comes from my good friend Doug Brignole.

A few years ago, I decided I wanted to get really fit, so I went to the gym and asked to be referred to a trainer. The guy they connected me with just wasn't what I wanted. Although he had muscle, he was also overweight and, worse yet, unhappy. He wasn't the kind of person I wanted to emulate. On the other hand, he did make me realize I should be modeling someone who is the very best at what they do. So I decided, *I want to learn from Mr. Universe!* I put the word out, and that's how Doug entered my life.

Doug grew up in Southern California in a first-generation immigrant family. He was a small kid, and he frequently got beaten up on his way home from school. At age 14, he decided he had had enough and it was time to improve his physique. He went to a local gym and asked, "Can I *please* join?"

He was too young to be a member, but Doug persisted. He worked out an arrangement with the manager to work part time and work out during his off-hours. He fell in love with bodybuilding and eventually got the urge to compete. By the time he was 17, he was a contender for Teenage Mr. California. Though he didn't win that year, he did place well, kicking off a lifelong career in bodybuilding. The rush of competing fueled him, so Doug set his goal higher: He wanted to become Mr. America.

He started out by making sure he was absolutely clear on his outcome. He is not only a bodybuilder, but also a world-class artist. One of his unique skills is his ability to draw the body and biomechanics in amazing detail.

Doug had a friend take a photo of him in a bodybuilder's pose, and he blew up the image. He then put tracing paper on top of the enlargement and drew, in very fine detail, exactly what he would need to look like to win the title. He illustrated the shape, size, and balance of each muscle group.

Once Doug was absolutely clear on what he wanted, he asked himself the following questions: *What do I need to do to achieve it? What could get in the way? How am I going to overcome each challenge?*

This was decades ago, before you could find 20 kinds of protein powder at the store and smoothies on every corner. Like other professional bodybuilders at that time, Doug prepared all his own meals, figuring out a dietary regimen that would enhance his workouts. He put that tracing paper picture of himself in a frame and set it on the table where he ate five times a day. With one bite, he'd point his spoon or fork at the picture and say, "That's what I will look like." And with the next: "I'm going to make that happen." He did this for months.

From time to time, Doug would have his friend take new pictures of him in the same pose, enlarge them, and lay the tracing of his goal body on top to monitor his progress. He adjusted his diet and bodybuilding routine based on the results. Pound by pound, muscle by muscle, he filled out the image, bringing a dream sketched on tracing paper to life.

Finally, Doug competed and won the Mr. America title in his division.

After the competition, Doug had his friend take one final photograph. He posed just like he had in the original, so many months before. He blew the new picture up and laid the original tracing paper on top. The photo and the original image he had drawn were identical.

Doug Brignole set clear goals, created a solid plan, checked his results periodically, and made necessary adjustments. He executed in a similar fashion for his other goals as well, eventually winning the title of Mr. Universe as well as Mr. America in the same year. Though he's now in his 50s, Doug is still competing; recently, he was the overall winner at the Muscle Beach International Masters competition.

We can all apply the lessons from Doug's story to turn our big ideas into reality and break through to the next level in our entrepreneurial journey:

✳ *Be clear on what you want.* Your goals must be specific and measurable. It's not enough to say, *I want to make $1 million.* You need to be much more specific: *I want to earn $1 million, in net income, by this date.* For your business, it's too vague to say, *I want to increase sales.* A better goal would be: *I want to increase gross sales to $1 million, per quarter, by this date, with this profit margin.* Clarity is power. You can't manage what you can't measure.

✳ *Make a list of what you need to do to get there.* Clear goals are important, but you must back them up with a solid strategic plan. I heard recently that having clear goals increases an entrepreneur's chance of success by 20 percent. But having clear goals and combining them with a well-thought-out plan increases your chance of success by *400 percent.*

It's important to break down what is required to accomplish your goal into small, manageable pieces. When you're finished, ask yourself, *Is this it? If I do all these things, will I reach my goal?*

Or are there other things I need to do? Odds are, there are more steps than you realized.

✳ *Identify what could get in the way.* To accomplish your goal of $1 million in gross sales, per quarter, by a specific date, with a specific profit margin, you may find several obstacles in your path. For example, you may need to tweak your product, refine your sales pitch, upgrade the people on your team, or find ways to reduce costs. Decide how you will overcome each obstacle. Make a list of everything you will need to do to break through each obstacle.

✳ *Find and study role models.* Learn what others have done to achieve the outcome you want. This helps you minimize risk and will save you money on trial and error. Study their beliefs, their strategies, and the order in which they did things. Then do the same things to produce the same results.

✳ *Create your strategic plan.* Having a big idea is a good start, but it's not enough to succeed. You need clear goals that are specific, measurable, and actionable. You need a plan that tells you what you need to achieve, what could get in the way, and how you will overcome each obstacle. By combining your big idea with clear goals and a strategic plan, you will put yourself on the right course to bring your idea to life in the next 90 days.

✳ *Sustain it.* Millions of people every year set out to achieve their goals; some get there, but many don't. Those who do can either celebrate their success and stop or continue on to maintain and even build on their success. Doug could have celebrated winning Mr. America and then stopped his bodybuilding routine and gone off his rigorous diet, but he did not. He kept doing what he had done to reach his goal and continued measuring himself to stay on course, which kept him in remarkable shape. He still competes around the world at the age of 50. Getting there is only half the battle; staying there is the rest. In Doug's case, it means a constant process of discovering which diet and exercise plans, and which tools and technologies, can help him maintain and improve what he has built. It means adapting to an aging body over time and adjusting his methods to help him stay on top.

In business, you can celebrate reaching that $1 million per quarter mark and let sales drop off—we've all seen that happen. It's like the person who goes to the gym, loses 25 pounds, and celebrates for a week, gaining ten of them back. Sustained success is difficult, but the most prominent business owners and the long-term success stories keep on measuring their success, pay attention to new ways of doing business, stay connected to market feedback, and set new goals and then strive to reach them.

Let the Numbers Tell Your Business Story: Start with the Last Page First

What is the first step in figuring out how to execute your big idea? Creating a working model for your business.

We've all been brainwashed into thinking that the best way to do this is to sit behind our desks and write a long, detailed business plan. You know the kind. It starts with a fancy cover and your mission statement and then describes your team, market, product, competition, and so on.

Most entrepreneurs spend a lot of time and resources writing their plan. Too often, they get feedback from all the wrong people. Their friends and family want to support them, but they are telling the entrepreneurs only what they want to hear—that they have come up with the next Google or Apple or Tesla (keep in mind, none of this feedback is coming from customers). By the time the entrepreneur gets to the last section in the business plan—the financials—he's totally sold on the idea. Sometimes the financial section is left unfinished or dropped entirely as the business is launched. Intrapreneurs face an equally dangerous problem: the temptation to take a basic set of assumptions and artificially inflate the numbers to get the support needed to move forward.

And why not? We are passionate. We are committed. We know we can't fail. So what are we waiting for? *Let's go!*

Here's the problem. Most entrepreneurs change their business model six times when working through the financial section of their plans. While running the numbers, they identify key distinctions with regard to income and expenses. They gain a deeper understanding of what it will take to break even and how to achieve free cash flow. As a result, they come up with better-informed strategies for attaining their desired financial outcomes.

The most important part of the initial business planning process, and the one people most often neglect, is getting your numbers to tell a story that makes sense for you and your investors. If you start at the beginning of the plan only to learn that your assumptions about the business don't add up once you reach the end, you've lost valuable time and money.

Regardless of whether you are in startup or growth mode or moving to the next stage of your business, mistakes can be costly, so here's what I recommend:

❋ *Start with the last page first.* Once I have a basic understanding of what I'd like to build, the market, my target customers, the business opportunity, and the product, I dig right into the numbers and create a simple one-page spreadsheet that clearly identifies how the money flows. Basically, I write business plans backward. I've learned that once the numbers tell the story you want, the rest of the plan will write itself.

❋ *Don't wait.* Don't make this process more difficult than it needs to be. Limit your model to one page. Create the simplest, most basic spreadsheet you can that identifies income, expenses, breakeven, cash flow, and the capital required to achieve your outcome. Use conservative assumptions, and do not rely on best-case scenarios.

❋ *Get out of the office.* You will learn more about your business by getting into the market than you ever will sitting behind a desk. At least 50 percent of your time should be outside the office gathering information that can be applied to your plan. That means contacting industry insiders to learn more about the market, talking to prospective customers about their needs, and testing your competition's products and services.

✳ *Be careful who you listen to.* When we have an idea we passionately believe in, we are convincing. It's easy for our family and friends to tell us we have a winner on our hands because they want to be supportive. But when you're modeling your business, the people whose feedback matters most are current and potential customers. Listen to what they have to say and apply what you learn to your model. Let their feedback, and not your enthusiasm, sway your projections.

✳ *Don't throw out negative feedback.* Sometimes it can be difficult to absorb negative feedback in a constructive frame of mind because we are so close to our projects and have so much on the line. We start rejecting and deflecting feedback that isn't in line with what we believe. But honest, educated feedback is like gold. Use it to open your mind and ask tough questions about your assumptions. You must be obsessively committed to asking what you can learn from this feedback and how you can apply it.

This is especially important for people entering new markets where they don't have prior experience. Getting feedback from others who have lived in the space will add to your perspective. Sometimes you will learn that there are things you don't know as a newcomer that would significantly impact your financial results. In fact, this holds true throughout your business' lifetime. The entrepreneurs I know who have built the most successful and thriving businesses are obsessed with getting constant feedback from the marketplace and adapting their businesses based on evolving market needs.

✳ *Be open to what the numbers tell you.* The worst thing you can do is try to manipulate a model to match your assumptions. You need to approach your financial model with a completely open mind. Recognize that it will probably take longer than you initially thought to get to market, generate revenue, create profits, and accumulate the cash flow you need to operate and further invest in the business. By being open, you will be able to make distinctions, apply them to your business, and set yourself on a path to success.

You need to be clear on where you want to go and put a simple and adaptable plan in place to help you get there. The clearer your vision is upfront, the easier it will be to back a plan to help you get there. Being obsessed with customer feedback will enable you to tweak strategy in a way that evolves with the market and helps keep you on top of the competition.

The One-Page Plan

If you're going to market quickly, you may not have time for a bells-and-whistles 90-page plan. I like beautiful charts and graphs as much as the next entrepreneur, but frankly, we don't often have the bandwidth to focus on that much information—and neither do your potential investors, partners, and team members. When I was young, one of my mentors used to say, "Give me everything I need to know, but keep it to one page." And he was right!

Once you've created a sound financial model, what you need next is a one-page "executive summary" that clearly describes your business.

An executive summary is one of the most valuable tools for both entrepreneurs and managers inside big organizations. It should highlight the company or project's team, mission, market served, target customer, problem being solved, unique value proposition, competitive environment, financial assumptions, exit strategy, and return on investment.

Now, just because the summary is only one page, that doesn't mean you don't have to do the work required for a bigger plan. You will still need to study the market and competition and have your arms around the financial drivers in your business. But today, markets move so fast, and new products and services are launched so easily, that having a clear vision for where you want to go, a flexible framework for how you will get there, and the ability to adapt is most important.

The executive summary should be clear and easy to read. Share it with your team to ensure that everyone is headed in the same direction. The summary can also be given to potential investors, partners, and customers to draw interest. And, yes, you do need to keep it all on one page.

Many people have said to me, "But I need more space!" My response? "If you can't explain what you want to do in a few sentences, then you don't really understand your business." And, by the way, nobody else will, either.

I didn't say this would be easy. In fact, when you ask most entrepreneurs to summarize their business in a sentence, on a page, or in a PowerPoint deck, they can't do it. Instead, they ramble on and on. In the real world, giving an investor too much information is as bad as giving them nothing at all. They'll throw your plan right in the trash.

That's why this tool is so valuable. It provides focus for you, your team, and anyone else that touches the business. When you get in front of your target investor, you will be prepared and you will stand out from the crowd. In today's world, that's what you need to get the deal done.

Why You Need an Exit Strategy in Place from Day One

You just read about starting with the last page when writing your business plan. A similar theory is true when starting, growing, or scaling your business. You need to create an exit strategy on day one and keep it in the front of your mind as your business goes through its life cycle. It's that important. Having a clear exit strategy will help crystallize your vision and business strategy. However, many entrepreneurs skip this step. They are either too eager to get started, firmly believe they would never sell, or concerned that focusing on an exit so early in the company's life cycle would be a distraction. Let me give you three reasons why *now* is the right time to begin thinking about an exit.

1. *Your investors will want to know how they will get a good return.* Will it be from an IPO, sale, or dividends? If your plan is to

get acquired, they will want to know who will buy you and why. How will you value the company at that time, and building on that, how much will they receive? Can you point to comparable recent acquisitions to support your case? Finally, how long will it take to reach that point and how will you fund the company during that period?

2. *Planning an exit is a way for you to think strategically about your business.* For example, what does your target buyer need that your business can provide (such as sales, new customers, new products, or new markets)? What metrics do you use when evaluating your business, like revenue, gross profit, net profit, or EBITDA? Who in those organizations buys companies, and how can you be proactive in building relationships with them? Knowing the answers may also help you determine the direction of the company in terms of plans, partnerships, and overall strategy.

3. *At some point, you may just want or need a way out.* Even if you self-finance or think you will never sell, many factors may surface that change your thinking. You may decide to cash out to capture a maximum return on investment; you may feel burnt out or just get the urge to do something else. Sometimes business goes sideways, or a major change in your personal life may make a quick sale necessary.

Consider this, too: If you don't have an exit strategy, you have an incredibly expensive hobby, not a business. If you need a hobby, I recommend fishing.

Below are a few ideas to consider when thinking through your exit strategy in the early days of your business. They can—and should—be considered as you craft your business plan.

✳ *Create deep relationships.* Businesses are bought, not sold. The best acquisitions at the highest returns typically come as the result of long-standing relationships or strategic partnerships. These give the buyer the opportunity to get to know you and your business and for you to sell yourself to them.

☀ *Keep your house in order.* You should always keep your financials and other business documents filed and precise. When the time comes to sell, you will need clean financials to attract buyers and the highest valuations. If your back office runs well, that will instill confidence and make the selling process move faster. Plan and execute from the beginning.

☀ *Get back to work!* Now that you've made your exit plan, stop focusing on your billion-dollar exit and put all your energy back into serving your customer. Go build a great business, and the rest will fall into place.

Not Every Problem Is Meant to Be Solved

While planning for the future is extremely important, you will inevitably run into some unanswered questions as you start out or try to grow and expand. In the world of business, you may find that some things are better left unchallenged as the solutions may be too difficult, too time-consuming, or simply implausible.

Like many entrepreneurs, I constantly survey the landscape and keep my eye out for opportunities. A few years ago, I spotted one—or thought I did.

Having made some good money in my Silicon Valley years, I wanted to reinvest part of my capital in something that would generate passive income. The answer, my new big idea, was self-storage.

I did some homework and found there are about 40,000 self-storage facilities in the U.S. But the fact that really got me excited was that the biggest owner, Public Storage, controlled just *3 percent* of the market. To me, this spelled opportunity, the chance to develop a national brand, roll up the market through acquisitions, and create efficiencies through scale.

It didn't quite work out that way. Instead, I learned an important lesson, an "aha" moment: If a problem looks obvious but hasn't been solved, there may be a good reason. In the case of self-storage, 95 percent of self-storage facilities are independent businesses. These family operations typically consisted of only one facility, and often the owners lived on the premises. At some, their kids worked the storefront. Why would they sell if their whole way of life revolved around the business? If they did sell, how hard would it be to get them to make the decision?

Another problem surfaced, too. Once you get the couple who owns the business to move away, you're faced with a new challenge because then you need to hire and pay someone else to run the business, an expense the previous owners didn't have because they'd been operating it themselves. The effort, time, and money it would have taken me to acquire hundreds, if not thousands, of family businesses and then rebrand them just didn't make business sense. I could spend a fraction of the energy in another industry and likely have better results.

After investing lots of time and money working on what I thought was an obvious winner, I realized that because of my lack of experience in the industry, I hadn't understood certain mechanics of the business.

This doesn't mean there weren't opportunities to build great companies in self-storage. The people who succeeded already knew you couldn't grow quickly through acquisition, so they developed from the ground up and worked to establish regional rather than national brands. When one of the very few portfolios of multiple facilities came up for sale, they were prime targets for acquisition with high values. That also meant the sellers were big winners.

There's a larger conclusion to be reached from this experience that you should consider. For generations, entrepreneurs have fallen into the trap of thinking that all businesses and industries are pretty much the same. Some think that just because they've been successful in one industry, it will be easy to duplicate their success in a new one.

That can be true, but never forget that every industry has its own character, and that business cycles change. No two moments or opportunities are ever identical. No matter how much you think you know or how good your business acumen, *always* walk into a new industry looking to learn. Do your homework before you take the plunge. That means talking to people who are close to the industry to help you understand the nuances of that particular business. It means poring through every piece of material you can find to seek out other companies that are doing, or have attempted to execute, the model you are contemplating.

If you find a high failure rate, don't fool yourself into thinking that your model is different or your team is smarter. Instead, pause, take a deep breath, and learn everything you can. If you have deep knowledge of the industry, you will be less likely to jump in feet first and try to make changes that simply won't work. You should also ask other people to weigh in on your plan, provided they have the background and experience to be a worthy advisor. Remember, be conscious of the difference between *opinion* and *counsel*. Opinions come from people who have no firsthand knowledge of something. Counsel comes from people who have direct personal experience in the area where you need guidance. Sound business planning requires input from the latter.

Not all business problems are made to be solved. If you look at a market, see a problem, and conceive a great solution, there may just be a good reason nobody else has done it. There could be something about the market or the industry that makes it a poor fit for what you want to do. That possibility makes doing your market research more than a matter of reading a book or a report. It means looking at the problem in a whole new way. The key is getting away from your desk and talking to people in the market as well as seeking expert counsel every step of the way. Coming into an unfamiliar industry with fresh eyes can sometimes work, especially if you're seeking to apply new technology to an old business. But beware: You may end up paying a high price to educate yourself, only to find out that your plan has been tried and failed before.

One of the most important jobs of an entrepreneur is *not* to take shortcuts. That means building a solid plan, strategy, and financial model that support your goals—and doing it *before* you start building your new business, product, or service. That critical step will help mitigate risk. Unfortunately, too many entrepreneurs, in their excitement to get started, skip right over it, their business gets started on the wrong foot, and they have to go back and correct all their mistakes. This costs them valuable time and money.

Remember, the best shortcut in life is taking a long-term view.

securing
your crew

When building a great company nothing is more important than the team you surround yourself with. As a leader, it's your job to ensure you have the right people in the right positions in your business.

Yet hiring good people is only half the battle. You'll also need to rally your team around your vision, build a great culture, and empower each of them to be their best.

In this chapter, we talk about getting your crew in place, but also about doing a self-assessment and handing off some of the work you do—aka delegating. The more you can take off your plate and hand over to trusted team members, the easier your life will become. I can always tell when I'm having lunch with a CEO friend who has hired and delegated properly. They are relaxed, they order dessert, and they don't feel like they must get back to the office before all hell breaks loose.

In this chapter, I focus on why hiring the right people matters, your role as CEO, delegating, assessing talent, outsourcing, and everything else that is important when it comes to securing your crew.

Know Your Strengths (and Theirs): How Having the Right People Can Make a Difference

Two friends of mine, born in the same place, work in the fashion industry. Over the years, each has gained access to very similar resources. Both have charismatic personalities and are natural leaders. Yet one of these women constantly struggles—her business is broke and may have to close its doors—while the other woman's company is now worth more than $1 billion.

The obvious question is: *With so much in common, what's the difference?*

The short answer is the successful entrepreneur had great self-awareness. Having her own "aha" moment early on, she recognized what she did well and, just as important, where she needed help. She knew from the start to build a team with the right skills around her and then get out of their way. Her strategy allowed her to work her strengths and hire her weaknesses. Her key tactic—and it's a good one—is to find people that *play* doing the things she considers *work*.

In effect, she fired herself as CEO, putting someone else in place with a track record of successfully building companies like the one she wanted to create. This allowed her to focus on product development, which is the work she does best and enjoys most. The company thrived.

In contrast, the struggling entrepreneur did two things wrong. First, she tried to do everything herself, from scheduling meetings to going on sales calls to making the product and shipping it to her customers. She was always so busy working *in* the business that she had no time to work *on* the business. Second, she put herself in the wrong role. Although she, too, was miscast as a CEO, she didn't have the foresight to hand off the executive responsibilities to someone better suited to the job.

An important element of your entrepreneurial success is to build the right team around you. What do you need to know about yourself and your potential crew to get your business to break through to the next level? Stop doing it all! C'mon . . . let's have a personnel breakthrough by learning to let go and trying the following.

Work Your Strengths and Hire Your Weaknesses

One of the best qualities an entrepreneur can exhibit is self-awareness. Know yourself. Are you a visionary? Do you like to take risks? Are you better at setting up systems and managing day-to-day operations than thinking big? Is there a specific area like sales, marketing, or product development where you excel? Get clear about who you are and how you can help the organization most, and then focus on filling the gaps by gathering the right people around you.

Sometimes entrepreneurs, perhaps out of pride, find it difficult to put someone else in the role of CEO. The same hesitation may also apply to other leadership roles. My advice? *Get over it.* This kind of limited thinking will only obstruct your path to success.

Aim to hire people more qualified and smarter than you and give them the tools they need to succeed. By the way, assigning somebody else a major role in the company doesn't mean you have to give up your influence or ownership. When your role is in perfect alignment with who you are, you will be able to contribute more and really enjoy what you are doing in the process.

Look at the histories of other companies. The most successful ones were started by people who brought in others very early in the company life cycle to raise their performance.

When Sara Blakely got started, she worked on Spanx at night, filling orders from home and personally going into stores to rearrange product displays. As the business began to grow, she recognized that, at heart, she's a visionary rather than a CEO. So two years after she founded the company, she hired Laurie Ann Goldman as CEO, a woman with ten years of experience running a licensing division at Coca-Cola. She played to her strengths and hired to cover her weaknesses. Basically, she knew what she didn't know and was OK with that.

Sergey Brin and Larry Page, the creative geniuses behind Google, fired themselves as CEOs after three years and hired an experienced executive, Eric Schmidt, to run the company. Schmidt helped engineer its exponential growth, while Brin and Page kept doing what they did best in development.

Be Ready to Substitute Players

As a company grows, people who excelled early on may not be the right fit down the road. One manager may be great at taking a product to market but not know how to grow the business beyond a certain point. I've seen people perform brilliantly at one level who can't shift gears to get the company to the next one; they're great at taking a business to $1 million or even $10 million in sales, but not $100 million. That's not surprising—different skill sets are needed at different levels—but you need to make sure you have the right people in the right places at the right time in your company's life cycle.

One key thing to consider is that employees, partners, and contractors need to be comfortable working in a fast-paced, resource-constrained environment where they will likely be asked to juggle multiple tasks. Also, because getting your business off the ground is so time-consuming at first, you must be sure the people on your team do not have any other major obligations during the critical go-to-market period. Once the business grows, you'll need people who not only know how to do the job but can also manage others effectively. In the beginning, everyone does a bit of everything, but later on, once people have defined roles, strong leadership and management skills become increasingly important.

Bring in the right people, ones you can trust, give them all the tools they need to succeed, and then get out of their way. Leverage your strengths and spend your days doing the work you enjoy most.

And, as you'll learn in the next section, get comfortable with delegating everything else. It could make the difference between going broke and building a billion-dollar business.

Identify Your Entrepreneurial Kryptonite

What comic book character best describes the entrepreneur? I think it would be Superman.

Entrepreneurs are the heroes of business. They start companies, execute tirelessly, and are on call 24 hours a day. In the early stages, they put their stamp on everything, assuming responsibility for all decisions. They're the driving force behind all that gets done.

But just as in the *Superman* comics, there's one thing that can knock the entrepreneur down. No, it's not kryptonite—it's the failure to delegate. If you want to grow your business and maximize its potential, it's important that you learn to hand over responsibility to others—and the sooner, the better.

I have two friends who started a chain of indoor playgrounds for kids. After operating the business for three years, they are generating plenty of cash and impressive profit margins for a retail business. Their goal is to grow the number of stores throughout their state and then take the business national. Will they get there?

I found that instead of focusing on growth, they still spend most of their time on basic administrative tasks. They have run into a trap that many entrepreneurs encounter: Because they are so close to the business, they think they can do every job in the company better than anyone else. They can't seem to loosen their grip, and, as a result, their business has plateaued. By simply handing over more administrative tasks (like answering the phone, taking orders, and cleaning), they could significantly increase the amount of time they spend thinking strategically and growing the business. Remember, as your business grows you need to spend more time working on the business, not in the business.

Consider two conversations I recently had with clients.

In the first, I spoke with a consultant who runs a good business and makes $100,000 a year. I respect her skills. I asked her what she was planning to do that day. She said: "I need to schedule a bunch of phone calls and meetings and fill up my calendar. Then I need to go buy boxes and packing material and tape and bring them back to the office and pack some marketing materials for prospects. Then I need to go to the post office and stand in line and mail everything out."

I asked her how long that would take. "All day," she said.

In the second conversation, I asked a good friend (also a consultant) about *his* day. He said, "I'll be out meeting with prospects and clients closing business in the morning, then I'm going on a 50-mile bike ride to train for the Ironman triathlon." I asked how he could fit such time-consuming workouts into his schedule with all the bookings he needed to make, along with sending out presentation materials.

"Why would I do that stuff?" he asked. "I leave it to someone else." He has a virtual assistant he pays $1,000 a month to handle all his administrative tasks. He makes more than $1 million a year.

It's pretty clear that the difference between the consultant with the $1 million business and the one with the $100,000 business boils down to delegation.

Every successful business owner will, at some point, realize he needs to get out of his own way and delegate more responsibilities to his team. That "aha" moment will free you up to do whatever helps you use your unique talents and contribute more to the business.

The most successful business owners spend their time on what is most valuable to growing their business and delegate the rest to others. I'd suggest my first client look into the following fixes.

Start by Valuing Your Time

By handing over more administrative tasks (like answering the phone, scheduling meetings, and sending out marketing materials), you can significantly increase the amount of time you have to spend on the big picture. When is the right time to bring in this help? Today.

I hear you asking, *How can I afford that?* Wrong question. Ask yourself instead, *How can I afford not to?* Your time is too valuable to waste.

☀ DELEGATION DOS

Try these delegation dos to clear your plate and make room for more big-picture breakthroughs:

- ☀ *Make a list of your tasks.* For one week, make a list of everything you do (both business and personal). Provide as much detail as possible. Circle all the administrative tasks—reading email, scheduling meetings, creating presentations, standing in line at the post office, returning phone calls—that don't require your personal attention and that you can hand off to someone else. Next, look at nonadministrative tasks and decide what can be handed off to other members of the team.

- ☀ *Use the same systems, platforms, and tools.* Get all your employees and assistants working on the same platforms and systems for email, contacts, calendars, project management, etc. Live in the cloud with shared folders stored in Google Drive, Microsoft OneDrive, or Dropbox. Use Skype for group video calls, etc.

- ☀ *Refocus your energy.* Get back to your role as entrepreneur CEO—or whatever position in the company suits you best. Spend your time taking advantage of your strengths.

You don't necessarily have to hire a full-time employee. Instead, bring on a virtual assistant you can pay by the hour. That person can handle scheduling, shipping, answering your phone, and responding to many of your emails for less than $10 per hour, perhaps working remotely from home. A small expenditure can give you the time you need to get in front of more investors, prospects, and clients.

I think of it this way: You either *have* a $10-an-hour assistant or you *are* a $10-an-hour assistant. As an entrepreneur CEO, is that all your time is worth?

Train and Trust Employees to Take on More Responsibility

When you start a business, you are the head of every department in the company. You are responsible for every job function. But as you add people to your team, be sure to fire yourself from those positions and let them take over.

For example, you hire a new head of sales. That's a good decision, one area of responsibility you can take off your list. Your new job is to let the person you have hired do their job. Get out of their way and redirect the energy you had put into sales back into your role as entrepreneur CEO. Your superhuman energies are better invested when they're focused on what is required to grow. By delegating, you will move your business further and faster with less effort.

Maintaining your altitude can mean making a series of small tweaks to your processes—or a complete overhaul of your team, systems, and strategies. But you will not know what needs to be done unless you take the time to step back and take a hard look at how you're doing in these first days and weeks of planning and getting your business off the ground.

Your Role as the Entrepreneur CEO

I often ask entrepreneur CEOs and corporate managers the following question: *What is your responsibility as the person in charge of your business?*

This is often met with a blank stare. Other times I get a vague response, something like, "Well, I do a lot of things. I guess my job is to keep the company or project moving forward."

These are not useful answers. It's no wonder that many CEOs just ricochet between crises without any real thought about how to proactively drive the company forward.

WHAT TYPE OF ENTREPRENEUR ARE YOU ?

The first step in building a great team is having a clear understanding of your strengths and weaknesses and then filling in the gaps. Which label below best describes you?

※ *Visionary*. You love dreaming big and inspiring people, but you're not crazy about day-to-day execution. You are a risk-taker. You have vision, you think big, but you also like the idea of rolling up your sleeves and building a business. You thrive in fast-paced environments and like handling multiple responsibilities. You're comfortable with limited resources and can multitask like crazy.

※ *Manager*. You're not a wild-eyed visionary and you don't want to take on all the risk. You like to add structure to an organization to achieve its goals. You enjoy overseeing a team, building systems, and best practices. You pay attention to data, details, and key business metrics and excel at execution. You feel most comfortable in a more stable environment.

※ *Sharpshooter*. You have a craft, a unique skill, or a basic knack for doing great things in a particular area. Perhaps you are an artist or salesperson. Do you excel at writing code? Have you mastered a skill that you just love to exercise? You may be less interested in being a CEO or manager because it would get in the way of you working on the things you enjoy most.

At the end of the day, whatever your style, this business needs you. It needs you to contribute what you are best at each and every day to help the business succeed. A fancy title doesn't mean anything. What's important is that you put yourself in the role you enjoy and at which you excel. And let others do the rest. That is the sign of a true leader and successful entrepreneur.

Before you assemble your team, you must be absolutely clear on what your role and day-to-day responsibilities will be leading the company. Knowing what to focus on will also help ensure you're not spending your time in other people's business and getting in the way of them doing their jobs.

Every CEO is different, but that doesn't mean we can't learn from the best. That brings me to my old friend, Mark Moses. He is the entrepreneur CEO I look up to most.

Mark is just a little competitive. On personality tests, he rates as a "super achiever" (on a scale of one to 100, he tests at 100). His life story reinforces the picture. Driven to succeed no matter the costs, he founded several successful companies; the last one, Platinum Capital, became a $1.6 billion business. Then, after "retiring" at the ripe old age of 40, he threw himself into Ironman triathlons. He's competed in 11 of those, even breaking the 11-hour mark, which is pretty impressive for the Ironman distance.

But let's go back in time. As a college kid in Canada, he started a company called Student Painters, a home painting company. In his first summer with the business Mark did $70,000 in sales and made an $18,000 profit, impressive indeed in an era when college tuitions topped out around $5,000. The next summer he did $120,000 in sales and cleared $35,000. "I thought, maybe I didn't want to be an accountant after all," he remembers. It was an "aha" moment for him.

Mark knew his results were good, but he decided to see what would happen if he went out and hired talented people, taught them how to model the system he'd built, and helped them grow prosperous businesses for themselves, for which he would get a small cut. With that in mind, he packed up a U-Haul and headed for California. There he eventually grew Student Painters to 250 branches with 3,000 guys and gals armed with paintbrushes. I was one of those painters. I became friends with Mark as a college freshman when I opened a branch for him in San Diego.

After four years in the business, he sold Student Painters for millions of dollars. Next, Mark went into the mortgage banking business. He was steadily building the business, but in 1997, he set himself—and his company, Platinum Capital—a new goal of lifting sales over $1 billion. To kick off the crusade, he rented a 2-ton elephant and rode it into the annual company meeting. He told his people, "If we think big and act big, we will be big. Let's do a billion dollars!"

Overnight the elephant became—and remained—the symbol of the company. The very next day, employees started bringing in elephant objects: paperweights, pictures, posters, and stuffed animals. By creating and reinforcing this shared vision, Mark created a rock-star culture. "People knew us as the elephant company," Mark says. "I was the elephant guy."

But Mark's ride in the mortgage business exemplified the ups and downs of entrepreneurship that every one of us faces. In 1998, when the Asian flu hit and lending dried up overnight, Mark was forced to lay off 230 employees. In 2000, his business was a day away from bankruptcy when an angel investor stepped in and lent the company the necessary capital. Mark then turned the company around, rebuilding it into a $1.6 billion business. Finally, in 2006, he sold it. Today, Mark is a coach for CEOs and entrepreneurs. He helps them figure out where they want to go and how to build a plan to get there. He also holds them accountable to make sure they execute along the way.

What I particularly respect about Mark is his ability to cut through the garbage and tell it like it is. One concept he works hard at is teaching his CEO clients the central role of the entrepreneur CEO. Given his diverse business background, his view may be surprising to you: He sees the job of the leader as very similar, whatever the business.

But being the head decision-maker is just the start. With a thank you to Mark, I want to share some of the most important parts of your day-to-day job description if you are in the role of CEO:

> ✳ *The CEO is responsible for the vision and direction of the company.* This seems straightforward enough, but it's more complicated than it sounds. When I ask CEOs where their company will be three years from now, fewer than one in ten has a good answer. This is inexcusable.

You have to look at the horizon and know where you want to take your company. This kind of vision differs from a goal on your mission statement; your vision is a measurable three-, five-, or ten-year view of where you want to be. I recommend starting with the sales and profits you hope to achieve and then working backward to see what it will take to make it happen. You'll need clear drivers, processes, and accountability to manage your company's progress toward your vision. In short, having a vision is worthless unless you can engineer the specifics to achieve it.

✳ *The CEO has the ultimate responsibility for cash.* You may think watching the cash is the CFO, accountant, or bookkeeper's job, but no.

For any company, cash and access to cash is its lifeblood, the air it breathes. If you run out of cash, you're done. You'd be surprised how quickly a fast-growing company with high profit margins can run short of cash. The reason, Mark says, is that "growth eats cash." You may have to use up cash to add to your working capital, build up inventory, or finance your accounts receivable. Managing the monetary ebb and flow is ultimately the CEO's responsibility because it is so vital to the health and survival of your business.

✳ *The CEO must ensure that the right people are in the right jobs at the right time.* "Lots of CEOs fall down on this one," says Mark. CEOs may be sentimentally attached to longtime employees who have been there from the beginning. They refuse to let them go or move them aside, even if they are no longer beneficial to the company.

As the business grows, you will need to make changes. The people who got you to one threshold may not be the people you need to take you to the next level. The CEO, hard-hearted though it may seem, must be dispassionate about hiring and firing. If you can only afford two salespeople, they need to be the two best salespeople you can find. Some people operate better in startups than in more mature businesses. Recognize your people's strengths and weaknesses, and don't wait too long to bring in new talent. The wrong employees will bring you down.

✳ *The CEO is responsible for key relationships.* The CEO must "own" the key relationships in the company, such as those with bankers, key vendors, the biggest customers, and shareholders. Any outsider with the power to alter the future of your company—by ordering, selling, lending, etc.—needs to have access to you (and you to them). You want them to feel comfortable calling you up at any hour of the day or night. Too often business owners hand over these relationships to high-level employees. But what happens if those employees leave and take the accounts with them? You cannot—and should not—keep control over every contact. But know who the key ones are and keep them close.

✳ *The CEO must have processes in place to continue learning.* You did your market research before you started your company, right? Back then, you didn't have anything invested. You had nothing on the line. But now that your life is tied up in your enterprise, be diligent about keeping up with what is going on in your industry, with your competitors, and with your customers.

Business changes faster than ever these days, and the annals of recent corporate history are littered with the bones of companies that didn't evolve or adapt fast enough to survive the rapidly shifting environment. Go to conferences, talk to consultants, and get to know your rivals. Use tools like Google Alerts and LinkedIn to help you keep track of what's happening in your field and outside it. Read trade blogs and ezines. Look to learn—as well as sell—when you're out in the field, whether it's one-on-one or at a convention with thousands of attendees or meeting customers at a small event. Hire a business coach and put together an advisory board to gain experience and wisdom from people who can help you stay current.

✳ *The CEO must be a cheerleader.* "The CEO has to be the chief energizing officer," Mark says. She must communicate what's going on to the rest of the team, explaining the company's results and getting employees onboard with her vision for the future. "If you want them to buy into what you're selling, then you have to align their best interests with your best interests," he adds. Often the best way to do that, he recommends, is through open and engaging communication. According to Mark, "Almost all corporate culture can be improved with communication."

Do you fit the CEO profile? Is this the kind of role you're prepared to play in your company? Are these the things you excel

 THE COMMANDER'S CHECKLIST

You'll find a wide range of CEOs, with different characteristics, styles, and personalities that set them apart. However, there are some important aspects of the job that I highly recommend all CEOs have on their list of priorities. They include the following:

- ☀ *Vision.* Do you have a clear, specific, and measurable vision?

- ☀ *Responsible for the cash.* You can't leave this task to your CFO. It's too important. Always keep an eye on your company's cash.

- ☀ *People.* You must make sure you have the right people, in the right positions, at the right time.

- ☀ *Key relationships.* What will happen if the person you hired to oversee accounts leaves? They will probably take those key relationships with them. You need to own the relationships that are most important to your business.

- ☀ *Learning.* Work at growing and educating your team. You also need to stay on top of the market, competition, and customer needs.

- ☀ *Cheerleader.* Don't forget, you are the chief energizing officer!

at? Just because you started and run a business doesn't mean you have to be the CEO—you can bring in someone else to be the CEO and do the work you enjoy most to benefit your business. And, once you have identified your own role, you can apply that same process to pinpointing the roles and tasks that best fit the other members of your team as you make hiring decisions and create the vision for your company.

Talent Assessment Matters

Having identified the role you will play in your business, as well as the tasks you want to take off your CEO plate, the time has come to think about filling in the gaps. Selecting top talent, identifying the best players, assigning them to the right positions, and making sure they clearly understand and excel in their role—these are the factors that separate championship organizations from everyone else.

In the world of NFL football, Stephen Austin is regarded as the expert of experts, a world-class evaluator of talent. Over 20 years, he built his company, Elite Pro Football Combines (since renamed the NFL Regional Combines once it was bought), Elite Football Services, into the leading private evaluator of football players in the world. (In 2011, after several hundred players vetted by Austin signed with NFL teams, the NFL bought EFS, making it the league's nationwide producer of combine showcase events.) Stephen's systems are so effective that they have been modeled by top sports organizations all over the world. The U.S. Navy SEALs have even enlisted his help in finding the next generation of elite warriors.

I asked Stephen, "What is it that separates the best players in the world, like Tom Brady, Jerry Rice, or Richard Sherman, from everyone else?"

His answer surprised me. He said, "It all comes down to this: three plays."

That's it. Three plays per game, three moments in which a superstar player does something just a little better than everyone else.

For a quarterback like Tom Brady, one play might be avoiding a sack. Another could be throwing the ball away instead of risking an interception. The third might be drawing an opposing linebacker offside with a change in cadence. Three things—often little things—may not seem like a lot, but multiply those three plays per game by 16 regular-season games, three possible playoff matchups, and ideally the Super Bowl. That's *60* plays a year that the other guy, who's also a really talented player if he's in the NFL, didn't make.

Stephen explained you can't tell whether a person will make those three plays based on how they perform at the combine. That's why Stephen's pro scouts watch hours and hours of game tapes to understand how their candidate has performed in the past. They spend time getting to really know a player before deciding, talking to former coaches and teammates and collecting references. Investing the time to gather this kind of intelligence is one of the hallmarks of championship organizations. That was the "aha" moment for me here: understanding the importance of taking the time to really get to know the people you plan to hand off so much responsibility to. And I've found that to be true at every level of the business, from the first assistant we hired to the president of our company. Everyone matters.

One of the greatest challenges for busy entrepreneurs is to find the time to learn enough about job candidates to make the best hiring decisions. When they don't take that time, they soon learn that one or two bad hires can really set them back. Finding the right people takes probably half as much time as it takes to unravel the mess that can come with hiring the wrong person, bringing in a replacement, and getting the company back on track. Since you want to find teammates who can make critical plays for you, here are some tips for hiring well.

Get Clear on What You Need

You don't have time to waste, so begin with a clear job description that specifies the job's exact requirements. This will save you more time and energy than anything else and will help produce the best results. The description should include the job title, a list of responsibilities, prior experience required, functional expertise, educational requirements, and how much you're willing to pay (being transparent about money will prevent both sides from wasting time). The more detailed the profile, the easier it will be for you to connect with the person you are looking for—and for your network to help you identify the right candidates.

From time to time, you will need to fill a position where you don't necessarily know all the day-to-day responsibilities or requirements. When this occurs, most entrepreneurs just try to wing it. Since that typically leads to a company's worst hires, I recommend you take a different approach.

For example, I once needed to hire someone in finance, but I wasn't sure what title, job description, and background would best fit my needs. I just knew I needed stuff done, so I reached out to a friend whose job entailed recruiting people for financial positions inside big companies and shared with her what my business needed. She started by mapping out a finance department's organizational chart, including a CFO, vice president, controller, accountant, and bookkeeper. She then gave me sample job descriptions and overviews of the day-to-day responsibilities for each one, what kind of background I should be looking for, and the appropriate stage and time to bring them into my company. From this exercise, I realized I needed a controller, so we tailored that job description for my business, sent it out to my network, and made the right hire.

By following this process, you should end up with a clear understanding of the roles and responsibilities associated with the position, as well as a profile of your ideal candidate. You may also learn that you don't really need that position after all. You might start out with one thing in mind, but discover you were on your way to hiring the wrong kind of employee entirely.

Where Should You Start Looking for Help When Making Key Hires?

First, talk to board members, investors, and other advisors to begin getting a feel for the position. Next, talk to people in your network who are already serving in the role for which you plan to hire. Ideally, they should work for companies of similar size and at the same stage.

Ask them about their role, responsibilities, and interactions with management and peers.

Don't Talk to Just Anybody

When you complete your job description and resumes start coming in, whittle them down. Only consider the people who meet all your important requirements. Especially in the first 90 days, you don't have the time, and your investors won't have the patience, for on-the-job training. *Test, test, test.* Take the time to really get to know your candidate. Does she match the job description? What do former employers, co-workers, and customers say about her? Have you and your team spent time with her?

Identify fast, test slow. When possible, start the candidate as an independent contractor instead of a full-time employee. This is a great opportunity to see the candidate in action and watch how she works with your team. You can ensure that the fit is right before pulling the trigger and giving her a full-time job. If it's not possible to start her as a contractor (she is employed full time someplace else, for example), give her a simple assignment to complete during the interview process. It will help you and your team understand how the candidate thinks and executes.

Never Settle

If you do make the hire and it just doesn't work, get rid of her as fast as you can! Hire slow, fire fast, and move on. There are plenty of great people out there. Be patient and wait for the right one to come along.

Document Your Employees' Performance

That way, when they move on you know what they have done well and how their job has changed over time. Once an employee has been in a position for a while, his role usually expands beyond your initial job description; documenting his role as it changes, based on company needs, technology, the growth of your business, and his learned skills, will help you determine your needs when the time comes to make

HIRE A BUSINESS COACH

Think you have all the answers? You might not—and a business coach can help you get a 360-degree view of your business—without the emotional baggage. Keep these things in mind when thinking about hiring a business coach:

☀ *The most important person on your team.* Former executive chairman of Alphabet and Google Eric Schmidt told *Fortune* magazine that the best business advice he ever got was to hire a coach. This is someone who brings out your best by providing support, feedback, and advice. "I initially resented the advice because, after all, I was a CEO," said Schmidt. "I was pretty experienced. Why would I need a coach? Am I doing something wrong? My argument was, how could a coach advise me if I'm the best person in the world at this? But that's not what a coach does. The coach doesn't have to play the sport as well as you do. They have to watch you and get you to be your best."

☀ *Hire someone with no formal or emotional ties to your business.* It is essential that your coach has no formal connection with your business (e.g., as a board member, investor, etc.). This is because a coach needs to be able to provide advice solely for your benefit and not theirs. If your coach has skin in the game, it is impossible for them to provide you with purely objective advice that benefits you alone.

☀ *Don't reinvent the wheel.* Remember, there are two paths to success: You can figure it out on your own through trial and error, which might take more time and money than you have to spare. Or you can find coaches, role models, and advisors with experience and add those people to your team. Listen to what they have to say, and apply the lessons you learn from their experience.

the next hire. Conversely, if a hire doesn't work out, you need to know what went wrong. Did you hire the wrong person? Was the job description unclear?

Repeat the Process as Your Company Breaks Through, Grows, and Scales

In today's fast-moving business cycle, you need to constantly re-evaluate what you need, create new job descriptions, and continue seeking out strong candidates, testing, and hiring the right people at every stage of your business.

It's great if you have people who do a good job, enjoy the culture, and stick around for a while, but always be prepared to replace your staff as needed and add new talent as you grow. As you'll read in the next section, sometimes that talent comes in the form of a partner.

The Perfect Partner?

Think of the greatest partnerships of our time: John Lennon and Paul McCartney, Steve Jobs and Steve Wozniak, Bill Gates and Paul Allen, Ben Cohen and Jerry Greenfield, Bill Hewlett and Dave Packard, Mark Zuckerberg and Eduardo Saverin. More than half ended in divorce, but some lasted a lifetime.

A business partnership is a lot like a marriage. It's a daily commitment, and in the early stages of a new venture, you will probably spend more time with your business partner than with anyone else, including your spouse. In some cases, business partnerships evolve organically from working on an idea from the start, as with Zuckerberg and Saverin or Lennon and McCartney. Often, however, it's a matter of deliberately choosing a partner, and finding that ideal partner, in business or in marriage, is not easy.

Potentially the most important decision you will make in these early days is whether or not to bring in partners to be co-owners alongside you. This could include searching for someone who complements your strengths and weaknesses. It could also include someone who informally brainstormed or created a rough business product or service idea with you. If you choose to go that route, you need to give as much thought to whom you take on as a business partner as you did when you decided whether to marry your spouse.

Some partners seem to have been made for each other. A man named Irv Robbins grew up working in his father's ice cream shop. Irv's brother-in-law, Burton Baskin, also knew ice cream pretty well; he enjoyed making it for the troops while serving as a lieutenant in the navy during World War II.

After the war, Robbins started Snowbird Ice Cream in Glendale, California. Burton Baskin, who had married Robbins' sister Shirley during the war, ran a menswear shop in Chicago. When he and Shirley moved to Los Angeles, Robbins convinced Baskin that selling ice cream would be more fun than selling clothes. Baskin agreed and decided to open his own ice cream store.

As Robbins once told a newspaper reporter: "I was about to sign a lease on a store in Pasadena, and I said [to Burton], 'You take it. You go into the ice cream business and do the same thing I'm doing. And as soon as we have enough stores open, we can open up a little ice cream factory together.'"

So two people in the same family opened two ice cream stores in the same neighborhood. They decided to compete rather than becoming partners because both felt that if they joined forces, the compromises required of a joint business venture might get in the way of their creative ideas.

Over the next few years, however, as each built a successful business, Baskin and Robbins started to recognize there might be significant benefits in banding together rather than competing against each other. They shared a similar vision and had several "aha" moments along the way. They agreed wholeheartedly to sell nothing but ice cream but make lots of different flavors. They also realized they had complementary skill sets, as one excelled in operations, and the other in sales and marketing. Both had networks that, put together, would enable them to reach out farther and faster when trying to grow.

They decided to become partners in their new ice cream venture and selected the order of the names in their new company, Baskin-Robbins, with a coin toss.

They were also early pioneers of one of the great retail concepts of the past century: franchising. This was by far their biggest "aha" moment, which led to their ultimate breakthrough—a chain of stores that has since grown exponentially. Because they were both well-versed in what it meant to operate a store and understood the pride of ownership, they determined that the best way to grow was to find managers who wanted to buy a piece of the business. Baskin-Robbins thus became what is believed to be the first restaurant chain to franchise their outlets. Within five years, they had 40 shops in Southern California; soon after, they trademarked their 31 Flavors concept. Today Baskin-Robbins has more than 2,800 shops in the United States and 5,000 worldwide.

There's no single model for partnerships, but the Baskin-Robbins story is a great example of how, with a shared vision, similar temperaments, complementary skill sets, nonoverlapping networks, and hard work, a partnership can succeed.

If you're thinking about seeking a partner to join your business, be sure to consider these factors:

- ✳ *Vision.* Your potential partner should share your vision or complement it with her own ideas.
- ✳ *Temperament.* Often one partner is a natural leader, while the other is more of a functional expert. Successful enterprises require a balance of both.
- ✳ *Complementary skill sets.* Partnerships work better if your skills diverge. Thus, a great salesperson and a great web developer may make a powerful team. Investors don't like to pay twice for the same position. Expertise in different aspects of business is a plus, and it helps when partners can approach problems from different perspectives.
- ✳ *Nonoverlapping networks.* You each have a network, and the less they overlap the better—enabling you to gain access to the widest range of possible investors, partners, and vendors.

PUT IT ON PAPER NOW!

Like marriages, not all partnerships work out; many end in divorce. That makes a partnership contract—the business equivalent of a prenuptial agreement—essential. Put it in writing and have it reviewed by your attorneys. At the very least, a partnership contract should address the following:

- *Ownership*. Who owns what percentage of the company's equity? It does not have to be a 50/50 split!

- *Financial commitment*. What will each of you put into the company? If more capital is needed, what's expected of you? Is the company financially responsible for contracts and accounts, or are you as individuals?

- *Time commitment*. How much time and effort will each side give to the company? If you're not expected to contribute evenly, then adjustments should be made in terms of ownership and compensation to account for that fact, unless you balance time investment against financial investment.

- *Cash compensation*. How much do you get and when will you get it? Is it based on hitting certain milestones or hours spent? Will compensation be in the form of salary or distributions? Do you have to take cash, or could you exchange it for more shares instead?

- *Expenses*. What's your policy on expenses? How much entertaining can you do? Who writes the reimbursement checks?

- *Voting rights*. If one person has more shares, does she make all the rules? If you've split them 50/50 and don't agree on

---

 PUT IT ON PAPER NOW!, CONTINUED

_____

something, how do you break the tie? Do all big decisions need to be unanimous?

✴ *Vesting schedule*. What happens when one partner leaves the business? Make sure you have a vesting schedule in place (a simple plan that outlines how equity is distributed.)

✴ *Buyout*. Under what circumstances can you sell your interest in the company? What will the terms be? You should agree upfront. Make sure you include a provision that one partner can only sell to another partner if the other partner expressly approves.

✴ *Experience*. You'd be better at your job if you had twice as much experience, right? Partners can pool their years of experience to create a deep well of knowledge and skill to draw from.

The breakthrough moment is one born of recognition. You realize that you both share a vision, your mission and operating methods dovetail nicely, your networks complement each other, and you share a foundational trust. You'll know when you have the right partner: You'll be able to finish his sentences, he'll be able to finish yours, and you'll have the chemistry to form a formidable team.

Outsourcing 101: This Is What You Asked For!

Sometimes you have to go outside your own business to get things done. Say your company wants to build something—a new product, a new website, etc.—and wants to do it fast. Having managed to scrape together enough money to add a couple of full-time employees to your team, you need to launch before your competition catches up. Due to your finite budget and time constraints, the realization dawns in a big "aha" moment: You need to outsource.

Cash-constrained entrepreneurs used to either write off the idea of outsourcing or look overseas to do it. But today, regardless of the size or growth stage of your business, odds are you'll want to outsource some functions. Outsourcing is often a critical part of scaling and growing a new business or product, but it's an area where many people fall down. Like all aspects of business, there's a learning curve.

A few years ago, my big idea was to launch an online marketplace in the health-care industry that would provide seniors with better prices and easier access to a variety of services. I wanted to get something up quickly to test the market response, but all the best developers I contacted were busy on other projects, so I reached out to a few friends, asking what they would do. One told me that to solve a similar problem, he'd hired a firm in India to build his company's website.

I decided to do the same. I contacted the outfit my friend had used, and we had a one-hour call to get acquainted. I shared my idea over the phone, and they responded with an overview of how they would execute my vision. We negotiated a price and signed an agreement. I was in business.

A month later, I got an email with a link to my new website. It was a disaster! The graphic design, the look and feel, the user experience, and the functionality were all wrong. To make matters worse, I had planned to use the site for an investor presentation later that week. Now I would have nothing to show. I was extremely frustrated. I just didn't understand why there was such a big disconnect.

In outsourcing, I had set aside everything I knew about hiring and running a project. I gave the contractor a general project description and expected them to fill in the blanks when I hadn't really thought through everything myself. I put my entire business in their hands instead of just giving them one product or feature as a test. I didn't check in along the way, so the first thing I saw was their finished product. As a result, I had no idea they were on the wrong track. Because I was so vague about what I wanted, they were forced to make decisions for me. While some were good, most went against my vision for the product.

When I asked them to explain themselves, they said, "This is *exactly* what you told us to build!" And, frankly, they were right.

How can you avoid some of the common pitfalls in outsourcing?

- ✳ *Take a disciplined approach.* Too many entrepreneurs abandon everything they have learned about hiring or dealing with consultants. It doesn't matter if you use an overseas developer or someone right across the street. Perhaps because the outsiders won't be full-time employees, or because they'll be on a shorter-term contract, entrepreneurs are less careful about whom they hire. Or maybe, as with my health-care site, they do a poor job of communicating what's really needed, resulting in a big disconnect between what is expected and what is delivered. There can also be language and/or culture barriers that need to be addressed. In addition, since the outsourced employees are not at a nearby desk or workstation, many entrepreneurs don't bother to check on how things are going. This is a big mistake—you must monitor essential steps throughout the process. This way, if your consultant gets off track, or you need to make adjustments to the original project, you can minimize your losses and get the project back on the rails before it's completed.

- ✳ *Hire right.* Do not take anyone's word about the quality of outsourced work. Operate with the same diligence you would use when making full-time hires. Check references to get a better picture of past performance. Agree on a very clear job description and, if possible, run a test by executing a small project together before handing over too much money or control. If you're not getting the results you want, don't waste time; cut your losses and move on. Even if people are referred by valued friends, be careful. I've found that most people are not very careful when referring consultants, who may be between gigs, out of work, or juggling lots of projects. Some are friends of the people making the referral, and the favor being done is for them, not you. Or the referrer knows them socially rather than through a business relationship.

※ *Be absolutely clear.* If you paint an incomplete picture of your intended outcome, you'll get something that only vaguely resembles what you had in mind. Many entrepreneurs have a vision but no concrete idea of how they plan to execute, so they hand the job over to someone else, expecting them to fill in the blanks. With a full-time employee, that can work. Your staff person can fill in the details of your broader vision; that's what you hired them to do, and since you're there, you can still exercise some direct control. They have the benefit of being in the office and getting feedback every day. They are also using your materials and tools and know how your company operates. Most contractors, however, only do what they are told. That's usually a good thing because if they start filling in the blanks, they could take things in an unintended direction.

This also means you need to have a comprehensive understanding of your desired outcome. Write down the details as you think through each step in the process. Pass on your descriptions and expectations.

※ *Make it a dialogue.* Continue the conversation throughout the process. Describe the specific look and feel you're going for. Try to point out comparisons since examples of like products can be used as models to provide a clearer picture. Think of this as similar to the process of building a home; you find houses you like and, ideally, walk your architect through one that is close to what you desire.

If you are developing an ecommerce site, for example, what is the specific user experience you want? What are the steps in the buying process? Can you picture them in your mind? The clearer you can be, the more likely you are to get the result you want. Point them to two or three comparable websites you like that they can use as guides when building your site.

※ *Manage against clear deliverables.* It is important to specify key milestones and delivery dates. That keeps both sides honest and up-to-date and helps ensure the contractor is making progress (you can't manage what you don't measure). Assign strong managers to oversee contractors.

※ *Payment varies.* Sometimes the supplier will want everything upfront, a retainer/kickoff fee, or payment at regular intervals. Many entrepreneurs I work with attempt to pay solely based on performance. But there are risks with this model. If people don't get paid, they fail to pay attention. As a result, the work does not get completed, takes longer than expected, or is of poor quality. Keep in mind, you do not always have to pay in cash. Trading services may have the same value as cash to your vendor. But unless there is an equal exchange in value, a project usually fails.

※ *Take responsibility.* If your first reaction on seeing your product is, *Hey, this isn't what I intended*, it's not the end of the world. That's just another reason we only build one thing at a time. Don't take your disappointment out on your contractor: How much of the fault was yours for not being clear or checking in? You may decide after seeing a prototype that you want something altogether different. Instead of losing your temper, outline what you like and what you would like to improve. Communicate this feedback in a constructive way to your contractor.

Once you've taken care of all your people points, from hiring and delegating to partnering and outsourcing, it's time to focus your energies elsewhere. In the next chapter, we'll talk about creativity and how it can help poise your business for a breakthrough.

unlocking creativity

I f you ask people what's changed the most when you walk into an office today, as opposed to 25 years ago, most people will tell you it's the technology. And while that may be true, there's another significant change that jumps out at you in many companies—the culture.

How many offices 25 years ago had ping-pong tables, foosball tables, basketball hoops, yoga classes, snacks, order-in team lunches, or teams assembled outside for meetings? Work was supposed to be the opposite of fun, but now they are fused together in many company cultures, and it's paying off with increased creativity in the workplace. In this chapter, we zoom in on office cultures and how to use them to unlock creativity and help fuel breakthroughs.

Culture Is King

In the middle of the dotcom boom, the market was hot. Companies were springing up almost overnight, and I was getting calls every day to help them get off the ground.

In 1998, I decided to test the job market with a series of interviews in Silicon Valley. I remember walking into beautiful lobbies with expensive furniture. People were moving around the office on scooters; one company even had a slide in the middle of their workspace. All these companies were trying to sell their cool cultures.

I was about to take a job offer at one of them when a good friend from my days at Quote.com called. He had gone off to become the first employee at Xoom.com, an online community and ecommerce business. They were looking to hire, and he knew I was in the market.

When I arrived for my interview, I found that Xoom's offices were in a beautiful landmark building off California Street in downtown San Francisco. But inside I saw torn green carpet and chipped paint peeling off the walls.

There was no receptionist. Instead, Chris Kitze, the company's founder and CEO, had an office near the front door and was the first to greet people as they walked in.

I soon learned that Chris had a vision, one that became the shared vision of everyone he brought into the company. He hired the best people, gave them access to the resources they needed—and then got out of their way. He was absolutely committed to seeing everyone on the team win: If the company made money, they would, too.

When I talked to the team, there was a pride of ownership that I hadn't seen anywhere else and a common purpose and sense of community that wasn't present in the fancier offices. I could see why many of the people I met at Xoom had followed Chris from one company to another.

The company had money, so I had to ask: "Why the torn carpet and chipped paint?"

"That's not important," Chris said. As an owner, he believed the best use of funds was to invest the money back into the company—into hiring the best people and building a great business. If he did that, the rest would take care of itself.

Unlikely as it may seem, that torn carpet and chipped paint became a symbol of pride everyone shared within the organization. It is part of what got me to join the company, and our team built a great business, took it public, and eventually merged with NBC to create NBCi/ NBC Internet.

The culture didn't stop at pride of ownership. It was also sales-driven. Everyone knew our number-one goal was to generate revenues. Without cash coming in the door, we had no business. Chris set the tone, signing all his emails with the tagline "Go Sell Something." Every day, in every email, those words reinforced the focus, and not just with the salespeople. Everybody in the company came to think of themselves as salespeople, which meant they thought about problems and about the product in a way that was very customer-centric.

Soon after I arrived, I saw how valuable the sales-driven culture could be. Times got tough in the second half of 1998. I returned from a vacation to find the stock market going sideways. As a result, we lost the investment bank we thought would take us public. We were nearly out of cash, but the culture Chris had established saved us. Even though many of our most talented people could easily have found great jobs in those days of the internet boom, nobody jumped ship. We knew we could sell our way out of any problem by generating the cash we needed to get through it.

What are the key factors in creating a great culture for your new business?

✹ *Vision.* Establish a clear and shared vision. That way, everyone runs in the same direction. How do you create a clear vision? Ask yourself this question: *Where do we want to go?*

The answer, written as a *vision statement*, should be a clear description of what you would like to achieve over a specific period of time. This creates a framework for the company and serves as a guide for choosing current and future courses of action. A vision statement is different from a mission statement. A vision statement answers the question *Where do we want to go?* A mission statement answers the question *Why do we exist?* A vision statement is shared within the company. The mission statement is shared with the outside world.

❋ *People.* Invest money in great people. Give them access to all the resources they need. Help them solve problems and remove roadblocks so they can do their jobs. Then get out of their way.

❋ *Commitment to seeing everyone on the team win.* From the top down, everyone must be absolutely committed to seeing the team win. As an entrepreneur (and the person taking on most of the risk), you are certainly entitled to earn more in the long run than anyone else. But shared ownership, structured in the right way, in which everyone knows their role and the impact they are having on results, creates a culture that can't be beat.

That may sound like a simple recipe, but too many companies fall short of it, and, as a result, they don't succeed at the level they should. And getting one or two of these things right isn't enough. As a leader, you need to be committed to all of them. If you do, you will significantly increase your chance of success.

Innovation, Creativity, and Building a Killer Culture

Building a culture of teamwork is only one part of the breakthrough equation. You also need to build a culture of innovation. How do you inspire people to open their minds in a way that unlocks the creativity within your organization and achieves the best results? Let me share a story about how a former colleague in the advertising industry attained legendary status for his ability to unlock creativity (and have a great time in the process).

His goal was to change the way products were marketed in his client's business. He knew everyone in the industry had been talking to their customers for years in the same old way, and he wanted his team to think in entirely fresh ways about their jobs and change the way their product was viewed. To that end, he took the whole creative and account team to Las Vegas.

He told them almost nothing about the trip. The team arrived in Vegas on the first day and partied, going to the best restaurants and clubs and doing some gambling. Some of the crew stayed up all night. No work got done.

On day two, he told his people there was nothing on the agenda other than having more fun. So they did more of the same: eating, drinking, gambling, clubbing.

Day three? Still no agenda. So they went at it again: the best restaurants, the best clubs, a nonstop party.

On day four, his tone changed. Over the past few days, his team had left life, stress, and responsibility behind. Now he wanted something from them. He gathered the group and told them, "We have a mission. We need to change the way products are marketed in this industry. We need to be creative, different, unique. We need to appeal to our client's core young male audience—and they play lots of video games."

While he was speaking, video game systems were being installed in team members' rooms. Each person was given two different games. For the next three days, he instructed, they were not to leave their rooms; their job had become to play video games. They were supposed to think about the whole experience of playing a game, including the graphics, the sounds, and the characters that appealed to the target audience. He wanted them to consider how game designers presented content, how they manipulated the look and feel of the product for the customer. He asked them to pay attention to the scoreboards, the sound effects, and every other little trick the game designers had devised. Most of all, he wanted his team to think about how his client could build upon video game innovations to make their real-life products win over a new generation of customers.

After three glorious days in the sun, his team wasted no time in unleashing their creativity and changing the way people used their client's products. In short, they came up with a unique look that separated them from everyone else in the industry.

Could his team have accomplished the same results playing games back in their New York offices? I doubt it. By taking his team to Las Vegas, he shifted them from *work* mode to *play* mode. He put people together who normally did not have much time to interact in a social setting. The days of partying in Las Vegas brought them closer, building camaraderie and a sense of teamwork. Two guys in a hotel room playing a video game see their jobs differently than they would seated in adjacent offices at their computers.

I'm not saying you need to take your team to Vegas (or anywhere else) for six days. But to foster creative teamwork, you need to find a way to get them out of the office mindset and break down their natural resistance. You need to tap the genius within each of them on a regular basis. Being creative applies to all aspects of your business, from building something cool to breaking down barriers when trying to sell your product.

Part of my former colleague's legacy is that creativity has become an essential part of the culture at his company. They are still thinking outside the box and building great products. You can, too, by following these recommendations:

- ✳ *Get groups together.* When you are launching a new business or product, team members are busy. All of them have their heads down, focused on what they are responsible for. Most of their time is spent working with other people in their department. The creative and technical people don't get much time to interact. There are ways to change that.

    At Xoom we had pizza and beer at 3 p.m. every Friday. People from different groups got to interact in a social environment. As the company grew, those Friday afternoons offered an opportunity to meet new team members, and together we evolved a shared vision of the company. Even if people with different responsibilities looked at the company in different ways, over beer and pizza we came up with some of our most creative—and collaborative—ideas.

- ✳ *Encourage risk.* You win some, you lose some. But people need to be encouraged to take risks and be creative. They need to know that even if something doesn't work, these experiences are all a valuable part of growing a business. The best way to do this is to make lots of small bets. That way, if they try something

OPENING MINDS

Your company culture will set up an atmosphere that either nurtures creativity and innovation (which is vitally important in an increasingly competitive world) or stifles growth. So how do you inspire your team to open their minds and be creative? Here are some ideas:

- ※ *Combine business with pleasure.* Take your workers out to play—to the ballpark, for some hoops, for a brainstorming session over beers. Bring pizza into the office on Friday afternoons, do something different on a regular basis. Taking your employees out of their comfort zones and getting them to interact with one another can open their eyes to new possibilities.

- ※ *Encourage experimentation.* Declare that for a few hours every month, no one is allowed to use their computer or smartphone. In place of screens, issue every employee a notebook and ask them to spend the time writing, sketching, and diagramming their thoughts and ideas on how to improve and innovate the business. The novelty of putting pen to paper will force them to think in a different way. After the exercise, encourage them to tear pages out of their notebooks and post them on a brainstorming wall.

- ※ *Make small bets.* Encourage your team to experiment with side projects. Many of these will fail, but odds are one of them may turn into your next big idea.

- ※ *If something doesn't work, still celebrate that your team took a shot.* People who are the most successful and creative are the ones who take risks. They try, they fail, and they learn from their mistakes. Create a culture where taking a shot at something new is celebrated as long as something is learned.

that doesn't work, there is no concern that it will put the entire operation—or the person's job—at risk.

❀ *Get out regularly.* Do something outside the office at least once a quarter. The activity doesn't have to be expensive or extravagant. You might schedule a happy hour, miniature golf, or go-cart racing. Whatever it is, getting people to engage in a new setting can build relationships and inspire creativity.

Once you've developed a sound business plan; put the right people in place to execute; and created a culture that encourages openness, innovation, and risk-taking, you will have built a great foundation for the business to succeed. You will also be in a great position to move to the next step in the process: raising capital.

What I Learned from Chase Jarvis on Harnessing Your Team's Creativity

Director and media maven Chase Jarvis cofounded CreativeLive back in 2010 to share free creative education with aspiring artists and entrepreneurs worldwide. In addition to his work creating campaigns for Nike, Apple, Red Bull, Starbucks, and other Fortune 100 companies, Chase is widely recognized for creating Best Camera, the world's first photo app to share images to social networks, which kicked off the mobile photography sharing craze. With a global social following, Chase Jarvis and CreativeLive host the world's largest live streaming creative education website, weekly live video podcasts, and *Chase Jarvis Live*, interviewing the world's best creators, innovators, and entrepreneurs.

I asked Chase if he thought creativity was something you're born with or if it is something that can be taught. Chase explained that he believes everyone is creative: "One of the things that differentiates us from other species on the planet is that we can put unlikely, disconnected things together to form something new and useful. We all have creativity inside us. One of the things that I've turned to recently is really projecting the idea of how we can make the world a more creative place. When it comes to sparking someone's creativity, I think there are a handful of things that can be done. First of all, it's important to recognize that creativity isn't some gift that's anointed. It is a process of putting something out there, of discovery and rediscovery. The act of creating, whether it's a photograph each day or creating music, rewires your brain to be able to create new solutions to other problems," says Chase, who also points out that the concept of creativity underpins the solution to every problem the world will ever face, from world hunger to climate change.

"If you think about creativity with a capital C rather than just the creative arts, such as photography, painting, drawing, etc., you start to understand that this is a really, really critical aspect of our culture. It is a way of thinking and creating solutions to all sorts of problems. This is something we should look to shepherd into each new generation so that we get the benefit of creativity from everybody. We should encourage creative thinking," adds Chase.

So how can we bring creativity to the workplace? How can we get more out of ourselves and our teams? Chase suggests a few ways to unlock your creativity. I've edited these down for length, but you can check out the full list at www.chasejarvis.com/blog/12-secrets-for-unlocking-your-most-creative-work/. They are:

❀ *Keep a schedule.* For example, Chase says this could mean "taking photos every day, writing first thing every morning, [putting] headphones on and painting from midnight to 2 A.M. every day . . . whatever works for you." But the more consistently you can schedule creative time, the better.

❀ *Meditation.* Chase asks, "You've heard athletes like Michael Jordan talk about seeing the game around them develop seemingly in slow motion?" Meditation allows you to slow down. Things seem infinitely more manageable and less likely to throw you off your game.

❀ *Regular exercise.* Chase says, "Just being active contributes hugely to my ability to kick ass as a professional artist. Staying fit and getting your heart rate up during the day has even been shown in studies to increase creative connections and cognitive ability." It turns out that even just a daily ten-minute run can change your mindset.

✸ *Get plenty of sleep.* The significance of sleep has only recently been recognized as vitally important. Chase says, "Sleep is like the wonder drug." It plays a major role in how well you function in your daily life. Don't underestimate the need for sleep.

✸ *Take breaks during your day—and take a walk.* "It's been shown scientifically that there is a link between taking walks and creative boosts," Chase tells me. He says the key is to turn your phone off and do nothing but observe. Look at the light, other people, and the world around you.

✸ *Get away.* "I try to take small steps far away from work as often as possible. I'll hit up the family cabin for a night, take a road trip, get out on our little boat for a couple of hours, etc." Chase advises. "Get some separation if you can, even if it's just for a few hours."

✸ *Read more books.* "I got into the habit of reading a lot about ten years ago. And I haven't stopped," Chase says, because books provide inspiration from others. Often, reading can be enjoyable and quite beneficial for discovering new ideas.

✸ *Hack your learning style.* Become an avid fan of self-learning. There are so many places at your fingertips to gather information: from books, webinars, podcasts, and online courses to simply experimenting with the things that interest you. "I got my start by teaching myself how to do what I do, and to this day, I'm an avid proponent of self-learning." Chase says he loves the challenge since, "learning is not passive. It's insanely active."

✸ *Visualize success.* "One of the best ways to stay creatively pumped is to do some visualization. It doesn't have to be rigorous." Chase advises that the key is to do so with intention. Visualize each step toward your goal and think of what you want the end product to look like or what the end result of your efforts will feel like. Your specific dream isn't really the point, Chase says: "it's about believing you can be successful at whatever you choose to imagine."

✸ *Immerse yourself in various forms of art.* "This is a big one," Chase admits. He recommends getting perspectives from creative people and their works, from painting to dance to photography to music or theater. Exploring the creative world can also take you outside your comfort zone and help you be different, if not better, at what you do.

※ *Make things every day.* "Science says it, and I experience it . . . Your brain pushes into new neural pathways as you create. Quite literally, creativity creates more creativity. The rote act of doing your craft —or *any* craft—is a primer for more creative mojo. Do not underestimate this."

※ *Find adventure.* Adventure can be stimulating. Chase says, "Putting yourself in a situation where you're being stimulated and taking information IN is a critical mode."

※ *Find quiet.* "Great ideas do not always come in the heat of battle," Chase says. They often come when your mind is relaxed. "This is why your best ideas often happen in the shower, right before going to bed, or when you wake up early . . . because there's less noise in your world at that moment."

While there are many people who allow their creativity to flow freely, there are even more who are intimidated by creatives and convinced that they do not have the "creative gift." But, as Chase Jarvis shows us, there are ways in which we can unlock, open the door, and break through to our own creative thought process. We just need to explore the possibilities. And while not everyone will find the time or energy to devote to their creative side, just recognizing and acknowledging it will add another tool to your repertoire. It will give you more angles from which to approach projects and even problems that arise inside and outside business, including the problem of work/life balance, which we'll address in the next section.

Creating Your Own Work-Life Balance

Courtney Brown is the CEO of Cents of Style, a popular fashion retailer that is a 100 percent online women's fashion brand, selling everything from shoes to apparel. Here's what's cool: The company is

✳ BEARD CLUB CULTURE

Chris Stoikos is a serial entrepreneur and founder of The Beard Club, which sells the must-have grooming oils and other products for today's beard culture. After starting and then selling a business right after school, he moved to Los Angeles, where he truly earned the title of serial entrepreneur, starting one business after another. His toolbox alternative, Coolbox, landed him on *Shark Tank*, and The Beard Club (originally dubbed The Dollar Beard Club) has seen meteoric growth since it launched in 2015. In the first 14 months of business, the company took in more than $14 million in revenue.

The big reason for The Beard Club's success is the culture Chris and his team created, and they work hard to protect it. As Chris describes it, "It's body, mind, business all wrapped into one." Chris also believes that a company is only as healthy as its unhealthiest employee. "Everyone needs to be taking care of themselves on every single level in order to be productive to the best of their ability every single day," he says.

The culture is what launched The Beard Club. "It's a cool culture. It feels good. You're always energized. The energy within the office is phenomenal. Everyone is always hyped, vibing on super high frequencies," explains Chris.

So how did they build this culture?

- ✳ When they first meet job candidates, they don't just want to know their prior work experience, but also what they do outside the office. "We want to know how they take care of themselves and the kinds of food they put in their bodies," says Chris.

BEARD CLUB CULTURE, CONTINUED

❋ They want to know how much these people read and the kind of books they read. "For us, not reading consistently is a real problem. You need to fill yourself with knowledge from books. People put their entire life into a book that takes you 6-8 hours to consume. You will find amazing amounts of stuff that people put in there in terms of their little nuggets that you can pull from and instantly apply to your life and to business," explains Chris.

❋ Chris and his team do not want them to sweat the small stuff. "I used to compare gas prices to save a few cents here or there. But think of how much time I lost on something that had such a relatively small impact on my life," explains Chris, who believes that sweating the small stuff gets in the way of discovering that big breakthrough that could make the difference in your life or business.

largely staffed by a team of talented stay-at-home moms. Courtney has not only succeeded in her mission to empower more women but has also created a multimillion-dollar company to boot.

From stay-at-home mom to CEO, Courtney gives a new meaning to the term "work-life balance." "At Cents of Style, we strive to facilitate balance with our employees by allowing for flexible work hours and locations. Everything from our customer care to our fulfillment of packages is done by women in the time that they have, often the odd hours, early mornings, and late evenings. And we put faith in our employees that they are self-disciplined and motivated enough to get their tasks done when they have the time," Courtney says.

What some companies would consider an inconvenience, Courtney views as her most valuable asset, and the results show.

With three straight years of 200 percent to 300 percent growth, Courtney has proved that success in business and family are not mutually exclusive.

It started when Courtney was a stay-at-home mom. "We had just adopted our first child, and after years of infertility and the adoption struggle, I thought, 'You know what? I have it. I have this beautiful, precious daughter and I'm set. I'm going to be a Utah Pinterest mom,'" Courtney says. "I got into it and I thought, 'This is wonderful, but I need something else where I feel like I'm contributing to my family, my community, the world, and myself.' I even hesitate to say that now, ten years later, because women get super uncomfortable when other women admit that perhaps motherhood isn't the end-all. Cents of Style came from that place."

As is the case with many small businesses, it began with the people closest to Courtney. In this case, she was surrounded by other stay-at-home moms. "As we grew in scale and found problems, we found ways to use this incredibly underutilized, talented workforce in the hours that they had available to scale our business," says Courtney.

Rather than working on the traditional 9-to-5 schedule, they worked with the time that stay-at-home moms have. This means starting work after the kids leave for school and working most of the day until the kids come home or get picked up after school. "Then we get back on at 9 and we work until midnight. We live in a digital age. We have technology that allows for all this. We have harnessed incredible software and incredible companies to allow us to connect remotely. Of course, it has huge challenges, but I am such a believer in this that we will work through those challenges," explains Courtney. It's not about how much time they spend at their desks; it's about getting the job done.

"Because we live in a culture where women's roles are so incredibly traditional, there are certain jobs and certain roles and responsibilities that are absolutely acceptable. If I chose to be a nurse or a schoolteacher, even a blogger or influencer, all those roles are acceptable. But I decided, you know what, I want to become the

CEO of a fashion company, and do it from home nonetheless," says Courtney about her "unconventional" choice.

"What if you could harness the power of that stay-at-home mom who's an incredible multitasker? Who yearns for something? Even if it's ten hours a week. Something she can put her name on and say, 'That's mine.' But who also doesn't want to sacrifice her home life and family. That is the workforce model we have built our business on," concludes Courtney, who recalls one year's "aha" moment coming in the span of 72 hours when the store did 20 percent of its annual sales.

"We had an item go viral," says Courtney, adding that she was terrified, but also that "the experience pushed me and required me to go beyond what I thought I was capable of. It also taught me that not only could I do this, but that what I was doing was needed and wanted. We could be a company of women who chose both career and motherhood. We would do both well and stand in the face of the myth of balance, leading lives bold and full."

Courtney's creative approach to solving the problem of work-life balance ultimately became the heart of her company, boosting the morale of her employees and creating a value-based culture that set the tone for others like it. Her breakthrough story combines two things that are vital in today's entrepreneurial environment: creativity and culture. Forget conventional wisdom. Forget the roles society wants to box you into. Ask yourself, "What do I want? What do I value? What do I have to do in order to achieve it?" Remember:

✳ Just because corporate America says you should work from 9 to 5 doesn't mean that has to apply to your business. The way Courtney sees things, it's not about how much time a person is sitting at their desk; it's about what they get done.

✳ When working with your remote workforce, be absolutely clear on what needs to be accomplished and when the project is due; then manage against those objectives.

✳ Leverage technology to connect with your team, manage goals, and set everyone up to win.

As we see in Courtney's story, answering these questions is vital to determining how you craft your approach to balance—both for yourself and those who work for you.

How to Have a Killer Culture

Let's talk a bit more about the role of creativity in corporate culture. Having heard about the success my good friend Sam Khorramian was having with Big Block Realty, one of the fastest-growing real estate companies in the United States, I decided to sit down with Sam and talk about his unique approach to real estate. Big Block had recently landed at number 31 on the 2017 Inc. 500 and had been named San Diego's best real estate brokerage four years running, so I knew Sam had to be doing something special . . . and I was right. Their model goes against conventional wisdom, which has turned into a financial windfall for the company.

As we talked, Sam explained that, for him, the key to success was focusing on creating the best work culture imaginable and putting his agents first. To provide agents with a full commission, Sam charges agents a flat fee of $300 per month or $3,000 yearly. Agents are not asked to then pay out to the firm from what they earn in sales. With a 100 percent commission on each sale, it's no surprise his agents love working for Sam.

But he soon realized it was more than just the commission that made the business work. After all, if he had given his agents a 100 percent commission and then dropped the ball on support, they would have been out the door as fast as they came in. With that in mind, Sam created an environment that gave the agents all the support they needed as fast as they wanted it.

Sam had his "aha" moment when he realized who his real customers were. "Our customers were no longer real estate buyers. They were the realtors themselves," says Sam. If they could meet the agents' needs and make them happy, the agents would take great care of the buyers.

"We started a broker hotline, which meant if the agents had any questions at any time, they could call. There would be real brokers in our office there to answer their questions. Then we came up with agent concierge, which is a service that provides support for agents when they need it," explains Sam. "For us, it's really just the idea of delivering the 'yes' whenever they ask, and we continue to do that. It's worked really well for us."

The most important steps to creating a killer culture in your business are:

✴ Creating an environment that everyone involved wants to be a part of
✴ Making sure the environment doesn't feel like every other business
✴ Making work more fun

When you walk into Big Block Realty, there's a foosball table, a direct reflection of the founders and the energy they infuse into the business.

"I think creating a welcoming, fun environment comes out of the basics. People like to have fun. People like to know that other people care about them. People like to know that when they need help, someone's gonna be there to help them," says Sam, who points out that it wasn't the 100 percent commission that got 600 agents to join the company—it was the culture. "If we only offered a traditional split but backed it up with love, a great culture, and great service, I think we could have similar growth, because people will pay when there's value," explains Sam.

"We learned that if you take care of the customer, actually love the customer, give them something they're proud to be a part of, then that's going to help you grow organically. That's what you're seeing from some of these big platforms, the social platforms. They blow up because they give people something they want to be a part of. Then they tell their friends, they tell their colleagues, they tell their parents, and that's what we've created here at Big Block."

A couple of other things Sam did at Big Block came from some of the concepts that online shoe retailer Zappos used to launch its culture. When creating their agent concierge, they decided to expand on the great customer service model Zappos used. "When we're recruiting agents and getting them to join our company, we tell them, 'Look, we wake up every day to work for you. Our job is to make your life as a realtor better and more enjoyable, and give you a better experience than you've had. So regardless of what you want, short of us paying your bills, you can call agent concierge and ask them for what you need, and the answer is always yes. If you want us to make reservations for you and your clients somewhere: yes. If you're running late and need some stuff printed so you can grab it quickly on your way through the office: yes,'" Sam says.

Of course, not every culture needs foosball tables. For some it's a weekly yoga class, after-work get-togethers, a lounge, or any other amenities that can take the people in your office out of the business experience for a little while and let them clear their heads. Your company's culture needs to fit the people, the brand, and the personality you want to express to your employees—which will then be passed along to your clients.

Creative Accountability: Finally, an Award for Screwing Up

I am always fascinated by my mentor and business partner, David Meltzer.

The 1996 movie *Jerry Maguire* was based on a sports agent named Leigh Steinberg. In 2008, Leigh hired Dave to be his CEO; while there, he helped negotiate over a billion dollars in deals. Today, Meltzer is the CEO of Sports 1 Marketing, a global sports and entertainment marketing agency he founded along with NFL Hall of Famer Warren Moon. Dave is also a co-host of the hit TV show *Elevator Pitch* and has a top-trending business podcast on iTunes.

Like other uber-successful people, Dave just does things a little differently. One of my favorite examples is the Stevie.

Every Monday morning, the team at Sports 1 Marketing (of which I am a part) holds a contest. Each employee shares with the office the biggest mistake they made during the previous week. We look for truly epic screwups! We call this award the "Stevie." Why? Because early on a guy named Stevie had a monumental mistake that was so big we named the award after him.

We do this exercise because the number-one problem people have in business is accountability. When they make a mistake, they use excuses to shift blame and justify their actions. What our culture does is encourage people to get better. We simply need to ask ourselves two important questions: What did I do, and what am I supposed to learn from it?

To win the Stevie Award, you not only need to share the mistake, but also which of the four core principles we teach at Sports 1 Marketing applies to that mistake. Whether their error was related to a lack of gratitude, empathy, accountability, or effective communication, Dave wants everybody in his organization to take responsibility for their slipups. He wants them to know that mistakes will happen and learn from them. He even rewards the biggest mistake each week with a bonus!

This is a great opportunity to reinforce your company's core principles and develop a culture of accountability. It creates a highly efficient and accountable culture. It also makes people recognize that it's OK to make mistakes. As a result, people are less afraid to take measured risks. They understand that if they screw up or fail, it's not the end of the world. The faster we can shine a light on their error, the faster we can grow from it, resolve it, and move forward. The recognition of mistakes and failure can also encourage creativity: If people are too scared to take risks, they will not dare to be very creative.

Success requires a willingness to take risks and make mistakes, but just as important, to shine a light on what didn't work. Sunlight is the best disinfectant. It helps you attack problems and create solutions. In Dave's "killer culture," people don't fear failure: They embrace it, they share it, and everyone can learn from it. They even grow from it. The result is a company that grows faster than they could have imagined.

raising capital

As an entrepreneur, I constantly find myself in conversations about raising money—people want to know where to look for funds and how to get them. But the idea that you must raise a ton of money to start a business is just not true. In this chapter, I talk about bootstrapping your resources and how to make things work on a small budget. Then I move on to the all-important art of getting funding. Whether you're seeking thousands or millions of dollars, you need to be prepared. This is crucial: The reason most people don't get funded isn't that they have a bad idea—it's that they don't know the right steps to take.

Bootstrapping 101

Most entrepreneurs start businesses from the same place: *nowhere.* Despite beginning with little or nothing, the best of them bootstrap, and through their own sheer will, hard work, and effort, they find ways to make things happen and pull together the things their business needs to launch.

As an entrepreneur, you have to keep pushing your business forward, largely by yourself. You have to take whatever you have of value and leverage, share, or swap it. That often means that founders of startups forgo paychecks, offer their services as consultants, give away products and services for nothing, and do lots of moonlighting, at least until they can generate enough cash flow to survive.

Intrapreneurs also bootstrap by adding the new project to their existing responsibilities. They effectively take on twice as much work with no additional pay to get their idea off the ground. They become masters of juggling not only their core duties, but also their new project responsibilities. Since management does not want to see either fail, intrapreneurs risk their job security as well as their reputations. Only once the new project hits certain milestones can the intrapreneur hope to get more resources and (maybe) a bigger paycheck.

Bootstrapping is more vital today than ever. Many investors are reluctant to put money into a venture until it is generating positive cash flow. They have far less appetite for risk than they did before the global economic crash of 2008, meaning most won't reach into their pockets until you've taken your business beyond the early stages and proven your model. As a result, new business owners have to bootstrap longer than in the past.

My first exposure to bootstrapping came compliments of Tony Robbins. I wasn't raising money for a new business, but it taught me how to be scrappy. I was 21 years old, and my title was field sales representative and national sales trainer. As an advance man responsible for filling the seats in Robbins' seminars, I would travel to a city where Tony was to speak, along with a handful of my peers, to promote his events. The primary program I sold was called "The Power to Influence," and it focused on sales and persuasion.

Before our team went into the field, we immersed ourselves in the content. We had to be passionate about Tony's message because our task was to drum up interest and sell tickets for his programs. We spoke to small groups, sometimes five times a day, seven days a week. We'd share a few program highlights, talk about what people would gain by attending, and try to sell as many tickets as we could to rack up sales commissions.

In retrospect, this experience not only taught me about sales and persuasion but also a bunch of survival skills that would later come in handy as an entrepreneur.

I spent two to three months at a time in cities like Detroit, Toronto, Vancouver, Boston, Houston, Seattle, and Los Angeles. No one on the team collected a salary, and we didn't have expense accounts. We paid for our own rental cars. Nobody even had a phone! Basically, we were given a plane ticket, a place to stay, and a couple of initial bookings. After that, we had to live off the land.

We did, however, have something valuable in our pockets: Our currency was tickets to Robbins' events. We learned how to barter tickets and our own speaking and coaching skills in return for what we needed. This was a key moment in my business education, a sort of Bootstrapping 101.

Here's how it worked. When we got off the plane in a new city, we would decide who was going out to search for what. The first priority was always cars and cell phones. We would split up and go to car dealerships, where we would talk general managers into giving us cars for a couple of months. In exchange, we'd provide in-house training and give their entire sales team tickets to one of Tony's events. We did the same thing at cell phone stores and gyms. One guy even bartered for time at a tanning salon.

Like a pack of lions, we had to work together as a team. And—aha!—we learned that as long as you have persistence and a deep supply of something with perceived value (in our case, Tony Robbins tickets), you can catch all the antelope (or cars and phones) you need to survive.

That same scrappiness applies to bootstrapping your own business. You have to be creative and master the art of trading with others. It's about offering value for value.

That's what I learned to do while working for Tony—identify my inherent value and leverage it to grow the business. Think a bit about how to identify your own value and how you can leverage that as you ramp up your ability to bootstrap. Here are a few questions to ask yourself before you get started:

- ❋ *Where do you need help?* What do you need that you can't afford to go out and buy? Do you need a website, design, marketing, social media, accounting, or legal advice? What will each of these things cost?
- ❋ *What's your currency?* What do you have of value to offer? Can you provide consulting help with their business, introduce them to key prospects, or provide another service they need? What expertise do you have that can benefit the other person?
- ❋ *Who are your trading partners?* Take a close look at your network and identify other entrepreneurs you can barter and partner with. What you will find is a trading economy you probably did not know existed. And don't be afraid to go to prospective customers. Often they will be willing to give you access to certain resources in exchange for being first in line when your new product or service is ready.
- ❋ *Where's the cheap labor?* Even if you can't afford to pay talented people to work for you yet, there are many people out there who will work for free in exchange for a promise of future compensation or even talented interns who work for college credits and some work experience on their resumes. These could include people who are out of work, in transition, or trying to find something part time. The opportunity to get in on the ground floor of something they believe in may be enough to get them started.

Create a list of the products and services you need most. Identify which people in your network offer those services. Then see if you can trade services with them in a way that helps both parties move their businesses forward. If you can do that, you've just broken through the bootstrapping ice!

CANNIBAL WOMEN IN THE AVOCADO JUNGLE OF DEATH

Like it or not, a new business sometimes requires a capital investment beyond the bounds of bootstrapping. Unfortunately, money, as the saying goes, doesn't grow on trees (even if, in reading about some startups, its seems like people can't give it away fast enough).

The hard facts are that less than a third of all businesses ever take any outside capital, and, of the ones that do, most have typically been in business for three years or more. Making your pitch to a series of potential money sources can feel like a distraction while you're trying to run a business. It will involve working your network, setting up meetings, putting together materials, following up, and closing the sale.

Raising capital takes persistence, whether you are an entrepreneur pitching to individual investors or an intrapreneur working inside to build consensus for funding within a big organization. Most investors probably won't agree to put money into your company, but that doesn't mean you stop looking. Go into each meeting with the objective of listening to all the feedback the investors have to offer and applying what you learn going forward. For example, your investors may have excellent ideas on how to improve your pitch, find additional revenue, reduce your startup costs, separate yourself from the competition, and find strategic partners. By listening and following good advice, you're bringing yourself one step closer to finding the finances you need.

I've always been inspired by my friend Gary Goldstein, whose story is a classic tale of persistence in. Gary started out as a

CANNIBAL WOMEN, CONTINUED

criminal defense attorney, but his real passion was storytelling. So, he decided to move to Hollywood and launch a career in the entertainment business. There, he managed young writers and directors before making the decision to produce films. Gary went on to produce some of the top box office hits of all time, including *Pretty Woman*, the highest grossing live action film in Disney's history and a beloved classic. But what stands out most for me is the way Gary launched his filmmaking career and the lessons it provides all of us.

When Gary decided to produce his first film, he didn't have all the money and resources he needed. He teamed with an up-and-coming writer. The two bootstrapped as long as they could. Then it was time to go and raise outside capital to get his film made. That part certainly wasn't easy, but Gary never thought about quitting. Making a film was his passion and, as he told me, "you have to chase your passion like it's the last bus of the night." Through Gary's persistence, and pig-headed determination, he raised $200,000 to make the film. It was titled *Cannibal Women In The Avocado Jungle of Death*.

In addition to having a tight budget, a scheduling conflict left Gary and his partner with only four weeks from the day they closed their financing to cast, film, edit, and deliver the final product. That may sound impossible to us, but it wasn't to Gary. He was committed to making this project a success. He did not believe in waiting for the "perfect time" or "perfect circumstances" to get started. Instead, he believed that being in the game was more important than waiting around on the sidelines. With that mentality, he devised a plan to spend two weeks preparing the project and two weeks for everything else.

CANNIBAL WOMEN, CONTINUED

But at the end of the first week, Gary was up against a real problem. The film had no cast and crew; it was just Gary and his writer. Instead of shutting down, Gary persevered because he believed that "success is far more likely when you choose persistence over doubt and inaction."

Gary and his writer hit the phones and called all their friends, and asked them to call *their* friends and invited them out to the set. They decided if someone showed up that dressed well, they were in charge of wardrobe. If someone had a camera, they would be the cinematographer. Casting consisted of seeing who would arrive on the set each day. This was guerilla filmmaking at its best. Somehow, that film, which ended up starring Shannon Tweed and Bill Maher, came together. It ran on cable for the next 15 years. The experience was successful enough that Gary was able to dissolve his management firm and become a full-time independent producer.

I asked Gary what he learned most from that experience. "You don't have to be a master at something to achieve something worthwhile," he said. "Just by sheer will and stubbornness you can accomplish anything you set out to do."

Where Will the Money Come From?

So where is all this money going to come from? If you want to go beyond basic bootstrapping, who's going to invest in you? There are several options when launching a new business or product. To help save time and get you to market faster, the following is a list of capital resources. To get started, put most of your energy into the source that best matches your business goals, stage, and network.

✳ *Friends and family.* If you are launching a new business or taking a new product to market, those closest to you are usually
the first source of capital you should consider. Your friends,
family, or company may make funds available even when your
new venture is still in the idea phase, while other professionally managed sources of capital may not be an option before you
have a product or prototype to show. Most friend and family
investments range from $1,000 to $25,000, and they may be in
the form of equity (ownership in the company) or debt (a simple
loan). Even though these are people you know and trust, you
should still hire an attorney and put everything in writing so
there are no conflicts down the road.

✳ *Angel investors.* Angels are wealthy individuals, often are experienced or retired entrepreneurs willing to help crystallize your
vision and business strategy, and may invest up to $250,000 in
new businesses they believe will succeed. Angels typically work
as individuals or through groups with other angel investors,
putting money into startups and early stage businesses. Apart
from monetary investments, they can also be great coaches for
the enterprises in which they invest. Their investment can be
equity or debt, and is typically in industries with which they are
familiar. Angels can be a great resource when it comes to bringing in new investors and strategic partners for additional rounds
of financing.

✳ *Crowdfunding.* This source makes use of online and off-line networks to attract informal investors (and sometimes professional
ones) to buy into an idea or company. The concept of crowdfunding is to raise small amounts of money from a large number
of individuals. There are many forms of crowdfunding, including donation-based (meaning donors don't get a share in the
company but receive some item or perk as a "thank you"). There
is also equity-based (when the crowd invests in an early-stage
private company in exchange for shares), revenue-sharing (when
the crowd's loan is paid back by sharing a percentage of revenue
until a target return is reached), and peer-to-peer lending (when

a company receives a form of debt financing without use of an official financial institution as intermediary).

✳ *Venture capital firms.* Venture capital is almost always provided in exchange for equity in your company. VCs are very sophisticated investors. Although they have a financial focus, many can also provide significant managerial, operational, and technical expertise. In return, they expect a bigger portion of equity, and sometimes even a controlling interest (meaning they assume more than half the equity and/or decision-making power in your company). Average investments from venture capital firms begin around $250,000 and go up to millions of dollars. They are typically looking to invest in businesses with a proven model and operating history.

Much to the surprise of many new entrepreneurs, the breakthrough does not come when you receive your funding. It comes when you truly understand how to *get* funding. Once you become adept at doing the necessary research, master the presentation, and know how to handle the follow-up (or callback), the lightbulb will go on, and you'll have that "aha" moment.

The "Big Meeting" Mentality: Winning Over Investors

When you've hung out with company founders as much as I have, you've inevitably heard the following line: "I have a big meeting coming up." Because the entrepreneur got the appointment, he's sure the investor has real interest. His growing enthusiasm leads him to think the money is in the bag—only to come back from the "big meeting" empty-handed and deeply disappointed.

For the typical entrepreneur, raising money is an entirely foreign experience. Given that you're dealing with financial professionals who have been doing this for years, your inexperience puts you at an immediate disadvantage. We need to get you up to speed quickly; there is no time to waste. Start by doing your homework to make sure you get in front of the right people.

Investors have a mandate to make money, and typically they have a specific formula to mitigate their risk. That makes it imperative that you understand their priorities. Some things for you to consider include:

✳ *Background.* What companies have your potential investors worked for? What's their functional expertise? Often they will only invest in what they know. For example, if they spent their career in real estate, they will have a deep understanding of how to analyze the true value of a real estate deal, how to get involved in ways that help the entrepreneur, and how to step in and help turn the ship around if things go sideways. Knowing the background of your potential investors also helps you customize your sales pitch—you want to appeal to their interests and address any possible concerns head-on if you want them to invest.

✳ *Previous investments.* Know the kinds of companies they have invested in before (for example, that real estate investor probably won't invest in software unless it is a program that helps realtors). If you pitch someone on a consumer internet business and they only invest in energy, it won't matter how good your idea is—she will likely pass. Also be aware that if you are dealing with a venture capital or professional investment firm, you could be in the right place but talking to the wrong person. Find out which individual investor inside that firm matches your deal best.

✳ *Stage of investment.* Does your potential investor favor seed or early stage companies, have a minimum revenue criteria, or have other key requirements before they step into a deal? If you present your business at a stage other than your investor's sweet spot, they probably won't be interested. That is true with both individuals and large firms. Keep in mind that many professional investors raise money from other investors with a mandate to invest in a specific type and stage of company.

✳ *Size of investment.* Ten thousand dollars? A hundred thousand? A million? Be certain that what you're asking is in line with what they put into individual investments, and explain why you need the amount you are requesting and what you plan to do with it.

❈ *Expected return.* Are they looking to get back two, five, or ten times the amount that they invest? Make sure your expectations and theirs mesh.

❈ *Investment horizon.* When do they expect a return on their capital? What time frame do they have in mind: to get in and out within one, three, or five years? Everyone needs to have the same understanding on day one.

How do you find these things out? Again, do your homework. If you can't find an answer to a specific question, just ask. Asking good questions will help you establish yourself as a professional and someone who respects a potential investor's time, which earns you bonus points as well.

Knowing these things in advance will help you operate with speed and efficiency, saving you valuable time and money. It will help ensure every meeting is with a qualified investor. That way your "big meeting" will be exactly what you expect.

One last thing: *Believe.*

Raising money is no small task. No matter how good you and your product are, it is a time-consuming and labor-intensive process. But when you've done your homework and go into a meeting with the right person, you will know that, at some level, they really want to invest. Their mandate is to find companies just like yours. They are hoping that you are the person who can deliver what they want. In fact, they probably want this meeting more than you do!

So be prepared, practice, and then get in front of the right people—and execute once you are there.

How to Keep Your Deal Moving Forward

Having spent years raising capital and investing in other people's businesses, I've been on both sides of the table. As a result, I've had more than a few "aha" moments watching deals go from "we're getting funded" to "the deal is dead." I've learned firsthand what to do—and what not to do—when presenting to an investor. There are certain mistakes you can make that will kill a potential investor's interest and send you packing right out the door.

I find entrepreneurs get locked in during their fundraising period. They spend so much time on their presentation and materials and work so hard that they miss the mark. If they'd just take a breath, they might realize that a few basic tenets will help them reach that fundraising goal. The breakthrough occurs when they step back and recognize a few core principles.

You need to avoid the mistakes below to keep the fundraising process moving forward and, ultimately, get the results you want. This, by the way, is true for new entrepreneurs seeking startup funding and for seasoned entrepreneurs meeting with investors and strategic partners about growing and scaling their business.

❀ *"We've worked at some of the largest companies in our industry."* Investors fund people, not ideas. They want founders and management who have deep domain experience. In the early stages, they like a background that includes running fast-paced, resource-constrained environments, and thus might see it as risky if, for example, someone from a Fortune 500 company were seeking to launch a startup or a technology pro shifted into real estate. If your background is not in alignment with the stage of your company, it can be difficult getting funded. Often, a founder will need to add complementary team members that match the company's current stage so investors know the right people are in the right positions at the right time.

❀ *"We are first to market."* As an entrepreneur, you may think this is a huge advantage, but such a claim can actually work against you. Typically, being first to market means you take on all the risk. You'll spend lots of time educating customers, and to an investor, that says *expensive*. Many would rather ride in the wake of the first company. Therefore, if you have something brand-new, find some comparables. Give investors a framework so your idea doesn't sound so abstract. Pull from another industry if necessary, and make sure you illustrate how your business solves a real problem.

❀ *"We have no competition."* This claim may be the most common mistake made by entrepreneurs raising capital. On hearing it, an experienced investor will roll his eyes and assume one of three things: that you are lying, that you don't really know your market, or that others before you have tried and failed. He will probably then toss your proposal straight in the trash. What you should do is find competitors—anyone out there who can take a dollar out of your pocket—and show how and why your product or service is better than theirs.

✳ *"We need a million dollars to get started."* Investors will do everything they can to minimize their risk every step of the way. They will want to know whether you can start with something smaller and more focused. Can you get to market faster and get enough feedback to get a sense that you're heading in the right direction *before* investing that million dollars into a product no one may want? Before asking for money, make sure you not only know how much you need, but are also able to explain how and why you reached that number.

✳ *"If I build it, they will come."* Maybe that works in movies, but I've never seen it work anywhere else—and neither has your investor. It takes time, effort, and money to build a customer base. For this reason, it's a good idea to get people using the product, ideally paying customers, before you ask investors for money. For example, you may be able to generate interest online, take pre-orders for your product, and get real-time feedback. You also want to have a solid sales plan explaining how you will generate interest, your cost for acquiring a customer, and who will execute this plan.

✳ *"We have more features than anyone else."* Who cares? An investor would rather know that you have one functioning feature that your target customer likes than ten untested ones. Do your research; show the investor what people actually want. One feature that hundreds of people are asking for is far more valuable than ten features that nobody cares about.

✳ *"The big companies are too big or slow to compete."* Not if they are serious, they aren't. If a market is big enough, there is a good chance someone in the industry is sniffing around. If they decide there is an opportunity, they have the resources in place to jump in. This doesn't mean they will succeed, but they could be disruptive. If they haven't entered already, it could be because they think the market is too small.

As an entrepreneur, you need to recognize that the larger, established players could jump in at any time. Be prepared to address it since the investors know this, and based on the product and pitch, they will be asking themselves how the big companies will react.

✳ *"We do lots of things well."* I always ask entrepreneurs what *one thing* their business is great at, the one thing that separates it from everyone else. Most of the time, they don't know. Instead, they rattle off three or four things they think the company does *equally* well. Saying you are great at everything tells the investor you don't really understand what business you are in. We're living in a niche-driven world. When we try to build for everyone, we connect with no one. Before you meet with any investors, know your single biggest strength: that one thing you do better than anyone else. That is the foundation your business will build upon.

✳ *"We do that, too."* If, during a meeting, an investor suggests additional products or services that might be a good fit or points to things the competition is doing, don't say, "Oh, we're on that, too." That communicates a terrible lack of focus. Instead, acknowledge that her suggestions may be a great addition down the road, but for now you're focused on this one thing.

✳ *"I can explain that."* Some entrepreneurs think they need to be an expert at everything. As a result, they try to answer every question that comes their way, even if they have no clue what they are talking about. If you talk in circles, that'll be obvious to the investor. Investors know that a new business or product is surrounded by uncertainty; assumptions must be made and lessons learned. One of the signs of strength investors look for in an entrepreneur is the understanding that no one has all the answers. Let an investor see that quality in you. Communicate that they can trust you to be straightforward

☀ RED FLAGS

A few additional red-flag factors that could affect an investor's decision regarding your business include:

☀ *High failure rate.* Some industries have significantly higher failure rates than others (restaurants and retail stores are good examples). That certainly doesn't mean you will not succeed, but you'll need to have a very clear plan with a strong location and a solid marketing strategy and provide customers with unique products and excellent service.

☀ *Dependence on legal or government regulation.* Industries that tend to be more litigious than others or that are heavily regulated may make investors hesitate. If your product requires a long government approval process or a bidding process, there could be additional cause for concern because of the potential drain on cash. Investment in such businesses is not for everyone.

☀ *Key operations in different places.* If your company is based in one place and key operations are elsewhere, that can be a cause of concern. Geographic separation can create an added level of complexity when managing a fast-moving business.

☀ *Small returns for investors.* Your potential investor may believe in the product and the market, even that you have the right team to execute and everything is in place. But your business still may not meet their investment criteria if anticipated returns are too low, or they may view it as a lifestyle business and think you will want to stay forever, leaving them with no chance at a big exit. Chances are,

RED FLAGS, CONTINUED

> though, what you're offering will be perfect for someone
> else, perhaps people you know on a more personal basis,
> who want to see you succeed, share a similar lifestyle or
> passion, and are happy with smaller returns. Keep trying.

The most important things you can do to address these concerns
are to first, create a target investor avatar that factors in these
risks. For example, someone with familiarity, a high comfort
level, and a track record of investing in successful businesses in
your specific high-risk industry. Second, illuminate the problem
upfront. Sunlight is the best disinfectant. For example, in your
pitch, point out at the beginning that you are in an industry with
a high failure rate or one that deals with excessive government
regulation, and here is how you are handling that specific issue. By
addressing it, you are telling everyone that you are already aware
of the problem.

and open to collaboration. If you don't know the answer to a
question, you can always say that you will look into it.

✳ *"It will appeal to everyone."* If you're asked who your customers
will be and you say "everyone," you'll get the same response as
when you say you have no competition. What an investor wants
to hear is this: You are focused on solving a single problem
for a very specific target customer; in other words, you have
researched your demographic audience. In Chapter 8, we'll
discuss how to build your target customer avatar. Remember,
if you build for everyone, you connect with no one. There are
riches in niches. Investors want to know what niche you will
dominate.

✳ *"Writing a business plan would just slow us down."* Investors
know that without a plan, you have not forced yourself to test

your model; you have no real sense of income and expense or of capital requirements and timing. That also conveys that everyone isn't on the same page. How could they be without a written plan to provide them with a singular focus? Keep in mind, we're talking about a one-page plan or a ten-slide presentation. That's it!

Through the years, I've seen tons of presentations, many of which contained all the common mistakes mentioned above. People are seduced by the prospect of money and overly focused on the results rather than how to get them. Mastering the presentation, however, is a breakthrough unto itself. Practicing makes it even better; sitting down with people who have listened to pitches on the other side of the table is also highly recommended.

The Callback: The Art of Turning Interest Into Capital

In the entertainment business, you audition. Your goal is to get invited to the next step, so you wait for the *callback*. The same is true in raising capital: With each interaction, you try to generate enough interest and momentum to move to the next step.

Here are a few tips to get investors to make that call:

✳ *Build a great team.* People invest in teams, so make sure you build a great one, from partners and employees to consultants and collaborators. Make it your mission to surround yourself with the best. Avoid being strong in just one area. Cross-functional expertise that sees the business in different ways adds perspective and gives your investors confidence.

✳ *Feed information in bite-size chunks.* This is a rule of thumb in direct-response marketing because the purpose of the selling headline is to get you to read the first line. Logically, then, the purpose of the next line is to get you to read another, and so on. Eventually you build momentum and close the sale.

In other words, don't send an investor everything at once. If you overburden them, they'll walk away confused. Instead, feed them digestible pieces. For example, pitch them in a paragraph sent by email. Then, upon request, give them a one-page overview, and, if they're still interested, follow with a ten-page slide deck. Every communication should build on the one before.

✳ *Tailor to your audience.* Each investor will ask different questions and have different concerns after each communication. Your job is to get all these questions and concerns on the table and then apply what you've learned in tailoring your next communication. For example, one investor has concerns about the market. At the next step, you build a short presentation that offers a strategy for how you will attack the market. That conversation should cover just that, nothing else. Once you get past that issue, move on to the next.

Another reason not to send everything at once is the materials need to be tailored for your audience. Information prepared for one person may not be right for another person, and you can shoot yourself in the foot. Take a cautious, step-by-step approach to learning, iterating, and then improving your presentations to suit each conversation.

✳ *Be open to feedback and ask for advice.* Don't take anything personally. Use every piece of feedback you get, positive or negative, as fuel to power you forward. No matter how much you don't want to hear it or how much you disagree, approach everything with a beginner's attitude. That openness and flexibility is a great sign of leadership in early stage environments. And for goodness' sake, don't argue your point. You may win, but you'll lose the investment dollars you came for.

Tricks of the Trade: What You Need to Consider When Striking a Deal

Bootstrapping and investor pitches or meetings can only get you so far. At some point, you'll probably need to think about how that capital is going to work for you. But where do you start? Well, capital-raising means you must not only focus on getting the money but, in doing so, you should seek the most favorable terms, trade the least amount of equity, and maintain control of the business.

As you prepare to meet with investors, consider these factors.

How Much Money Do You Really Need?

You won't need as much as you think if you limit the focus and draw upon all the resources you can. Then again, you may need more than you think since the launch will likely take longer than you hoped it would. My advice is to raise just what you think you'll need, and then a little more. By running lean, your team stays focused, and you'll make better decisions and avoid waste.

Early stage investors will want a big piece of your company. They probably deserve it for assuming the risk of investing in a business or product that still has a long way to go. They build that risk into what they charge for their capital, demanding more equity, higher interest rates, more control, or other terms. That also means that the more money you raise upfront, the more of your company you will have to give away in the form of equity.

Be thrifty. Take in as little money as you can and give away as little of your business as possible. Prove your concept, and then go out and raise more money when your company has earned a higher valuation.

Loans

Loans can be guaranteed or nonguaranteed. Will the interest be simple or compound? How much time do you have to repay the principal?

Equity

How much equity will you give away? Will your investor(s) be active or passive? How much control will you relinquish? Do your money sources wish to be involved in big decisions or do they plan to leave those to you and your team? What kind of return are they expecting? When do they plan to see this return?

You don't want to give too much of your business away. It's easy to give up 40 or 50 percent of nothing early on when your business barely exists. But odds are, if you raise money once, you will need to raise more down the road. And if you give away a high percentage in the first round, you are likely to lose control of your business the next time around.

Entrepreneurs are optimists; they tend to focus on their current round and often significantly underestimate their long-term capital requirements. As a result, they part with a lot of their company's equity early, thinking they will not need to give much more away. So they spread it around to investors, employees, contractors, and advisors. Later, when they go out and try to raise more money, they may end up with a minority share and lose control of their business. Keep in mind that it's common to have to seek money two or three times.

The decisions you make early will have a lasting impact. If your company is performing well, anticipate that each round will cost you between 15 and 30 percent of your equity. If things go sideways, capital could become much more expensive. To avoid giving away too much, demonstrate proof of concept. Show investors that you can execute and customers will pay for your product. This will help mitigate their risk and create significantly more value for your company. Every little percentage point will make a difference down the road.

Preferences

Investors typically have certain rights that supersede the entrepreneur. One is preferences.

Preferences are special return scenarios regarding what happens to the money when a given financial event occurs. For example, should you sell your company, investors may demand their principal gets repaid first, after which the remaining money is divided by everyone else on a pro rate basis. Alternatively, an investor may have outlined that they receive two or three times their investment before everyone else splits the remainder. The lesson? Focus not only on how much equity you give away, but also the preferences built into investor agreements.

Control

Even if you own most of the company, you may not be in control of it. Many investors fight for contractual provisions that give them the power to make decisions on certain aspects of the business. Be sure to understand how much control you are ceding. Try to always maintain at least 51 percent of decision-making power.

Value

Beyond cold cash, what else does your potential investor bring to the table? Does he bring industry or operational knowledge? Will you gain someone skilled in team building or who has contacts for strategic partners? Balance their overall value with the capital they bring to the table.

Raising capital is often a requirement to launch a new business, product, or service. It's hard work that takes time and dedication. The biggest reason entrepreneurs fail to raise the funds they need is they don't have a road map, so they waste time. They get in front of the wrong people. They say the wrong things. They overburden their target with too much material. When they finally do get an offer, they don't know how to negotiate the best deal.

If you follow the steps in this chapter, you can steer clear of these problems and set yourself on a path toward success.

breakthrough three

TAKING YOUR IDEA TO MARKET

getting in the game

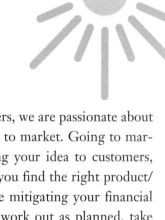

As entrepreneurs and business leaders, we are passionate about the products and services we take to market. Going to market successfully means introducing your idea to customers, getting valuable feedback, and adapting until you find the right product/ market fit. The trick is to do all of this while mitigating your financial risk every step of the way so if things don't work out as planned, take longer than planned, or go sideways, you haven't gone through all of your resources and can adjust.

The good news is that bringing your idea to market is easier today than ever before thanks in large part to technology, the tools available to entrepreneurs, and the reduced costs associated with running a business. This is a far cry from the past, when people would have a dream but would have to put in on the back burner because the costs were too high and the risk was too great for most people to take a shot.

Now, you're finally ready to move forward. You're clear on what your big idea is. You've decided to stay focused, really nailing that one thing before moving on to the next. You are clear on who your target customer is and the value they will derive; it's time to go to market. What you will need to focus on is how to do it in the most efficient and statistically successful way possible. The following chapter will get you ready and provide the breakthrough ideas necessary for you to launch successfully and move forward with sustained success.

Find a Way to Simple First

A few years ago, I attended a conference on the Big Island of Hawaii. The organizer, David Hornik, of venture capital firm August Capital, calls the invitation-only meeting "The Lobby." Almost everything leading up to the arrival was secret; no one knew who else would be there. The philosophy is that a confidential environment helps everyone to open up and grow.

On the first day, the organizers issued the participants different-colored T-shirts and told us to go find other people wearing the same color. These people would be our team for the day. Mine consisted of Dick Costolo, who became CEO of Twitter (a position from which he stepped down in 2015); Sarah Lacy, founder of PandoDaily, the number-one Silicon Valley news site; and Bill Tai, a leading venture capitalist. But we were still missing one person from our team. Looking around, we finally found our man: Stanley Burrell, aka MC Hammer. Rapper, dancer, actor . . . *and* entrepreneur.

Don't think for a second that the legendary rapper was invited to the event for his entertainment value. Hammer regularly attends tech gatherings and has invested in notable tech startups, including Square and Bump Technologies. He's lectured at Stanford and Harvard on the uses of social media and has a promotional deal with iPad case maker Zagg. He's also launched businesses of his own. In 2007, the creator of hits including "U Can't Touch This" and "2 Legit 2 Quit" launched DanceJam.com, a sadly short-lived YouTube-like site for dancers to share videos.

Needless to say, I was psyched to be on his team.

We all got in a big white van. Our job was to go on a scavenger hunt, competing against other teams to be the first to solve a series of puzzles. We were a savvy bunch, and I could sense the competitive energy surging. We got to the first site, read the clues, and looked at the materials. Dick, Sarah, Bill, and I looked at each other; we were confused and couldn't figure out how to solve the problem. And Hammer wasn't helping. He stood a short distance away, talking on his cell phone, looking at the ocean.

"Hey, Hammer, can you help us out?" we asked.

"Yeah, sure, give me the clue," he said.

Our task was to take a pile of rocks, a couple of sticks, and a piece of rope and turn it into something. Hammer took one look at the clue, thought about the problem for a minute, and then stacked one item on top of another, completing the assignment. Problem solved and task completed.

We went to the next clue. The same thing happened—four of us working hard to solve the problem and Hammer talking on his phone and gazing at the ocean. When we asked him for help, he walked over, took one look at the clue, and again solved the puzzle. We moved on to the next clue. Guess what happened? He solved it again, quickly. I think Hammer solved every problem on the scavenger hunt for the team that day.

We didn't end up winning (we found out later the other groups were getting ahead of us because they were sharing clues on what was then a new online service—Twitter—as cofounder Evan Williams was another participant in The Lobby). But a little in awe, I went up to Hammer later at the bar and asked how he had managed to solve every problem so quickly. What was his secret?

"The problem with you entrepreneurs," he said, "is you start off with these big goals, but you make things complicated, more complicated than they need to be.

PLATEAUS

Most people believe that once things start taking off for them, as long as they put in the work and follow the recipe, so to speak, they'll continue to grow exponentially. When we're young, we really tend to fall into this trap. We don't understand that success is not like an elevator ride straight up, but more like taking the stairs, with plenty of landings—or plateaus—along the way.

I first learned this lesson from writer George Leonard, one of the leaders of the human potential movement. Here's what he shared. Let's say you want to learn how to play tennis. What's the first thing you do? Well, you probably go out and hire a coach. On your first lesson, that coach is going to teach you to hold the racquet, stand on the same side of the net, and lob balls to your forehand. Your job is simple. All you have to do is step into that and hit the ball over the net. But what happens is you fail over and over and over again. Why? Because you have to think about what you're doing, and thinking gets in the way of smooth, graceful movement. Until one day, boom. You hit the ball perfectly. It's like you've always known how to do it.

Here's the problem. Up until now, the coach has been standing on the same side of the net as you, lobbing balls to your forehand. Now you have to learn how to move side to side. So you had a slight increase in your performance, and now that you have to learn a new skill, you're going to have a decrease that takes you down to a plateau that's a little higher than the plateau you were on before.

As entrepreneurs, we have to learn when we're on a plateau. We really have to put in the work because that is where all the growth and progress takes place. Sometimes being on the

> ### ☀ PLATEAUS, CONTINUED
>
> plateau feels like we are stuck, but we're not. We're learning. So here are three things you can do to take advantage of this period and get yourself unstuck. I think of it this way: Plateau and GO!
>
> - ☀ *Rearrange the energy around you.* How do you do this? The simplest way is to put yourself around new people who can offer a different perspective. Remember, the knowledge that got you this far won't take you where you want to go. So change the people around you to find new perspectives.
>
> - ☀ *Eliminate the need to be right.* Open yourself to all possibilities during this period.
>
> - ☀ *Be grateful for what you have achieved and be excited about where you are going.* I've always found that plateau periods are good times to take advantage of healing. Rest your body knowing you are doing the work needed to succeed.

"I have a philosophy in life and business," he said. "I always find a way to simple first."

That was a big "aha" moment for me. When I think back on it, I associate his insight with the paper clip, the sticky note, the clothespin, the thumbtack, Scotch tape, the BIC pen, the disposable razor, and thousands of other products that have one thing in common: They're incredibly simple. And they were invented only in the past 150 years. Look around your home or office. You're surrounded by simple inventions that are easy to use, solve one problem, and solve it perfectly well.

The same is true with businesses: Simple businesses are thriving everywhere. Coffee shops. Sandwich shops. Dry cleaners. Lawn-care services. Bars. It doesn't have to be complicated. Every day entrepreneurs take a tried-and-true business idea, apply some differentiation and branding, and voilà! Of course, there are other factors—the right location or the know-how to make awesome coffee or sandwiches—but there are thousands of business owners making a great living by doing simple things well.

Take Stanley Burrell's brilliant insight as an order, a compulsion, a rule for your life—f or your whole business, in fact: Your concept, structure, and rough financials need to be so succinct and simple that you can fit it all on one page or explain it to someone in 30 seconds.

Narrow your focus. Narrow the problem. Narrow the customer. Narrow the geography. Get the whole idea as simple as you can make it, and work out from there.

Remember: *Find a way to simple first.*

The Power of Doing One Thing

As you find your way to simple, you'll learn that Hammer's lesson applies to many areas of going to market. The most common mistake entrepreneurs make when launching a new business, product, or service is trying to do too many things at once.

I call it hammers-and-nails syndrome.

Let's say I give you one hammer and one nail. Your job is to hold the hammer in one hand and the nail in the other. All you have to do is drive that nail into a piece of wood. That's it—just nail that one product or service. You may miss the first time or even the second, but eventually you'll succeed.

So let's say I give you two hammers and two nails. Now you have a problem. Your job is to drive both nails at the same time into that piece of wood. Who is going to hold the nails? Let's say you find someone crazy enough to volunteer. Odds are you will miss again and again. Eventually you may get it right.

Finally, let's say I give you ten hammers and ten nails. I think you get the point: This is exactly how most entrepreneurs launch their businesses. They simply try to do too much at once in the belief that going to market with "more" is better.

It isn't. During your initial launch period, or when relaunching new products or services, "more" means additional risk. More also means unnecessary complexity, as well as additional time to market, so more capital will be required. Often the initial breakthrough product or service is something simple, straightforward, and easy to get excited about. The add-ons, features, and advances come later. How do you decide what comes next? Don't guess; ask your paying customers.

Below are some important things to remember as you prepare to take your product to market.

Pareto Principle: Focus on the Right Things and Don't Lose Your Focus

I have a good friend who raised $2 million in a very tough market to start a consumer internet business. Finding that much money to start a new business was amazing, and I congratulated him on a big win. He was ecstatic and told me he couldn't wait to get to work on the site.

One year later, I ran into him again and asked how it was going. He sang the blues. He said he was doing terribly. In fact, he was on his way to his attorney's office to shut the company down. They had launched a few months before but had already run out of money. I asked how that was possible, and he talked about his big vision, how his company aimed to provide everything their target customer could possibly want to buy in the category. Their goal was to be a one-stop shop. He and his team invested all their time and money building something big and comprehensive, confident their target customer wouldn't want to go anywhere else once their website was up and running.

When the company got started, they were solving one problem for one target customer. It was a simple concept. But when the money came in, everyone started working on other "great ideas" and "shiny objects." So they kept building and building and building. They went from solving one problem for one very specific target customer to building a one-stop shop that did a lot of things for a lot of different people. Then they started running low on cash, so they decided to push the product out.

After the launch, they learned, much to their surprise, that about 95 percent of their users used just 5 percent of the site! And that 5 percent was the original product to solve the original problem.

So that means 95 percent of the time and money invested was essentially wasted. What can you learn from this?

Focus on One Thing, The Simplest Thing

When kicking off a new product or service, put all your energy and focus into that product or service. Focus on one thing at a time. It should not be the hardest thing; it should be the simplest, what we'll call the *minimum viable product* (MVP). The MVP provides the opportunity to learn the most about your customers, with the least amount of time, money, and effort. The MVP puts you in a position to go to market quickly, collect valuable feedback, and not waste time building things customers don't want. This strategy significantly mitigates your risk and helps avoid the trap my friend fell into. Remember, Amazon started just as an online bookseller.

Follow the 85 Percent Rule: Good Is Good Enough

Striving for perfection is the enemy of any product launch. As a rule of thumb, when the new business or product is 85 percent of the way there, you are ready to go. In my experience, the level of effort required to reach 100 percent is not worth the additional time and expense at this stage. You would be much better off getting something into the market and beginning to test.

Be Great at Collecting, and Learning From, Feedback

Once you have launched, listen to and learn from your users. Develop feedback loops to learn everything you possibly can. What do users like and dislike about the product or service? What features would they like to see added to enhance their experience? Which features don't work or generate little interest? Do whatever you have to do to engage with your users. That may include offering incentives to get feedback on surveys or in focus groups, reaching out on social media, or generating outbound calls to learn more.

The hardest part of this process for many entrepreneurs is to be completely receptive to what customers tell you. Given your passion

BREAKTHROUGH PRODUCT LAUNCH STRATEGY

Here are a few suggestions to help your product launch process reach the next level:

✳ *Focus.* Launch your new products and services fast and often, but always focus on one thing at a time. Don't start with the hardest thing, but the simplest thing, the minimum viable product.

✳ *Listen.* Launch quickly, but as you do so, develop feedback loops that enable you to listen to what your customers have to say and what those in the pipeline report.

✳ *Learn.* Make incremental changes and improvements based on feedback. Launch again, and continue the process of iteration, making it an ongoing part of your culture.

✳ *Move on.* Once you have found the right product or market fit and given your customers what they want, move on to the next one (that is, to the second hammer and the second nail).

and all the time you have spent on the project, you may not want to hear negative feedback. You may be inclined to think the customer just doesn't get it. But feedback is the most valuable tool you have as an entrepreneur. So listen, consider, and use what you learn to iterate, improve, or even throw out some of what you have built or planned.

Avoid the Shiny Ball Syndrome

As you start developing your MVP, you must fight "feature creep" at every step. You, your team, partners, and everyone else you share your vision with will have ideas about what should be added. While many of them will sound good at the time, they are instead shiny objects that distract you. Your job is to stay focused on one thing, get it to market, and *then* deliver the next thing. By focusing on one thing at a time, you can get to market quickly, learn a great deal about your product or service from actual customers, and make changes based on their feedback And if your launch doesn't fly, you have significantly mitigated your risk.

Speaking of not working, what if the product falls down or is simply a bad product or a poor market fit? Kill it. To mitigate your personal and financial risk, choose to fail fast rather than allowing a bad product to die a long, slow, very expensive death.

 WHO KNOWS MORE, YOU OR YOUR CUSTOMERS?

The truth is, your customers may not always be right, but they know what they want and what they are willing to pay for.

I sat down with Gary Vaynerchuk from VaynerMedia and asked him, "What is the biggest mistake you see entrepreneurs make?"

He replied, "Disrespecting the market. I'm just stunned that people think they're more right than the consumer when the consumer is the judge and the jury."

When Gary launches a product, he doesn't assume it is just going to work out. Instead, he told me, "I let it go out into the wild, and then I counterpunch. If I see that we've got some opportunity here, then we build on it and iterate. But I'm also very comfortable with putting something out and recognizing that even if we spent nine and a half months on this program, and the product or service is not going to work . . . we need to get out of this." He listens to his customers, and you should, too.

Riches in Niches: How to Grow Further and Faster With Far Less Capital

My early career was spent in the broadcast world. I worked for the TV and online divisions of media giants like CBS, NBC, and Fox. During that time, I sold advertising to global brands and marketed their products to the largest possible audience. The goal was to cast the biggest net and see how many fish you could pull in. I believed in the power of mass marketing.

For today's business owner, there's a problem with this model: Inevitably, you'll spend a lot of money telling your story to the wrong people. That's no way to build a business today. You need to be razor sharp in cutting up the marketplace, making dead sure that every dollar spent communicating to your target audience gets a good return on investment.

The good news is that this can be accomplished now in a way we couldn't dream of 20 years ago. Instead of living with a handful of TV channels (like the world I grew up in), there are now literally millions of targeted ways to connect with your customers. You can find your audience on one of thousands of TV stations that appeal to your niche. You can pinpoint your market on the internet and target them using social media. Today's consumers conveniently self-sort themselves into groups based on shared interests and desires. The key is to find your target and market very specifically to that audience. This is true not only when you first break through with your product, but throughout the life of your business. Your market may or may not change, but you need to know exactly who your customers are at all times.

Start by thinking of an ideal customer—one person or group—to whom you wish to sell your single, simple product. I call this your *target customer avatar*. Develop a very specific profile that includes everything you can learn about that ideal customer and what about your product appeals to them. Determine what your target customers talk about and learn the lingo they use to speak to each other. Learn what issues they care about, their spending habits, and where they shop.

Once you have a deep understanding of your customer, market your product or service to that specific market. Instead of broadcasting to a wide audience, go narrow and deep. There are riches in niches. The more you integrate yourself into that group (especially via social media sites like Facebook, Instagram, LinkedIn, etc.), the faster word will spread about what you have to offer. If you talk to the right people at the right time in the right way, and you deliver a product they value, you will soon have an entire community spreading the word, essentially functioning as your marketing team. On the other side of the ledger, if you misfire, everyone will know. Bad news travels fast.

I came to truly appreciate the power of targeting a deep, narrow niche when I worked with a direct marketing business a couple of years ago. The owners had acquired a database of more than 15 million buyers of a certain type of product. They had names, physical and email addresses, and a lot of personal data about each of them. Their initial plan was to use the list to market new products via email.

When they sent out their first direct marketing campaign, they cast the widest possible net, sending the same offer to all 15 million people. With that much distribution, how could they lose? They found, however, that only a tiny percentage of people actually responded to their emails; most of them got caught by spam filters. The majority of the people on their list simply weren't interested in hearing what they had to say.

We brought in a data analysis team and broke down the 15 million names into 100 groups we called "buckets." We learned that although all the people were on this list because they bought a certain kind of product, their individual makeup was very different. Not everyone was interested in the same products or wanted to be marketed to in the same way. We needed to sharpen our focus and tailor our message.

We decided to learn everything we could about one bucket at a time and developed targeted products and services for that specific niche. That meant we ignored the rest of the names in the database because sheer volume wasn't what we were after. I would rather have 15,000 buyers I know are interested in my product than 15 million people who are not.

The original—and unsuccessful—offer had been for a health-related weight-loss program. So we took a look at a segment of the people who had bought one product that could be loosely categorized as spiritual, such as Christian-themed products. Then we looked at the predominant gender of the people in that bucket, narrowed our age range, and found that our target demographic was women aged 45 to 55.

We kept adding filters: married; has children; empty nester; caretaker for a parent; pet owner. Now we were getting somewhere. All these requirements might seem like we were creating an overly narrow niche, but we still ended up with a list of more than a million names.

Then we went to work learning everything we could about our prototypical customer (we named her Christina). She was a 50-year-old mom with grown kids who owned a dog and was caring for her elderly parents. We joined Christina's online communities, found her on social media, and had real conversations with people just like her. We learned what drives Christinas and the kinds of products and services they were interested in.

We developed just the right product for this ideal customer. In this case, we built a spiritual program (in the form of prayer books, newsletters, and audio and video recordings) that touched on issues experienced by caregivers who also owned dogs. The response to this highly targeted campaign was amazing. Many Christinas bought the product, became part of the community, and referred other friends like themselves (and gave us their email addresses). In one month, the company achieved a much greater response—because we had connected with the market.

Here are a few suggestions for creating the perfect product/market fit:

❋ *Pick one very specific niche.* Instead of casting a wide net, focus on solving one customer need at a time.

❋ *Develop your avatar.* Create a very detailed representation of your target. I suggest writing down 25 of your target's characteristics. Who are they? What is their age, gender, and location?

What do they care about, what do they read, who do they hang out with, what do they watch, which products do they buy, and where do they buy them?

☀ *Engage in conversations.* Find the specific places they hang out (both in daily life and on the internet). Join their communities. Learn what concerns them, what drives them, and what lies under the surface emotionally that gets them to make decisions. Chime in when appropriate.

☀ *Continue doing what you do well as you grow.* As your business grows, you may want to offer additional products or services to your audience. Keep doing your research and keep the conversations going. But make sure to stay in your wheelhouse. For example, the airline parts manufacturer EMTEQ (now part of Rockwell Collins) had the idea to branch out into bus and train parts. They had the finances and the manufacturing facilities. What they didn't realize was that even though it was all part of the transportation industry, the clients had completely different needs and there were all sorts of new regulations they would need to learn. They nixed the plan and instead shifted to other areas within the interior of airplanes, such as adding wifi, which was a new product for a familiar audience.

Those Girls Don't Surf!: Authenticity Is Everything

One of my good buddies is Brian Smith, founder of UGG. You all know UGG as the iconic sheepskin boots worn all over the world, but Brian did not have an easy road to success when he got started. With every hurdle he had to jump, he learned an invaluable business lesson, and despite his rocky path, he built UGG into the behemoth it is today.

After spending years as an accountant down under, Brian made the move to California because he saw all the big trends were coming from there. "I was going to find the next big thing and bring it back to Australia," says Brian, who, after a few months of looking around for inspiration, noticed there were no sheepskin boots in America even though they were seen everywhere in Australia. "I decided to stay in California and started importing boots. I thought I'd be an instant millionaire, but people in America did not understand sheepskin the way Australians did," explains Brian, so he decided to start Ugg Imports (now known as UGG Boots) with a $20,000 loan, which he used to buy 500 pairs of boots. Want to know how many he sold in his first year? Only 28 pairs!

"Looking back, that experience shaped my future theme in life and business," says Brian: "You can't give birth to adults." Every business goes through infancy; it doesn't matter if it's a product or a service. After that first disappointing year, Brian knew he should have given up. But he still had inventory, not to mention investors' money tied up in it. So he started hitting swap meets with a van full of products. "Every time I surfed at Malibu, I had a little retail store going out of my van," recalls Brian.

The next year, he sold $10,000 worth of boots, which gave him enough money to start advertising. "I hired some models and posed them on the bay, choosing a perfect pair and clothing and having the boots front and center in the ads," says Brian, who made only $20,000 and couldn't figure out what he was doing wrong. So he started asking his surfing friends and others in his target market, "Why aren't you buying these boots?"

"I was having a beer with one of the owners of a surf shop when I asked why my boots weren't selling. When we returned to the store he asked a few grommets, 'What do you guys think of UGG?' And every one of them just came out and said, 'Oh, those UGG boots, man, they're so fake. Have you seen those ads? Those models? Those girls don't surf!'"

And that was the problem, right there—there was no authenticity in those ads.

"I instantly realized I was sending the wrong image to my target market," explains Brian, who knew it was time to pivot. He caught up with a buddy who was running the National Scholastic Surfing Association, which promotes surfing for middle school and high school kids.

This was the "aha" moment for Brian Smith. Instead of hiring an expensive fashion photographer, he took his little Canon Sure Shot and got shots of the teenage girls at Black's Beach and Trestles, both iconic spots for surfers. "When I started running those ads in the surfer magazines and action sports magazines, business exploded from $20,000 to $220,000 in sales," Brian recalls.

This is a perfect example of what it means to recognize your target customer and understand how to reach them. He shot an authentic ad with somebody who really embraces the brand. Super cool. And that authenticity is critical for every single person trying to build, grow, or sustain a business. If your audience does not resonate with your marketing, they will not be influenced to buy your products. If you try to pretend you are something you're not, your customers will find out, and you'll be toast!

That authenticity was the birth of what is today a billion-dollar brand.

Lessons From Buck's Pancake House: Building a Business Is Like Following a Recipe

When I first moved to the Bay Area in my 20s, I found my first business mentor, Bill Pick. Bill was a legend at *Wired* magazine and its digital counterpart, *HotWired*. As a driver of that effort, Bill was a pioneer of online advertising. In fact, many people credit him with selling the first online ads (HotWired was the first company to sell banner ads). While at Infoseek as head of business development and sales, Bill created keyword advertising. He worked tirelessly behind the scenes (though everyone knew Bill) to help create some of the online advertising that is part of our daily lives.

Every week for years, we met for breakfast at Buck's, a pancake house in Woodside, California, in the heart of Silicon Valley. We watched so many deals get made in front of us. Many of the people getting funded were super smart and had great ideas. Still, so many of their startups failed. They'd begin to execute, do a lot of great things, and then run out of cash. I wanted to know why.

Then Bill taught me one of the most important lessons of my life.

He told me that building a successful company is like making a cake. You start with a great recipe, but to bake that cake correctly, you have to add the ingredients in a certain order.

Then he took out a napkin (entrepreneurs love napkins) and drew a big triangle. He called it a success pyramid.

He said launching a successful company is not just a matter of doing things right, but doing them in the right order. Just like baking that cake, there is a recipe. If you do things out of order, your cake just won't turn out right.

Here's how that applies to business. The triangle looks like the one in Figure 8.1, from bottom to top.

The key when launching a company is to focus your energy sequentially on each step. If you don't, the pyramid will collapse.

For example, if I start to sell before my product is working, I've created a problem for myself. If my company starts to market a service before it's ready, driving a lot of traffic, the site could crash, forcing

*Figure 8.1—***Success Pyramid**

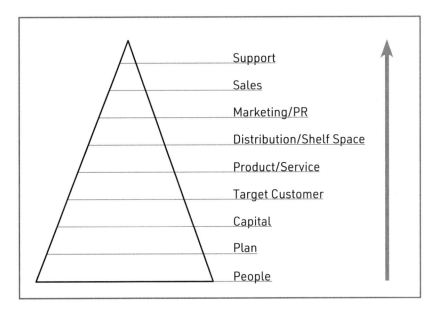

Support

Sales

Marketing/PR

Distribution/Shelf Space

Product/Service

Target Customer

Capital

Plan

People

customers to go somewhere else. You can apply this lesson in each step of the triangle. So start at the bottom and work your way up. Nail one step down firmly before you move on to the next.

Speaking of moving on, in the next chapter, let's take a look at marketing your business as you enter the marketplace—one step that you absolutely must nail down firmly to ensure your breakthrough success.

speaking to your customers

aking your idea to market is a multistage process, as illustrated in the triangle graphic in the previous chapter. An essential component of that process is marketing and how you break through to reach your potential customers and lead your business to the next level. While this isn't necessarily a book about marketing, you've probably noticed that how entrepreneurs communicate to their customers is baked into almost every breakthrough story I've mentioned. There's a reason for that—solid marketing is a vital key to your success. This quick chapter speaks a bit more to that concept and looks at some out-of-the-box ways to maximize your marketing reach, starting with leveraging partnerships to grow your business.

Crickets: How to Leverage Partnerships to Grow and Scale Your Business

Many entrepreneurs convince themselves that "if they build it, people will come." You may have believed in your gut that what your product offered was exactly what the market needed and that once you launched, customers would flock to you in droves. But when you opened your doors (either literally or online), all you heard was the sound of crickets. No footsteps, voices, or cash-register noises. Just crickets.

You might have the best product that no one has ever heard of. Or it might be that the folks that have heard of it just don't know where to find you. This is one of the most common problems I encounter with entrepreneurs, and it occurs for several reasons. First, there is wishful thinking (*I know people will come!*). Then, there is spending too little money on marketing or having no workable strategy for driving traffic in your direction. It is just as common with intrapraneurs, who place exaggerated confidence in the success of past launches or the strength of their company's brand.

A client recently came to me with a great idea for an online business. His product addressed an obvious need in the marketplace, and he had spent a year and $75,000 out of his savings to build a beautiful website to sell it.

"How's business?" I asked, expecting a happy answer. "How many people are coming to your website? How many units have you sold?"

His answer: none.

He had almost no traffic to the website and few buyers exposed to the product. He felt the business was doomed. To make matters worse, he had exhausted his cash resources building the product and promoting the launch.

But, as I told my client, there was hope. What he needed were partners. Not business partners (as we discussed in Chapter 5) but partnerships with other businesses, specifically ones with a similar customer profile.

In nearly all the companies I've been involved with, a key to the successful distribution of our products and services has been the

breakthrough three • taking your idea to market

partnerships we established early on. By hitching your wagon to a bigger, more established business, you can get a lot further faster, and with much less money out of pocket than by traveling the road alone.

My first lesson in partnerships was with Quote.com, which in 1995, was one of the first companies to get permission from the stock exchanges to put stock quotes on the internet. It helped create and define the market and was the leading brand in its field. Today, with hundreds of places to get stock quotes online, we take for granted how easy it is to find them. But back then, it was one of a kind.

Quote.com had a great product in an exploding market, but we had to move fast to keep our first-mover advantage. At the beginning, we had very little money to work with (I had to use my own frequent-flier miles to go see a customer). Since we had a small marketing budget, we needed to find other ways to grow. We needed partners. Though we felt we had something valuable to offer, we had to figure out how to structure a deal where both sides would win.

We approached sites that had a similar target customer. These other companies wanted to create more awareness; they believed that offering more value would drive usage. They wanted applications that kept users on their sites rather than surfing off to explore other places on the internet. And, ultimately, they wanted to find ways to monetize this traffic.

We offered to integrate our product onto their website, giving users a reason to stay on their websites longer. We proposed cobranding the pages to create branding and awareness for both companies. Once we figured out how to monetize the pages, we'd share revenue.

In just a few months, we built a network with more than 100 sites, some of which were among the largest consumer websites at the time. As a result, people began to see us everywhere.

We applied the lessons we learned about partnering to advertising as well. One of our key early advertising partners was what is now Ameritrade. Its founder, billionaire Joe Ricketts, knew that different kinds of investors liked different kinds of brokerages, so he offered four of them: Accutrade, K. Aufhauser & Co., Ceres Securities, and eBroker (these consolidated under Ameritrade in 1997). Each one had a different marketing angle to appeal to a different kind of investor. Joe advertised Ameritrade because he knew if our customers wanted a stock quote, they were likely to have a brokerage account, making advertising with Quote.com a no-brainer. Everyone was a winner, and ultimately, Quote.com became one of the largest ad revenue-generating sites and number one in its category. The company eventually sold to Lycos. The whole experience serves as a great lesson in growing a company quickly with limited resources through partnerships.

I've seen the same model applied again and again in my career: SportsLine USA and CBS became CBSSports.com, Xoom.com and NBC became NBC Internet, Lycos and Fox Sports became FoxSports.com on Lycos (which later ended up with Microsoft), and most recently Smart Charter and Virgin (which became Virgin Charter). In each case, a scrappy, early stage venture with limited resources applied the same formula and created a win-win opportunity with partners to achieve its goals.

How do you apply partnerships to your business to amp up your marketing efforts and growth potential?

- ✳ *Decide what you need.* What does your business need most at this stage? Capital, resources, access to potential customers, credibility, marketing, and promotion?

- ✳ *Follow your target customer.* Where do they spend their time? What businesses, websites, organizations, associations, or groups do they visit? A key is having a common target customer with nonoverlapping products.

- ✳ *Create a win-win agreement and execute.* Ask yourself, *How can I create a win for the person with whom I am looking to partner? How can they look like a hero to their business?* Find out what's most important to them. I go as far as trying to learn how my partner is evaluated in their job position and what I can do to help them look like a star. Once you've learned about what your prospective partner needs and gotten some feedback, tailor your partnership ideas. Create revenue sharing, where applicable, that benefits both companies.

One final lesson on partnerships? I believe that businesses are bought, not sold. Many of the best financial exits are the result of businesses that started as partnerships and then grew into something

 PARTNERSHIP PLANNING

Here's a quick look at how to prepare for and find a good partner who can maximize your market reach:

- ☀ *Be patient.* The wrong partner, or a big partner, will only expose your flaws faster. Build a great product first.

- ☀ *Calibrate your needs.* Determine what you want from a partnership—capital, resources, technology, marketing, distribution, emotional support, sales support?

- ☀ *Understand their needs.* What problem can you solve for your partner? How can you make your internal champion look like a hero?

- ☀ *Sell what they need.* Focus the conversation on addressing their needs vs. what you think is cool about your product.

- ☀ *Shop around.* Talk to as many potential partners as possible to be sure you find the right one.

- ☀ *Find an internal champion.* Because smaller companies and new initiatives can get lost in the shuffle, you need an internal champion in the business you're partnering with to take ownership of your project and drive it internally. As an entrepreneur CEO, it's important for you to maintain a relationship with this person.

As you think about what person or company might partner well with your vision, remember to not compromise on these points. A partnership should be a long-term relationship, so choose wisely!

more. Many who partnered early on with the right businesses followed through on what they agreed they would deliver. They built deep relationships and ultimately had the largest financial exits.

How to Build a Business Empire One Bottle of Wax at a Time

Barry Meguiar took his grandfather's brand, Meguiar's car care products, and transformed it into a household name, and he did it all with little to no advertising. Instead, Barry focused on demonstrating his products at car shows and educating the customer on how to properly use them. Today, he travels the world for his TV show, *Car Crazy*, to find others who share his passion for the automobile. The show is not about car wax but about people with a major car hobby. Barry has worldwide success, but who would've thought it all started with a simple question: Would you like a polish?

Barry went out and found his target customer at the car shows and brought them little bottles of car wax. He and his team would walk up to the car enthusiasts standing next to their hot rods and ask if they'd like a little polish. They weren't trying to sell something, simply to add value. All Barry would ask for in return was if they liked the way the wax worked on their cars, would they put a little sign up against the windshield saying that they used Meguiar's? And they did. He would also give them that tiny bottle so they would remember what to buy at the store.

So by the time the show opened, every car—the Cadillacs and Mercedes and all the rest—would have a little Meguiar sign on their windshields!

It's almost like an old-school version of what we call a tripwire, which is using a simple offer to get people into a sales funnel by giving something away. I really believe it's never been more difficult than it is today to get a customer into your business and get them to make that first purchase. However, it's never been easier to get them to buy from you the second time. Barry simply put his product in front of his target customer in the same way you might offer someone visiting your website a free report or discount in exchange for registering.

Today, Meguiar's has the best reputation in the industry. What I really love about Barry is the approach he took to building his call center. It starts by hiring people with an absolute passion for cars. "You call our company and ask for the call center, you got a problem," says Barry. "'I got score marks, I got scratches, I got water stains, I got acid rain.' Whatever the problem is, our call center representatives, who are extremely passionate about cars and our products, will stay with them for a half hour if necessary. They'll say go and use these products and call me back, let me know if that works." And they're not trying to sell anything. These are car guys with a passion who want to help people. People are starving for help, so they overwhelm them with help, which creates a tremendous relationship.

What Barry started all those years ago still reverberates in how we sell our products and services because this is exactly how people are using social media to build relationships, by listening to people's questions and providing answers. It's better than selling a product—it's creating a relationship. People become loyal to companies with whom they have established a relationship.

Let Social Media Be Your Sales Force

Sometimes the mirror takes a while to clear so that we can see what's right in front of us.

Ever since college, I've been surrounded by computers. I've worked and invested in several internet companies. I've been an early adopter of new technologies. But there was one area in which I dragged my feet: I was late to embrace social media as a means of growing a business.

I was guarded with my privacy. I had very little spare time, and keeping up with Facebook, Twitter, LinkedIn, Tumblr, Pinterest, Google+, and everything else seemed overwhelming. But everything changed when I saw the potential value of social media in launching a new business.

I learned that lesson after consulting with a bootstrapping software company. The business had no marketing budget and very little money to hire salespeople. As a result, the founders suffered from one of the most common problems experienced by entrepreneurs: not having enough feet on the street. They couldn't afford to effectively market their product and hit sales targets the traditional way, so they turned to social media. It is estimated that more than 65 percent of purchase decisions are made before the buyer gets to the store. They talk to their friends, go to websites, look at reviews, and check on social media. As a result, the most effective companies build fans first and customers second. With fans coming first—this is the best part—you can effectively crowdsource your sales force and build a virtual army of thousands of people telling their friends to buy your product. And it costs you nothing. You have the crowd sharing your story, giving personal referrals, and selling on your behalf. Social media can also be an excellent tool for market research, brand development, product development, and customer feedback.

With social media, you can reach virtually anybody you want. Thanks to laptops and smartphones, you can connect with anyone, anytime, anywhere. This is an enormous shift in our ability to access others. Not so many years ago, it was impossible to make contact with most people if you didn't know them personally. Today, a new set of rules applies. There are no longer gatekeepers standing between you and the top businesspeople, athletes, and entertainers in the world since many of them manage their own social media accounts and respond to followers. If you would like to start a conversation with someone who might make a difference in your business, just send them a tweet.

Even though I was fired up, I had never executed this strategy on my own. As a result, in my first attempt to crowdsource my sales force, I did everything wrong. I built a fancy profile but didn't devise a plan for reaching out and engaging the community. Instead, I waited for people to come to me. I wasn't clear on who I should connect with, the conversations I needed to be part of, or the communities I needed to join.

Another mistake was aiming to *get*, not to *give*. When I pushed out information, there was no engagement. Gradually, though, I learned that by jumping into the conversation, by contributing to the community, I was able to build connections and relationships with my prospective customers. As a result, they opened up, providing me with great feedback, product ideas, and even offers to help promote me to their social networks.

At the start, everything I put out there was too highly produced. I felt everything needed to look and feel perfect, but I soon learned another lesson: Authenticity is key. Being yourself is what people want, and if you try to be someone else, they'll know. If what you put out comes off as scripted and highly produced, the customer will see it as a violation of trust.

Social media has placed one of the best sales tools in history at our disposal. It's a great advantage, one that entrepreneurs didn't have 20 years ago. So how do you make it work for your business?

Pick One Channel

In social media, you must not only engage but also engage consistently. There are several services available to help you post a message to multiple sites at once, and many of them provide great information you can use to optimize your posts and their responsiveness. But the key to building meaningful relationships is to engage and connect, which means you must join the conversation. By reaching out to people in your community and responding to their comments, you can set the agenda.

Pick one platform to start with, whether it's Facebook, Twitter, LinkedIn, Instagram, or another from the growing list of choices. Learn a little about the channels before you decide. They do have different characteristics and are therefore somewhat different in how you can best present yourself. For example, LinkedIn is more popular in the business world and has a very large international following. Meanwhile, Instagram is more visually oriented. Twitter is very newsworthy, with quick comments and responses, and Facebook has many businesses, but the approach is more social. Each also has slightly different user demographics. But most important, find out which social media platform is the one your customers spend their time on—because that's where you need to be. Go find them and engage.

Be Authentic

Be yourself. Share and tweet and post the things that interest you. Don't try to be what you think others want you to be. And don't work too hard to make everything perfect; if you do, you will either never put anything up, or worse, you'll break trust with your customers. Whether it's Instagram, Facebook, or Pinterest, what matters is that you're genuine. Post things that genuinely interest you and your community.

Engage! Engage! Engage!

The primary goal on social media is to build relationships and add value. This is where most people fall down. They work so hard to create content and push it out but then fail to step in and engage with their audience.

That means don't talk at people but post what you think is cool. Talk with people and really engage. Respond to comments. Jump into communities. Share your perspective and point of view.

Document; Don't Produce

Overproduced content tends to turn people off on social media. Plus, you need so much content (video, audio, blog posts, quote boards, pictures, etc.) that most people don't have the time and resources to put it into production and make it look fancy. People don't care. And they don't care about what you did last week. They want to get to know you, experience your day with you, and relate to you. As a result, it is much more powerful to document your life in real time than it is to take a bunch of time honing and polishing one piece of content to a high sheen.

Don't Oversell

You know that guy at a party who always wants to sell you insurance? Don't be that guy. Get to know people, engage honestly, and join in the conversation . . . don't dominate it. Giving advice and offering suggestions will make you seem helpful, knowledgeable, and trustworthy. Get people to ask you about yourself, rather than telling them about yourself, and they will be more receptive.

Commit Yourself to a Daily "Hour of Power"

Getting started with these technologies is quick and easy. Opening an account costs nothing, and posting is free. In a few minutes, you can be up and running. Within an hour, you can reach out and connect with friends, co-workers, and customers.

Spend one hour per day during your launch engaging with the community. That's it. In one hour a day, at zero cost, you can build an army. The cost in time and money is negligible, but the potential payback in exposure and attention is incalculable.

Monitor and Protect Your Brand

Make sure to regularly frequent the sites, feeds, and pages that discuss your industry, product, or service. Look for posts that mention your company. Respond to comments and complaints, using them as opportunities to engage, build trust, grow your brand, and collect market research. If you pay attention, you can get ahead of potential problems.

Invest in Sound

If you are posting video or audio content, keep a couple of things in mind. Even though your color, background, and production values may not be perfect, good sound is very important. Buy a lavalier microphone for quality sound, and, whatever the source of your video, be sure there is enough light for people to see you clearly. You don't need to spend a lot of money, but this is one detail you should invest in.

Tell Them How to Reach You

Make sure your fans know how to get hold of you. If possible, give them your web address, email address, phone number, and social media handle. If possible, use the same handle on all social media platforms.

Social media offers you the chance to build a massive sales force that will be more effective than anyone you can put on staff. Your crowdsourced sales force will be out there telling other people who are interested in your product or service all about you. People are much more likely to trust your brand and make a purchase based on a friend's referral than by listening to anything you have to say.

Your Buyer Blueprint

In the end, it's all about the customer. You can break through and take your product to market, but you can't make them buy it. Therefore, you need the right product for the right buyer.

Twenty-five years ago I learned this valuable lesson while working for Tony Robbins and teaching his material. I learned that the biggest mistake salespeople make is selling the wrong thing. They either push what they think is most important about their product or service or what their boss has told them to sell. When the prospect says no, they don't understand why. It's because the seller never asked what the prospect wanted—he didn't understand their *buyer blueprint*.

Although I should have known better, I've fallen into this trap myself. One example was while I was at Virgin Charter. We had a smart, educated team. We were confident we understood our customer's problems and knew how to solve them. So we created a product road map, listing the features planned for development and ranking them in the order we would build them. With a hundred features on our list, I had the sense we were on the right track. Then, after spending lots of money building and going to market, we discovered a problem.

People just weren't using our service in the way we thought they would. Our team spent its time building features on the back end of our website: creating efficiencies, automating systems, and developing the technologies to enable a buyer to purchase and manage their trip details online. But customers spent their time on the front end of our website, doing searches and viewing profiles of all the available aircraft.

When they were ready to buy, most just picked up the phone and asked our team to process the order.

We needed to go back out into the market, so our sales, product, and technical people gathered in rooms with customers.

We soon learned that some of the functions people wanted most weren't in the current product or in the top ten things to build in our product road map. Some weren't even in our plan at all. Obviously, we had too many hammers—and not enough of the right ones.

The challenge is to create a solid buyer blueprint before you do anything else. You can do this by asking two very simple questions:

1. *What is most important to you?* Many times if you ask a customer this question, the answer you will get is *I don't know.* But try responding with *But if you did know, what would it be?* You'll find that usually elicits useful answers, and the person will start listing the things they value most, perhaps without even realizing it. Take notes, and once they're done, work with them to rank every item on their list to identify which features are most important to them.

   For example, if you could only have this feature or that one, which one would you choose? Continue to rework and refine their answers. A potential buyer may say, for example, that their top priority is that a food item taste good or that a tech service is easy to use. That's a start but not all you need to know. This leads you to the second question.

2. *How do you know you are getting what you want?* Nearly everyone forgets to ask this question, and it may be the most important one. Why? Because the definition of "good taste" or "easy to use" is different for everyone. Your job is to not only find out what your prospect values, but also what rules they use to determine whether they are getting what they want. That makes follow-up questions essential: *How do you know it tastes good? Do you crave sweet or sour, crunchy or smooth? How do you know it's easy to use? Do you need to access it online? Would you require it on a mobile device?*

With an early understanding of what your prospect wants, and how they know they are getting what they want, you will be able to build and sell products and services that match your buyer's blueprint, leading to big success for your business.

A word of caution, though: Just because a customer says they want something, that doesn't mean they will buy it once they have a chance to use it. We found that out at Virgin Charter. What customers told us they wanted before having access to the product was different from what they wanted once they had a chance to play with it. Sometimes buyers don't know what they want. It's not that they are trying to deceive you; they can only know so much until they have a chance to experience what you have to offer. For that reason, it is essential to do two things.

First, build one thing at a time rather than everything at once. That way, if your customers start using your product and realize they want something slightly different, you have not wasted too much valuable time and resources. Second, get customers to use the product as soon as possible and collect as much feedback as you can (remember the MVP, the most viable product, in Chapter 8?). Then iterate, redeploy, and scale.

Constant interaction and communication with your users and ongoing reevaluations of your product and priorities are the best ways to keep moving forward. Established businesses often make the mistake of thinking they know exactly what their customers want because they have been successful for many years. Times change, customers change, and their needs change. Keep asking for feedback to stay current. If you stop asking for feedback and stop learning about your customers, your competition will eventually crush you.

GROWING AND SCALING FOR THE LONG TERM

the entrepreneur's road map for lifelong success

aunching a business is a long, tiring process. If you've been
fortunate enough to get your business off the ground, you
have really accomplished something—especially in the face of
so many companies that fold before they become a reality. The challenge
is planning, preparing, executing, and navigating the twisting and turning
road that is building, growing, and scaling a successful business.

In this chapter I'll share the simple ideas to transition from launch
to growth, help you avoid common mistakes made post launch, how to
scale effectively, and monetize your business in ways you may not have
considered.

Training with Navy SEALs

A few years ago, I had an opportunity to train with Navy SEALs in San Diego, California. It was an amazing and grueling day. We started out with those beach and water exercises you see on TV, all of us with our arms locked in the ocean, with the waves crashing over our heads. Then we learned how to storm a building, rescue a hostage, and capture a prisoner. We learned how to shoot assault rifles. At the end of the day, we learned that everything up to that point was in preparation for our final assignment, which was to go into a mock village at night to capture a prisoner and rescue a hostage.

So that's where we began. The Master Chief, who was the most senior officer of the Navy SEALs group, walked in and filled us in on our mission. He showed us a map. We studied the terrain. We looked at aerial photos. Each of us was given an assignment, and we practiced again and again in great detail. Take five steps this way, take ten steps that way, and so forth. We spent more time practicing for our mission than on any other exercise, or even several exercises combined.

When we got to the village, it was amazing. There was a real helicopter built into an elevator. It was open on one side so you could practice landing and disembarking from the aircraft. Now here's the thing. When we went in, we had the map, right? But they told us that no matter what happened, if we got lost, we could just look at the tower in the middle of the village to reorient ourselves.

So once we were dropped in the village, we realized the map wasn't the territory; it was just a *representation* of the territory. It didn't matter how much practice we had put in; there would be variables we couldn't have anticipated. There were people walking along the streets. There were noises coming from inside the houses. There were banging sounds and other things that captured our attention. Just as I started to feel like I was losing my bearings, I looked for that clock tower, and at that very moment, an RPG (rocket-propelled grenade) went over my head and blew it up. This really threw me off-center—it just wasn't something I expected, and I needed a moment to process it. It was a lot like the feeling you have when you first get into a market. You may have the perfect plan and the perfect team, and you may execute your plan flawlessly, but once you get out there, you find things aren't what you expected.

I continued to adapt and adjust to the constantly changing conditions. When I felt lost, I went back to my training.

Eventually we succeeded. We rescued the hostage and captured the prisoner. We were able to do this because we didn't stay locked into our plan. We had the awareness to identify when conditions had changed, things were not working, and we adjusted accordingly.

Here's what to do when that happens as you grow and scale your business:

* *Take inventory of your business.* Work closely with your team to take inventory of what you learned during launch. Here's an opportunity for the group to contribute—for all of you to learn together so you have the best chance to improve. Did everything work out as planned? Did you focus too much on one area of your launch to the detriment of another? Did your supply lines, feedback loops, and financials perform the way you expected them to?

* *Be open to remaking or remodeling the business.* Sometimes even a new house needs some remodeling. The same is true in business. When you built your initial financial model, it was filled with assumptions. Now that you are in business, you have left the hypothetical for the real world. Go back and apply facts and figures from your launch to your model. Look at your income and expense projections, the time and resources invested, and the capital that was actually required to reach your goals.

  Sometimes busy entrepreneurs don't take the time to do this, but it's important to identify whether income, expenses, timing, or all of them were off and how these results will affect your need for capital going forward.

So now you've taken your idea to market. You've listened to feedback and iterated and improved on what you have. You've done two of the most important things at this stage: You've identified and amplified what has worked and killed off what hasn't, and you've made incremental progress toward growing a solid business. But what if you want more? What if you want to move from incremental to exponential growth? How do you do it?

My career was spent launching businesses from the ground floor. Many of those businesses took off early and experienced phenomenal growth. But many of the strategies we used back then just don't work today. There are a new set of rules and a different set of models that lead to the biggest wins.

So after I wrote *Launch*, I decided to find people who were the best of the best at growing and scaling businesses—people who were creating strategies and systems that worked. I interviewed the top business innovators and entrepreneurs for *Entrepreneur* and *Inc.* magazines. I also partnered with the best person I've ever met at creating exponential growth and replicating the process across multiple industries: Roland Frasier. Roland is the cofounder or principal in four current Inc. 500 fastest-growing private companies in the U.S. He's founded, scaled or sold more than a dozen businesses ranging from $3 million to $337 million in sales. He is a principal at Digital Marketer and advisor to more than 100 companies, including Pepsi and McDonald's. His focus is on exponential growth. Together, we laid out the framework we use when coaching companies to achieve outstanding results. I'm confident if you apply these principles, which you'll read about later in this chapter, you'll be on your way to creating an amazing business. First, though, let's talk failure.

Three Reasons Why Companies Fail

I was interviewing David Meltzer, and we were discussing common pitfalls of entrepreneurship: why companies fail.

According to Meltzer, the first reason for failure, regardless of whether you're in your 30s, 40s, 50s, or 60s, is because entrepreneurs forget the number-one rule of entrepreneurship, which is to stay in business. Every day, every entrepreneur should think about how to take care of themselves to guarantee that they're in business the next day.

Second, many people don't understand the difference between innovation and entrepreneurship. Innovation is the process of taking imagination and making it real, while entrepreneurship is the

 HOW TO TURN AN INDUSTRY ON ITS HEAD

When it comes to disrupting an existing industry, there are a few different ways to approach it:

- ※ *Start with one person.* In a big market, look for one customer who already has his wallet out but is unhappy about something in an existing product or service. If the market is big enough, odds are lots of people agree with him. Fix that thing.

- ※ *Make things simple.* The more complex your industry's common practices are, the greater your opportunity to disrupt by simplifying them. It may not be easy, but if it were, everyone would be doing it. Solving the hard problem gives you a great opening.

- ※ *Slash prices dramatically.* If you use new technology or other systems that significantly reduce your costs relative to the competition, pass those savings on to your customers. Entrenched players may not be able to compete because their infrastructure does not allow it.

- ※ *Get close to your customer.* Build a better relationship with your customers than anyone else in the market. Translate that relationship into new products and services that better address their needs and desires.

- ※ *Be yourself.* Be authentic in everything you do and stay transparent to the marketplace.

action of monetizing innovation. Great entrepreneurs don't need a creative process other than *How do I monetize my ideas?* or *How do I monetize somebody else's ideas?* According to David Meltzer, successful entrepreneurs are always asking two questions:

1. *What do you need?* Successful people will know and have a list.
2. *What are you willing to pay for it/What are you willing to pay if I can make that happen for you?* Successful people are happy to pay for what they need.

In fact, the most successful people I know always—always— know their answers to these two questions. The same day I started asking these two questions was the day my life changed. It was a big breakthrough for me. I stopped trying to create and instead started to listen and provide value where it was most needed.

I connect with millions of people through my work each year. After a speech, I may have 75 to 100 people come up, introduce themselves, give me their business card, and tell me what they need. In a group of 100 people, maybe one will share what they are willing to offer me in return. So whose needs do you think I prioritize?

So when someone asks you what you want, make sure to let them know what you will give them in return if they make it happen.

Biggest Mistakes Companies Make When Scaling Their Business

When you work with as many entrepreneurs as I do, you see the same patterns in terms of mistakes that business owners make once they are starting to grow and scale. Once a business gets past the initial stages— which come with their own set of mistakes—it moves into a new phase, which is growing and expanding what you've worked so hard to launch. As is always the case, a new phase in business, like in life, comes with its share of missteps, and I see owners and CEOs making them time and time again when scaling a business. The following are the most common mistakes companies make during the growth and scale periods and how to avoid them.

Refusing to Hire a New Team to Replace Original Employees

The people who got you this far may not be the ones who can take you where you need to go next. When we start a business, we are juggling a ton of responsibilities. We're typically cash constrained, which forces us to hire lower-cost generalists to help us. They don't necessarily excel in one area of the business, but they are good enough and flexible enough to help wherever we need it. But as the business becomes more mature and we approach a period of growth and scale, it's important to bring in specialists to run each department, such as a head of sales, marketing, or technology. It's also important to bring in people who have previous experience taking a company where we want ours to go. For example, if you want to build a company that does $10 million in sales per year, you need to hire a head of sales who has taken a company near your size and grown it beyond your $10 million target.

The problem is that often entrepreneurs feel loyalty to those who joined their business prelaunch and fought through early battles together. They tend to hold on to them for too long, stick them in the wrong roles, and hope they will succeed. It takes a very different type of person to run companies with 10, 20, 50, 100, or 200 people. So the number-one job of an entrepreneur, at every stage in business, is to make sure she has the right people in the right roles at the right time.

Not Understanding the Economic Drivers of Your Business

One very common mistake for entrepreneurs at this stage is that they don't understand the numbers behind what is truly driving the business. So they don't make decisions based on data and they wind up investing in areas that don't make the most business and economic sense. This is an especially common mistake for companies that are overcapitalized. They overspend. So it's crucial to slow down, make sure you have identified a true product/market fit that makes economic sense and a proven system for acquiring customers, and then decide to invest in scaling.

Being Stuck to the Product Road Map

It is very common for entrepreneurs to get past the launch phase and be stuck in their own business product cycle. We'll discuss how to avoid this below.

Focusing on the Wrong Opportunities for Growth

This occurs for one of two reasons. The first one we mentioned above: not understanding the economic drivers of your business. The second is being stuck to the product road map. Our team makes a list of what it will build next, prioritized and placed in order. But sometimes we get so caught up and wed to the road map that we forget to listen to the customers. As a result, we launch what we want instead of what they need. When preparing to scale, focus on data, feedback, and what your paying customers are telling you they want most. Build a product road map around their wants and needs.

Finally, we run into companies that do a great job getting to market, build great products, and have momentum. However, they are not sure how to take what they have and scale quickly. They get tunnel vision and can't wrap their heads around how to increase lead flow, profits, and valuation. We'll talk more about valuation shortly.

Being Brave: Thinking Out of the Box

Every year, I take each of my daughters on a special father-and-daughter trip. I work with the girls and let them choose where they want to go and what they want to do. We also pick out a theme. And for me, this is an important time because I plan to reinforce that theme throughout the year. The first time I did this was with my older daughter, Lily, and our theme was "Whatever your dream, you can achieve. How? By being like Merida with practice, practice, practice." A Disney movie called *Brave* had recently come out, and the main character was named Merida.

Lily really loved this movie, and she loved Merida, an archer who dreamed of big goals and wouldn't let anything stand in her way.

So we picked a location and I got a hotel room. Then, before check-in, to surprise Lily, I'd taken several cardboard boxes and made them into a castle like Merida's so we could play. I even pasted targets on the wall for her to practice her archery.

After dinner, we went into the room. Lily was really surprised by my setup, and we got behind the cardboard castle and started to play. So we were looking at the wall and the targets like they were our enemy, and I said, "Lily, use your archery skills and go get them just like Merida." And with her toy bow and arrow set, from the Disney Merida collection, she did. She started to shoot, and she missed. She missed again and again.

So what did Lily do? She started to run outside the box, the fortress I had created.

And I said, "Lily, get back in the box."

So she did, and she missed. Then she got out, she shot, and she nailed it.

And so I said, "Lily, get back in the box." After all, the game was all about shooting from inside the box I'd created (oh, the irony!).

She got back in again, and she missed, and she got back out and shot.

And finally I said one more time, "Lily, get back in the box." And then Lily stopped. She took off her bow and arrow. She threw it on the ground. She looked at me, and she said, "Dad, how can you ever hit your target if you don't get out of your own box?"

Wow! She was only 6 years old at the time!

Lily saw what I couldn't see at the time—that you need to step out of your comfort zone and try hitting your target in a different way instead of staying in one place where you feel safe and the outcome seems dependent on that perceived cover of safety. As we move forward, I'll ask you to step outside the box and let go of any limited beliefs and thinking. I'll share how to scale farther and faster than you ever thought possible.

5X Your Company's Valuation

Now that we know about the biggest postlaunch/growth and scale mistakes, it's important to avoid them, and for that, I turn to Roland

Frasier. As I mentioned in Chapter 5, partners should complement each other, and while my strength has always been the launch, Roland has been most proficient during the growth and scaling part of the business cycle. In this and the next several sections, I talk about my experiences with Roland, who had such an impact on helping me move clients through the business cycle. It was through watching Roland in action at these stages of business that I had my own "aha" moments. For example, I recall a client Roland and I had who thought they were ready to sell their company. They even took it to a bank to get a valuation. The bank looked at the company's books and saw it was doing $10 million in annual sales. The bank took that income and split it in half. One half was labeled monthly recurring revenue/subscriptions (MRR), and the other half was static/one-time transactions.

On recurring subscription revenue, the bank was willing to give four to five times valuation. So on $5 million in annual sales, the company could get a $20 million to $25 million valuation. On static revenue, the bank would only give an even valuation. So on $5 million in sales, they could only get a valuation of $5 million. That is up to a $20 million difference in the value of the company. So our client asked themselves, *How do we convert a higher percentage of our income from static to monthly recurring subscription revenue?* Here is what they did:

- ✳ Ended one-time, à la carte sales
- ✳ Asked what existing non-MRR products can be converted to MRR.
- ✳ Turned one-time sales into subscriptions, worth five times more to the bank

It's a short example, but here's how you can apply it to your business:

- ✳ *Convert to MRR.* For example, if you have a pet food business, instead of selling food one bag at a time, offer a discount to join a club, get them on monthly auto shipping, etc.
- ✳ *Add MRR services.* Continue to sell your core product, but add other products and services to give you monthly recurring revenue. So if you have a content creation service, you begin

offering marketing services, like posting the content you create on social media.

✳ *Turn one-time sales into auto-ship or box.* Go from a one-time payment to a monthly one. You can also create service packages that include monitoring, updates, and/or support. These service payments could be as low as $5 to $10 per month, but they could mean a fivefold increase in your company's value.

✳ *Create memberships, associations, and buyers clubs for your industry.* Start an association and get others in your industry to pay you.

✳ *Add certifications to what you do.* These could be professional certifications, trainings, etc.

So as you think about valuation as it pertains to growth and scale, Roland recommends trying this exercise:

1. First, write down your top five income streams.
2. Next to each one, write down whether they are static one-time sales or MRR.
3. Finally, write down what you can do with each one, referring to our suggestions above, to create MRR.

Here's a final tip from Roland: Don't be afraid to do several things per income stream. For example, monthly recurring service, auto-ship, etc.

Turn Expenses Into Profits

I create a ton of content for partners, social media, blogs, and so forth. To manage this, I kept adding people and resources, and it started getting expensive. Unsure how to control this added expense, I asked Roland for advice. He told me to look at Amazon's Jeff Bezos and study how he turned expenses into profits, and encouraged me to apply the same process to my business.

Bezos had faced a similar problem at his company Digital Marketer, which had built an overseas content team that was costing $50,000 per month. So he set a dual goal: first, to have it pay for itself, and second, to turn it into a profit center.

What he found was that the workload was inconsistent. Many people on the team had extra time on their hands. So he asked himself how they could use that extra time for clients. The solution was to create products that would generate monthly recurring revenue. This meant creating content for others and charging a monthly fee on a 12-month contract. In less than 90 days, the company not only paid for itself but turned into a profit center.

How can you apply this thinking to your business?

1. *Identify your biggest expenses.* Make a list of all expense line items.
2. *Determine what products and services you can sell.* Look at each line item and ask, *If I were to offer this service to others, would they find value? If so, what would they pay?*
3. *Convert expenses to profits.* Offer these new products or services.

For example, if you have a development team, you could offer third-party development to others. You could charge a fee, get equity in companies, etc. If you have a supplement company, could you buy in bigger bulk and formulate for other companies? If you have a large office space, maybe you could host events or rent that space out to others when it's not being used. For example, some New York City restaurants that don't open until dinnertime rent out the tables during the day to people who need temporary workstations. Maybe that extra income will even cover your rent.

What services could you offer to convert expenses to profits? It could be lead generation, social media support, customer service, facilities, content, fulfillment, sales, etc. Finally, keep in mind your biggest expenses, whether they can be converted to monthly recurring revenue, and who would pay for it.

Create Bolt-On Businesses (BOBs)

In Chapter 5, we talked about the power of a team. I said the first step in creating one was to identify your strengths and hire your weaknesses. But what if we took this idea a step further? What if we asked how to take our company's strength and bolt it onto someone else's weakness?

For example, I work closely with Digital Marketer, the number-one company teaching businesses how to attract and convert customers online. At its core, Digital Marketer is great at creating content that generates leads for its training programs and converting those leads into paying customers.

We wanted access to more leads. We were looking for scale to grow. But that can get expensive. So we searched for companies that were great at what they did and had the same target customer but a nonoverlapping product. However, generating online content—our specialty—was either not their core competency or something they needed help with.

Once again, Roland provided us with a solution and an "aha" moment. He suggested that we offer to create content for them at no cost. That would generate the signups and leads they were looking for. We did this both with big companies like Microsoft and smaller brands.

As a result, they got great content and leads, and in return, we got distribution to millions of target customers, which became leads that we could convert to customers *at no cost*.

It was a total win-win. They benefited from highly engaging content that their customers found value in. They got new leads to convert. We got new leads as well.

Roland filled me in on how you can apply this thinking to your business:

1. *Identify your superpower.* What is the one thing you are best at, the thing that would be simplest to use to create a bolt-on business?
2. *Define where your target customers are.* Are they interacting with certain brands? Which of these brands needs the most help from a superpower like yours?
3. *Match your superpower to their needs.*

Finally, working with big brands can take time. They tend to move slowly. People are busy juggling multiple tasks. How do you accelerate the process? Find a bridge. A bridge is a person that has a deep personal relationship inside your target company who will bring you in. I recommend offering the bridge an incentive to ensure they feel a burning desire to help you get in and close the deal. The incentive could be an affiliate commission, a broker-type fee, or even equity, depending on the deal.

Become a Brand Ambassador, Social Influencer, and/or Contributor

I'm always looking for ways to expand my reach, build an audience, and convert that audience to sales. I've found that building that from the ground up can take a lot of time and money. Also know that on the way up, gaining your audience's trust is key.

When I wrote *Launch*, I was beginning to transition out of technology and back into training. I started to feel a disconnect. I was doing a lot of work, selling one book to one person at a time. It seemed totally inefficient. I was used to building internet companies that scaled to millions of users. I wondered what would happen if I sold my content to one company that would distribute to millions of users rather than one person at a time.

So I asked myself, *How can I leverage content to grow my brand, build awareness, increase my reach, and build credibility quickly?* The answer was getting connected to larger brands that were embraced by my target customer.

I decided to do this in three different ways: as a brand ambassador, social influencer, and contributor. You can also apply this to your business brand as you grow and scale. You can make a name for yourself as an expert in your industry, which helps scale up the rest of your business profile. There is a lot of overlap across the three roles. In many cases, a deal includes all three of the things listed below:

   ✳ *Brand ambassador.* A person who is hired by an organization to represent a brand in a positive light, and by doing so, help increase brand awareness and sales. This is a top priority for big companies today because people are more likely to buy after a recommendation from someone they trust rather than from anything a brand has to say about itself. So brand ambassadors can be a highly effective mouthpiece in certain communities.

✸ *Social influencer*. A person who has built or has access to a large audience on social media and can persuade others by their authenticity and reach. Today, more than 65 percent of purchase decisions are made before a person gets to the store. They go to websites, look at reviews, and listen to what the people they follow have to say on social media. Because social media influencers can have millions of followers in a specific niche, they can be a valuable mouthpiece for brands.

✸ *Contributor*. A person who contributes content to a media outlet or corporation. Today, media companies and organizations can't seem to create their own content fast enough. Big websites like Yahoo!, Huffington Post, Entrepreneur, etc., need to post hundreds, if not thousands, of new articles each and every day for their sites to look fresh. Because the cost doesn't make sense, many organizations have turned to third parties to contribute content for free in return for distribution and promotion across their channels.

Back to *Launch*. I asked myself:

✸ What media and corporate brands are most aligned with my content?

✸ Where is there the biggest overlap with my target customer?

✸ What problem do these brands have that I can solve with my content?

What I realized is that content is a powerful tool used to attract, convert, and retain customers online. It can position you as an authority and build credibility. For me it is all about content; for your business, it could be something totally different.

I spoke to several companies and the founders of a major business magazine. They typically deal with later-stage businesses, rather than those that are launching. But they wanted to explore offering this type of early stage content to potentially expand their customer base. So we created a new channel for the publication. I developed a step-by-step program that guided entrepreneurs through the process of taking their idea to market. Instead of putting content in front of one person, as with my book, it became a channel on the magazine's website, which was accessed from the homepage. This association with the magazine's brand gave me and my book another level of credibility and provided more awareness to sell books to thousands of people rather than one at a time. So it was a big win for me. It was also a big win for the magazine. They got a great channel and several hundred pieces of content.

Next came Microsoft, which needed content for small businesses. I created the content. They distributed it and provided huge reach. This was literally seen by millions. They got the content they needed, and I got the views, traffic, implied credibility, and endorsement by evangelizing their products and services.

So how do you apply my branding breakthrough to your own business? Try this:

1. Pick ten brands you love and use every day.
2. Pick ten brands your customers use.
3. Make sure there is a heavy overlap with your target customer, but that they are noncompeting products.
4. Offer to represent the brand, share and promote it via your channel, and/or become a contributor.
5. Get paid via cash, trade, access, etc.

Make your own mark as a brand, and it can have a ripple effect that naturally helps the rest of your business scale up—all while you are bringing in additional profit.

Pace Yourself: Growth Kills Cash

The doors are opened to your new venture, and as far as you can tell, you're doing everything right. You have customers coming in the door, and orders are flowing. You're beginning to feel like that crazy idea of yours might actually work!

Hold it right there. Before you begin to take it for granted, I want you to hear about my friend Marty Metro.

Marty got his MBA from the University of Arizona at age 23. He went into consulting, working at Andersen Consulting and then later at a boutique firm. A few years in, he was a supply chain technology expert. When the dotcom boom turned to bust, Marty got laid off.

He decided to start his own company selling recycled cardboard moving boxes. The idea came out of his own experience since he refused on principle to pay retail price for new boxes when he moved into a new house in Los Angeles. Instead, he would go around town grabbing used ones from liquor stores. It wasn't that he couldn't afford them. He just didn't like spending money on things he would use once and then throw out. Marty figured he wasn't alone.

Leveraging his background in logistics, Marty started a company called Boomerang Boxes, selling used boxes for half the retail price. The business was eco-friendly and was written up in *Entrepreneur* magazine. Life was good.

Then he went broke.

"In three years, I had spent every penny I had," says Marty. He had self-financed the business, and when it needed more capital, he reached back into his own pocket. He burned through two lines of credit at $100,000 each and maxed out three credit cards at $35,000 apiece. The whole thing came crashing down.

Worst of all, his wife didn't know half the story—he hadn't told her he had actually invested more than she had agreed. The crash changed their lives. They had to sell their BMW and Land Rover, and Marty drove around town in a dented 1986 delivery van. (Adding insult to injury, the van had "Boomerang Boxes" painted on the side.) He got a day job as a telemarketer. Sitting in a cubicle all day, he was miserable working as a cog in someone else's system.

At night, he kept trying to figure out where his business went wrong. He just couldn't understand why it seemed the more boxes he sold, the worse things got for the business.

Marty's problem was one I've seen again and again: *Growth kills cash*.

This may seem counterintuitive, but it is remarkably easy to grow yourself out of business. Say you buy a product for $5 and sell it for

$10. That means the more orders you can get, the more profit you can make, right? Not necessarily.

When you're small, you can afford to maintain a low level of inventory. If someone wants to buy a dozen widgets, you've got them on hand, and once they're gone, you'll order another dozen to replace them. But what happens when a customer orders 500 widgets? You think, *Hey, that's great!* You go to your supplier, buy the widgets, and sell them to your customer. But the question you should always ask yourself is: *How am I going to finance this inventory?*

You may have enough cash on hand to buy the 500 widgets from your supplier, but what if your customer says he wants 60-day terms? That means that to do the deal, the cost of those widgets will be tied up in your inventory, diminishing your pool of working capital. If you don't have enough cash on hand to float your business until your customer pays you back, then your business may grind to a halt.

Back to Marty. Once he figured that out, he was convinced that if he could manage the cash flow, the box business would work. He decided to try again.

He did a tour of banks and venture capital companies, hoping to interest people in funding a new version of his idea. When they asked what had gone wrong, he explained how his growth had outpaced his cash requirements and what he would do differently this time around. Remember, showing potential investors your failures (assuming you've learned from them) can be as helpful as a string of successes.

Not only did he raise the money, but Marty and his investors rethought their entire approach to the business. Instead of operating a retail store that sold one box at a time, the new model involved buying cardboard boxes by the tractor load from big Fortune 1000 manufacturers. In the past, these companies would just crush and recycle the boxes. Instead, Marty and his team sorted, inspected, and packaged them into moving kits for sale to regular folks or back to other big businesses. The new model is akin to what dairies used to do with milk crates and bottles. When you got your milk from the milkman, you were only buying the milk; the empty bottles went back to the dairy to be washed and reused.

It worked! After succeeding in Los Angeles, Marty quickly replicated the new company, Usedcardboardboxes.com, around the country. The lesson from Marty's experience is this: As your business starts to grow, don't forget to pay attention to two very important factors.

1. *Growth eats cash.* When you're launching a business and strapped for cash, big orders may do more harm than good, and a booming business can actually cannibalize itself. Before processing disproportionately larger orders, be sure you understand the impact, positive or negative, that fulfilling them could have on your business.
2. *Invest from cash flow, not profits.* When reinvesting in the company, base your decisions on cash flow, not profit. Have a clear understanding of what big capital expenses might be around the corner so you don't run into a cash crunch.

Now that you know these lessons, don't be afraid to take a second bite at the apple if your strategies didn't work the first time around. If you have been a part of a venture that went belly-up, be honest with yourself about what went wrong. Seek the advice of others, learn from your mistakes, and try to imagine how you would correct them in a new business.

Don't be afraid that investors will not be open to you the next time around. If you can clearly demonstrate what went wrong and the lessons you took away from the experience, you may be surprised at how fast people jump on board.

Not Connecting With the Market? Find Your Core Message

Last year I shot an episode of *Business & Burgers* with world-class entrepreneur Summer Felix. Summer cofounded The Draw Shop, a company that creates animated whiteboard videos to help businesses find their core message so they could effectively and efficiently relay that message to their target audience. The Draw Shop's clients include Eric Schmidt, Arianna Huffington, Tony Robbins, Tim Ferriss, the

United Nations, and more. Nobody is more qualified at helping a company find its voice.

One of the things we discussed was how a business can have a fair amount of success during the launch phase, followed by a leveling off, or stalling out. Summer pointed out that entrepreneurs push very hard through the launch, growth, and scale phases. In some cases, just to get a business off the ground, they put on blinders and focus only on their plan and getting their idea to market.

Then, when they step back and start thinking about growth, they find out there is a disconnect between what they think they do and the value they bring and what the customer believes. In some cases, their message is murky and the market is confused.

Summer shared that many entrepreneurs have a very hard time telling their story and communicating a core message. She explained that the reason is they have so much going on, so much that they've accomplished, and so much to be proud of, as they should be. But when they describe what they do, they want to put it all in: every service they offer, how they can be the best coach, the best financial advisor, etc. What they really need is to be more selective.

According to Summer, people really want to feel a connection and trust in you. To do that, you need to talk only about a few things and keep them simple and clear to understand. That is how you gain an immediate rapport and trust. People digest smaller pieces of information more easily, which is why it's better to have a one-page bio, a good elevator pitch, and a concise business plan.

Some people get caught up in what they think about themselves and their business. But there is often a disconnect between the way they see themselves and their results in the marketplace. I guide these business owners through a discovery process that is healthy for a company at any stage.

Instead of having you focus on all the things you think your business is great at, Summer suggests you reflect on these seven questions:

1. Who is your target customer?

2. What do you do? What do they *think* you do? (If you don't know, ask.)

3. What is the one thing you do better than anyone else that your customer will pay for?

4. Can you communicate that value proposition in three words?

5. What is your target customer skeptical about when it comes to working with you?

6. What objections could they have?

7. How will you overcome those objections?

These questions work both in the early stages of growth and the later stages of a business that is looking to expand and/or reposition itself in an ever-changing market. At any stage, you must know who your customer is, what they want or need, what they don't like, and so on. The answers will change as the company grows, times change, and new needs arise. But the questions will stay the same.

what to do when things go sideways

N ow, as we move into the final chapter, I want you to take a moment to digest everything you've read so far: the success stories, the "aha" moments, and the breakthroughs. Then take a deep breath because like my ride with the pilot at the beginning of the book, we're going to circle the plane around one last time and talk about what happens when you *don't* nail that landing on the first try. We're going to talk about what to do when things don't work out the way you planned. In short, we're going to talk about failure.

Panic Faster: Before It's Too Late

Jack Welch, the legendary former CEO of General Electric, once offered a sound piece of advice to aspiring entrepreneurs. After he spoke at the

Entrepreneurs' Organization, the largest global network of its kind, somebody asked Welch what his number-one piece of advice to an entrepreneur would be.

Jack's response? "Panic faster."

Entrepreneurs are by their very nature positive, confident, and sure of their business. These are all great qualities to have when promoting your venture, but when things don't happen as planned and the business begins to go sideways, those same traits can work against you.

Entrepreneurs can get caught up in their own story. They can get so busy reading their own press that they don't see what is really happening around them. That means they may not react to danger signs soon enough.

Out of fear of the unknown, entrepreneurs sometimes freeze or pretend things aren't happening. They put off the inevitable, not wanting to make hard decisions like letting people go or cutting expenditures. Their emotions interfere, and the result is inaction.

Then, before they know it, they're out of business and have lost everything.

So here's some advice on how to avoid that worst-case scenario. These are some basics that can make the difference between reaching the breakthrough point or failure. They are lessons for every stage of business because things will inevitably go wrong from the time you launch until you retire, and even after you're gone. If you know how to deal with adversity, it will not stand in the way of your next big breakthrough. Try these tips listed below.

Focus on the Solution

Like Jack Welch said, you can't stand around hoping for conditions to improve. When things start to go wrong in your business, drop everything and identify where your problems lie. Spend 20 percent of your time on the problem and 80 percent on the solution.

Control the Dialogue

It's important, especially in small, early stage companies, to control the message. By the time you start panicking, odds are the rest of your team is doing the same. Remember, in their day-to-day responsibilities, your staff may be closer than you are to market conditions, sales trends, and financial matters. Good times or bad, they may know what's going on before you do and be more willing to believe it than you are.

When problems occur, you need to get out in front of your people. Your team will be wondering three things: *What is going on? How does this affect me? Will I lose my job?* You can answer those questions, but it's just as important that you redirect their focus in a constructive direction. You need to challenge them to learn something from this experience to help turn things around and take advantage of this situation to capture more market share.

Get Everyone's Input

You have a smart team in place. Leverage that talent to help diagnose problems. Often employees have already identified the problem and come up with a solution before you're even aware of it, but they're just not encouraged or motivated to speak up. Team problem solving should be part of your culture. Get everyone involved, and encourage them to take ownership.

Leverage Your Network

Whether it's formal or informal, you should have a board of directors, a group of mentors, a team of experienced advisors, and perhaps investors. You've consulted with them and asked their advice over the years because they are good at what they do. They know young companies run into challenges. Don't think you're losing face by asking for advice in a difficult time. Don't be embarrassed or afraid to admit failings. They've been there before, and they are here to help.

Experienced entrepreneurs are typically eager to lend a hand to a fellow business owner who sincerely asks for it. One of the most important lessons I have learned is that the people who are the most successful are usually the most accessible. They are also part of a community of other successful people who will help each other out when necessary.

Get in Front of Your Customers

At times, you will be far more effective getting out of the office and into the market. Get on a plane and go see your customers. Learn about their business and the changes they are facing. Perhaps they have a new need you can meet that is a pivot from your existing product or service. Even just making your presence felt will assure your customers that you are committed to their wants and needs.

Be Transparent

If your business is having problems (and even if it isn't), it's important to be transparent with your customers. You want to control the dialogue about any problems with your business, rather than let someone else, like a competitor, define those difficulties for you. By being upfront, you will create trust. You may even find your customer can help you design a solution.

Cut Fast and Cut Deep

If you're really in trouble, either with your financials or by not having the right people on board in a crisis, it may come down to trimming your team. Laying people off is one of the hardest jobs an entrepreneur has. You may not only feel you have failed in managing your business, but also that you've failed in providing for your employees. But you can't let that paralyze you. You have a deeper responsibility to your partners, investors, family, and the rest of your employees. Sometimes you need to cut off the limb to save the patient.

When you see that layoffs are inevitable, don't delay. Furthermore, never make these cuts incremental. Small cuts will kill your business because everyone will waste their time looking over their shoulders wondering if the ax will fall on them next instead of focusing on their work. When you have to cut, do it fast and deep. Later you can reorganize, rebuild, and start hiring again under better circumstances.

Keep Your Eyes on the Horizon

It's easy to get bogged down in the trenches, to be so distracted by the bullets flying overhead that you forget to survey the battlefield and take in the big picture. Doing so will help you anticipate and find the right path to take you out of this tough period.

17 Days, the Value of a Mentor, and the Importance of Being Brutally Honest

Most entrepreneurs seem to have one response when others ask, "How's business?"

Everything is great!

Many either believe that to be the case, or simply want to project that their business is making big headway, when nothing could be farther from the truth.

Entrepreneurs need to be positive and project an image of strength to attract investors, partners, and the best talent. That attitude inspires confidence and keeps your family and loved ones at ease.

But what happens when things are not going as planned? What happens when the image you are trying to portray does not reflect what is happening inside the business? In other words, what happens when that "breakthrough" is actually a wake-up call? How do you react?

Many entrepreneurs simply turn inward. They are afraid to talk to their investors because it will make them angry. They don't want to talk to their partners because they don't want to kill the deal. They don't want to scare their employees into looking for new jobs. They want to keep their spouses isolated from the emotional roller coaster. Perhaps most of all, entrepreneurs don't want to admit to themselves that something is wrong, maybe very wrong.

Instinctively, what many entrepreneurs do is try to hide from the news. Meanwhile, the problems eat away at them and their business. That's the wrong response, of course—the answer to all these problems may be just a phone call away. But as I pointed out earlier, you need to be open to the possibility of help by reaching out to the people inside and outside your business.

As my friend Michelle Patterson says, "We don't want to show that we're vulnerable. But when we do, it leads to amazing things." She should know.

Since its founding three decades ago by then-Governor George Deukmejian, the California Women's Conference has been bringing together women from all over the world to learn and to grow from each other. For most of that time, the event was organized by the first lady of California, the governor's wife. But in 2011, Governor Jerry Brown's wife decided to discontinue the event due to the state's budget crisis.

Mrs. Brown's decision inspired Michelle. As an experienced producer of large-scale events, she decided to take the conference over full time, determined to keep it alive. She locked down a venue, built her team, developed a plan, and started to execute. Over the next few months, she signed up thousands of attendees, brought in a slew of more than 250 exhibitors, and secured more than 150 speakers. Things were off to a great start.

As the event grew closer, two big things affected the conference and its bank account. The teams responsible for sales and marketing had inflated their projections and misled Michelle in their reports. In fact, she learned they were not even close. Not only were revenues short, but expected funding also failed to materialize.

The event was in danger of being canceled, and Michelle had just 17 days to save it.

She was also deeply embarrassed. She was supposed to be an expert in putting on this kind of event, and now it was in jeopardy. Like many entrepreneurs, her first instinct was to tell no one, to remain positive on the outside while she struggled to figure out how to make ends meet. But everything came to a head at once when a payment came due for the venue and the money wasn't there. The organization was $1.8 million in the hole with only 17 days to go before the event, and Michelle had no idea how to find the cash.

She broke the news to her husband first. He was nothing but supportive. He told her, "You would never forgive yourself if you cancelled this event. There has to be a way. You know a lot of very successful business leaders. Why not ask for help?"

The next day, Michelle made a phone call that changed her life. She reached out to the mayor of Long Beach, where the event was to be held. They met that day at the city's convention center, and she explained her financial problems. In response, he asked her one question: "What's your favorite flavor of ice cream?"

"Strawberry," Michelle said, confused.

With that, the mayor took her to get some strawberry ice cream. He encouraged her to take a deep breath. Then he said, "Let's dive in and tackle this together." She now had a partner to help take on this problem.

It also renewed her confidence. She realized that by getting her ego out of the way and opening up, people would respond in a way that would benefit the event. She went home and made a list of people who she thought might help her out of this mess. She called everyone on the list, and the response she heard most was not *How could you do that?* or *How could you let that happen?* Instead, everyone wanted to know *Why didn't you tell me earlier?* or *How can I help?*

Together with this team of advisors, she executed. In 17 days, she went from being told to shut down and consider bankruptcy to reducing what was owed from $1.8 million down to $100,000. The event went on as planned—and it was a big success.

The lesson is clear. When things go wrong, don't try to hide it. Instead of letting fear take hold, take action immediately. When you ask for help, sincerely and honestly, you will get it.

It may not be easy, but here are a couple of ways to, deliberately and with your eye on the horizon, dig yourself out of a business hole:

1. *Illuminate.* It's been said before, but it's still true: Sunshine is the best disinfectant. The more light you shine on a problem, the easier it is to tackle. Get it all out on the table. Don't hide from anything.

2. *Ask for help.* We have all been there. Letting go of ego and asking for help is one of the greatest signs of leadership and

strength. And there will be times in your entrepreneurial life when you feel like you're at the end of your rope, just dangling there with nothing to grab onto. But everything you could possibly need might be just a phone call away.

If you must choose between your pride and saving your business, that's no choice. Get over yourself, push down that ego, and ask for help. You'll be amazed at how eager people will be to come to your aid.

No entrepreneur starts by thinking about what she will do if her big idea, the one that she's worked so hard on, goes sideways. But you need to keep these lessons in the back of your mind.

Nothing in life worth achieving ever comes easily. Sometimes you need to fight for your dream. Sometimes you need to let your sheer will and persistence carry you through.

But remember this: You are not alone. There are people out there who have walked in your shoes. Find them and seek their counsel. Don't be afraid to open up about what you are experiencing. The more they know, the better they can help guide you out of a problem and into an opportunity.

Everything you need to turn that situation around is in you now or within your reach. Don't hesitate to reach out to people at any point in the life of your business. Many of the biggest breakthroughs have come from a little assistance or guidance that puts you on the right path. This can be anything from motivation to believe in yourself (which is always important) to someone reaching out to their contacts to help you find someone with the necessary expertise to help you solve your dilemma.

We're Out of Toilet Paper: Why You Should Never Quit

Sometimes things go wrong. No matter how much passion and hard work you invest in a new venture, you may hit a point where everything is on the line. The future suddenly looks like it holds nothing but failure. So why not quit?

Being an entrepreneur can be very rewarding, but building a successful business is certainly not easy. When things get tough, your business will fail if you don't have a deep sense of purpose tied to it. Without a clear reason to stick it out, it's just too easy to walk away. My friends Dr. Kristi Funk and her husband, Andy, are a perfect example.

After completing medical school and a grueling five-year residency of 80-hour weeks, Kristi looked forward to starting her surgical career. She was a resident at Virginia Mason Medical Center in Seattle when she was asked to join the Cedars-Sinai breast center in Los Angeles.

Breast surgery was still evolving as a specialty, and Kristi felt this new position wouldn't take full advantage of the surgical skills she had spent so many years developing, so she turned down the offer. But she soon realized the opportunity had less to do with performing surgery, and much more to do with making a positive impact on the lives of many women. That surging sense of purpose changed her mind. She soon called back and accepted the job.

By the time Andy Funk entered her life, she had already become a well-known and respected breast cancer surgeon. Although Andy was heir to the largest privately held German insurance brokerage firm, which his family had founded more than a century ago, Andy wanted to forge his own path. At 19, he had forfeited his inheritance, moved to America, started his first company in California, and promptly fell $250,000 in debt. Instead of heading home, Andy fought hard to turn things around. Within five years, he had sold three businesses and established Funk Ventures, a venture capital firm that soon became a pioneer in socially responsible companies. He had overcome big odds to make it from his early disappointments; this experience would come in handy later.

Andy became the youngest member of the board of governors of Cedars-Sinai Medical Center (a connection he would soon share with Kristi). Not long thereafter, Kristi and Andy met and married.

Kristi had, by this point, become one of Los Angeles' go-to breast cancer doctors. Her high profile attracted much media attention and helped draw many patients to Cedars-Sinai. But this success meant longer hours for Kristi. She and Andy felt like they had no life to themselves, let alone time to build a family, a dream of theirs. To make matters worse, Cedars rejected her request to hire any additional support to reduce her workload. Kristi and Andy agreed that things needed to change, fast.

As a medical and wellness investor, Andy had been intrigued by the thought of opening a facility with Kristi for some time. The center, the first of its kind, would not just allow them to hire more doctors to reduce Kristi's workload but also treat patients more effectively and with better technology. With their own facility, they would have the opportunity to change tens of thousands of lives and have an even bigger impact on people. A strong sense of purpose was born.

The plan came together quickly. They founded the Pink Lotus Breast Center and lined up their financing by recruiting other physicians to partner with them. In fall 2008, they leased thousands of square feet in a Beverly Hills medical complex, which would soon cost them more than $30,000 per month. Within weeks of signing the eight-year lease and personal guarantees, the U.S. economy went into free fall and all their financing disappeared. Lines of credit vanished, credit cards were canceled, and the physicians who had committed to join the venture began to get cold feet. When they thought things couldn't get more complicated, they found out Kristi was pregnant—with *triplets*!

But Kristi and Andy were determined to build their company. The Funks opened their facility in March 2009, on the day the Dow Jones hit its lowest point and just three months away from the impending birth of their triplets. Even though the business plan was designed for a minimum of three surgeons, Kristi was the only doctor on staff. When they couldn't make rent—because they were quickly running out of cash—their landlord sat down with Andy and offered him two options: get out of the suite or get sued. Andy and Kristi had no interest in leaving and had faith that their vision would come to fruition.

Just like at Cedars, Kristi was back to working 16-hour days to make ends meet while Andy was trying to hold things together on the business front.

Without other surgeons in the practice, Kristi and Andy maintained full ownership of the business, but they were also missing out on much-needed revenue. In addition, delayed payments from insurance companies meant cash often came in six to nine months after Kristi and Andy had to pay their expenses. Cash flow soon became impossible for Andy to manage.

Kristi was forced to go back to work only a few months after giving birth to find out that key members of their staff had quit, not believing the center would be around for much longer. Pretty soon, they started running out of everything at the office, even toilet paper. When Kristi asked Andy why they were out, he didn't have the heart to tell her they couldn't afford to buy any.

It was clear that, despite their best efforts, it just wasn't working. The children's arrival also meant a bigger house and two nannies so Kristi and Andy could work. With all the odds stacked against them, why not just close up shop, declare bankruptcy, and start over?

It wasn't that simple for Kristi and Andy. Although they faced incredible difficulties in their business and much uncertainty with a newly expanded family, they had a *purpose*, one they believed in so strongly that they knew they were fighting for something that was much more important than their short-term challenges.

Their persistence eventually paid off. Despite sliding into more than $2 million in debt, Kristi and Andy had built a center with a vastly improved approach to breast cancer care, a business that ended up doubling in size each year. Kristi's continued TV appearances provided further visibility, and breast cancer survivor and Pink Lotus patient Sheryl Crow soon lent her name, opening the Sheryl Crow Imaging Center at Pink Lotus. To top it off, General Electric selected Pink Lotus to be first to introduce a revolutionary mammography technology to the country. New surgeons joined the team, the business started to recover its losses, and expansion became a reality for the first time since the company's launch.

After a few years on the brink of financial collapse, Pink Lotus was not just headed toward success—it would soon be regarded by many as one of the top breast cancer treatment facilities in the world.

In May 2013, Angelina Jolie announced that she was having a preventative double mastectomy to decrease her risks of breast cancer.

As a celebrity with enormous resources, she could arguably have assembled a dream team of physicians and chosen any facility in the world to undergo her surgery. However, her dream team was right in her backyard: The multiple procedures were all performed at the Pink Lotus Breast Center, under Kristi's diligent medical care.

Be it Angelina Jolie, Sheryl Crow, or one of the many thousands of other women who come to Pink Lotus for their breast health care each year, Pink Lotus was soon regarded by many people as the number-one breast cancer treatment facility in the world. Kristi and Andy are making a huge impact on many women's lives.

Many entrepreneurs don't realize how close they are to breaking through just before they give up. If you are on the edge and thinking about shutting down, here are a couple of things to consider:

- ✳ *Get advice from experienced entrepreneurs.* Be open about what you are experiencing. The most successful people are usually the most willing to talk about their struggles and help others work through their own. It's a kind of initiation into the world of the successful entrepreneur, like a secret handshake.

- ✳ *Join entrepreneur clubs and organizations.* For added support, join entrepreneur peer groups like the Entrepreneurs' Organization, the largest global network of entrepreneurs. The mission of such groups is to support and help other entrepreneurs grow. One of the best ways to get through tough times is to talk to people who have already been there. I've found again and again that people who understood what I was going through could help me stay positive and navigate forward.

As Kristi and Andy demonstrated, if you have a strong enough reason *why* you are doing something, you will figure out *how* to make it happen. To live your dream, sometimes you need to combine that sense of purpose with pigheaded determination and persistence.

Staying Calm During Chaos: Learning How to Crash

Being an entrepreneur is a lot like driving a race car. When building a business, you move very fast, avoiding all obstacles along the way. At times, you may feel you are about to lose control and crash, almost like you're steering right into the wall.

Recently my good friend and business partner Greg Reid and I decided to learn how to drive race cars, so we headed to Las Vegas Motor Speedway to take a course. The instructors helped us get familiar with our cars, and we strapped on our helmets. I was driving a brand-new Ferrari 360 Modena with the instructor in the passenger seat. Even before completing my initial lap, I got my first big lesson.

When driving on a racetrack, you start with your head up and eyes focused on your goal: where you want to go way down the road. But as your speed increases and more things come at you, you feel a new type of pressure. It's all mental. The natural tendency for drivers at that point is to narrow their focus, drop their eyes, and look down, right over the hood. In skiing, you would call this looking over the tips of your skis. As a result, you get tunnel vision, seeing every little bump in the track, drop of water, and piece of shredded tire. And you start making lots of quick turns and sharp adjustments.

On the racetrack, tunnel vision can get you killed. Steering around lots of small bumps is one thing when you're going 15 miles per hour, but at these speeds sharp movements could lead to a crash.

The same thing is true in a fast-growing business. You need to keep your eyes up and focused on the horizon. Only with a larger view can you pick the best line to take around the corners. The little bumps in the road won't throw you off. Instead, the wider view will allow you to stay in control and reach your goal.

Another thing they teach in racing school is how to crash. When you least expect it, the instructor tugs lightly on your steering wheel. Of course you panic, feeling like you will spin out of control. And what's the first thing you focus on when you or your business feels out of control? You focus on the thing you fear most. On the racetrack, that is the wall. And so your eyes dart to the wall, and that turns your head, and your shoulders, and your hands—and the wheel—right where you don't want to go: the wall! Having jerked your wheel toward disaster, the instructor does something else surprising: He puts his hand up against your helmet and applies a little pressure back toward the track, so your eyes—and head and shoulders and hands and wheel—go back to the road, and back where you want to be.

In business, you'll speed into similar twists, turns, and hard corners. From time to time, you may feel you are losing control. Remember: Your job is to keep your eyes focused on the right path, without ever losing sight of the big picture.

If you feel like you are heading toward the wall, here is a simple list of things to focus on:

- ✳ *Move.* When we feel stuck or headed toward a wall, we tend to lock up. The first thing you should do is get out and move. Clear your head. Go for a walk, run, hike, whatever! Motion creates emotion. The way you move will change the way you feel. So get the blood flowing, and put yourself in a place you feel good.

- ✳ *Shift your perspective.* Whatever we focus on will determine how we feel. How we feel will determine how we behave. How we behave will determine the results we get in our business. Now, what we focus on is determined by the questions we ask ourselves in difficult times. For example, most of us get this voice in our heads. It's like an endless loop, asking things like, *What is wrong with me? Why do things like this always happen to my business?* Remember, our brains are like Google, so whatever we ask, we get a million answers for. So repackage every experience and ask a better question: *What can I learn from this to help me move forward?* The answer will shift your focus to where it needs to be.

- ✳ *Customers.* Get out of the office and talk to your customers. Get honest, unfiltered feedback. Find out what they want and how much they are willing to pay for it.

- ✳ *Mentors.* This is the perfect time to reach out to your mentors. Again, limit your outreach to people who have already achieved what you set out to do in business. These are people who can provide real counsel based on their firsthand experience; stay away from others just giving their opinion. The odds are these mentors will have already walked in your shoes and will know exactly what you should do.

✸ *Don't be afraid to tear it all up.* Markets change, and customers' needs evolve over time. What looked like a great idea today may not work tomorrow. So don't be afraid to modify your plans based on changing customer needs.

✸ *Be obsessed with learning.* The most successful people today have an absolute passion for learning. They know that business moves so fast that the thing that was a winning formula five years ago probably doesn't work today. So commit to learning. Make it part of your company culture.

Finally, and this is a big one, always be grateful. No matter what position you're in, gratitude changes everything. Simply saying thank you twice a day, once in the morning and once at night, will shift your perspective. I have an alarm set for 7:30 A.M. and 7:30 P.M. as a reminder. I do the same for my kids as well. It will force you to focus on what you have, rather than what you don't have, and put you in a much better mindset to succeed.

final thoughts: fill your cup first

Breaking through in your business is a lot like flying. When the air around you is turbulent, it's not always easy to break through to where the jet stream is flowing in your direction. But when that choppy air finally gives way to calm winds and you reach your desired cruising altitude, the sky's the limit.

In the introduction, I talked about how landing on an aircraft carrier is a lot like being an entrepreneur. Despite best-laid plans, you don't always hit your target on the first try. Sometimes, you have to pull up, circle back around, and give it another go. Other people depend on you nailing that landing, too, from your employees and family members to fellow entrepreneurs in your community. That's who I want to focus on as we end this breakthrough journey—the people around you. And the best way for you to help them and make a lasting impact as a breakthrough entrepreneur is to put your mask on first.

Just as the flight attendants suggest during their safety lecture at the beginning of each flight, you can't help anyone else if you're not breathing, so put on your own mask first. Or, to use a different metaphor, consider motivational speaker Les Brown's words. He likes to say, "Fill your cup first. Let what spills over feed others." In other words, make sure your own business is solid, and then use it to serve others. That's the final breakthrough—making a lasting impact. If you take this approach, you will not only create stability for yourself, but also abundance that can be shared with the world.

Some people get it backwards. I have worked with many entrepreneurs whose primary driver for starting a business was to create a vehicle for serving others with the goal of making money second. Or they focused on giving every bit of themselves away before building a business that created a reliable cash flow, leaving them spent personally, emotionally, and financially.

While I admire their passion, I also know that focusing on giving first and creating a sustainable business second usually leads to failure. That's because without a solid business that generates real cash flow, they are more likely to go under. As a result, they are not able to have the long-term impact they had hoped for.

If your goal is to create a platform that gives back, I think that's awesome. But have your priorities in order. First, create a fundamentally sound business—one that generates profits and sustainable cash flow. Once you have reached that threshold, use what you choose to give back.

Now, if you've reached a point where you can afford to give back but are looking for the right cause, I'd suggest this:

Give to other entrepreneurs.

When you're in orbit, and you look down and see someone who may be struggling, reach out and give them a hand. Maybe it's in the form of cash to help them get through a tough period, or maybe it's by offering advice or being a sounding board. When given the opportunity, invest in new businesses. Serve on boards. Assist entrepreneurs in launching new and innovative products and services. Remember, it's these dreamers who keep our economy moving and create jobs and growth.

Use your position to fuel the entrepreneurial spirit that is the heart and soul of America. Support others who are going down a road you have already traveled. You know they must take their own wing walks, fly a trapeze, and race around tough corners. If you can keep them from falling or hitting the wall, you'll be giving back in a way that can benefit us all.

> *"Life doesn't wait.*
> *Launch!"*
> — SCOTT DUFFY

your business breakthrough checklist

The Business Breakthrough Checklist is designed to help individuals interested in launching new businesses, products, or services. I've used this tool as a guide with my clients for years. Its purpose is to help you begin thinking about the process of launching and to gain insight into some of the critical decisions you will need to make along the way.

Directions

Start with "Get Your Personal House in Order" and work your way down the list. Make sure to follow this ten-step process in order. Think of this sequence like building a house. Without the proper foundation, everything could collapse. When you are finished, you will have a very good sense of the key decisions you will need to make as you launch and grow your business. You will be in a much better position to eliminate blind spots, reduce your risk, and be poised to succeed and have a breakthrough! If you get stuck or have trouble with anything below, don't worry. This is all a process, and you're on your way to building the business of your dreams.

1. Get Your Personal House in Order

❑ How much capital are you willing to risk?

❑ How much time can you dedicate to this project?

❑ Do you have a good attorney in place to set up your business correctly?

❑ Do you have a bookkeeper in place to set up your books from day one?

❑ Have you discussed your plans with your spouse or significant other? Are you on the same page? Have you both agreed to how much money you can risk and how much time you can dedicate?

❑ Do you have the right people around you? Are they people who have already achieved what you are setting out to accomplish?

❑ Do you have people who will pull you up and help guide you?

❑ Does your environment breed success? Do you spend your time with people and organizations that push you and demand you get more out of yourself?

❑ Is your personal brand a reflection of who you need to be to achieve the results you want? What do your daily habits tell others about you? Do they send the message you need to succeed?

2. Create Your Plan

❑ Have you built a financial model for your business? How much time and money will it take for your business to generate profits? Are you being overly optimistic in your assumptions?

❏ What are all of your potential sources of income? Have you factored in your costs of sales? Have you accounted for all of your expenses?

❏ Have you used your financial model to create the framework for the rest of your business plan?

❏ Have you summarized your business plan in a single page that highlights every key aspect of the business?

❏ Have you shared this business plan with your investors, team members, consultants, partners, etc., to ensure that everyone is on the same page and running in the same direction?

3. Build Your Team

❏ What are your core strengths? What is the one thing you do really well? What is the one thing that you really excel at or have been working to become great at?

❏ What are your weaknesses? What are the key areas in life and business that you have trouble with or simply don't enjoy doing?

❏ Would you describe yourself as a visionary (someone with big ideas who likes to hand implementation to someone else), a manager (who likes to take a vision and implement it), or a sharpshooter (who excels at a specific skill like design, development, or sales)?

❏ What is your plan for working your strengths and hiring your weaknesses? What is the best role for you in the company? What is the role where you can add the most value?

❏ Have you considered taking on a business partner? If so, do you have complimentary temperaments, skill sets, networks, etc.?

❏ Have you put a partner (prenuptial) agreement in place?

❏ What is your plan for creating a winning culture? What are the key values that your business will stand for that will permeate through the business?

4. Accumulate Your Resources/Raise Capital

❑ How much money do you need to get started? How can you scale down the first version of your business to get to market with the least amount of capital required?

❑ Will you bootstrap, borrow, or raise outside capital? If bootstrapping, what do you have of value to offer? Who are your trading partners?

❑ If you plan to raise outside capital, who is your target investor?

❑ What is their area of expertise? What are their investment requirements? What stage must the company be in? How much is their average investment? How long before they want to see a return on capital?

❑ What is your strategy for moving an investor through the sales cycle? Do you have your 30-second elevator pitch, one-paragraph business summary, and a one-page overview in place?

❑ What are the critical things you need to focus on during each meeting with an investor? What should you absolutely avoid doing or saying at all costs?

❑ Will you be selling equity in your business? Are you asking for a loan or convertible note? What are the terms?

❑ What are you negotiating for? Are you trying to hold onto equity, limit preferences, retain control, have the power to make key decisions, etc.?

5. Leverage Technology

❑ Have you made it easy for your team to do business? What tools do you use to communicate with others (email, contacts, calendars, video conferencing, document storage, etc.)?

❑ Is every member of your team using the same tools and technologies?

6. Create Your Product or Service—Go to Market

❑ What is the one thing your business is great at? What are you going to do better than everyone else? What is different about what you have to offer? Why will you stand out?

❑ Who is your target customer? Tell me 25 things about them.

❑ Who are they? Where do they hang out? What communities are they a part of? What do they care about?

❑ What is the one problem you are solving for this one target customer? Do they know the problem exists? Do they want the problem solved? Do they care?

❑ What is the simplest form of this product you can build to solve your customer's problem and get to market in 90 days or less?

❑ How will you collect user feedback once launched?

❑ How will you keep your team from suffering "shiny ball syndrome"? How do you keep them focused on delivering that one thing for that one target customer without adding a lot of unnecessary bells and whistles prior to launch?

7. Partnerships/Distribution

❑ What businesses have target customers that are identical to yours?

❑ What problems or issues do those businesses have that you can help them solve? Who is your internal champion within each potential partner business? How can you make them look great?

❑ How can you work together to cross-promote one another and provide resources to help both sides grow further faster, and with less capital required?

❑ What is your strategy for getting your product or service in front of potential customers? Do you plan to distribute through retail channels or online?

❑ Will you hire an internal team or outsource to third parties to help get distribution through your target channels and providers?

8. Marketing, Advertising, and Public Relations

❑ What is your strategy for marketing your new business, product, or service? Do you plan on mass marketing? Do you plan to focus your initial effort on a region or local area?

❑ Can you target your product to a very specific niche? If so, what is that niche? Why have you chosen it? Write down everything you know about it and why your product solves a need in that area.

❑ Do you plan to use social media? If so, what is your strategy?

❑ In which social media networks will you place most of your effort (i.e., Facebook, Twitter, Pinterest, etc.)? Where does your target customer spend their social networking time?

9. Sell! Sell! Sell!

❑ What is most important to your target customer? When was the last time you asked? What systems or feedback loops do you have in place to help you better understand their unique needs?

❑ What has to happen and how does your target customer know they are getting what they want? What are the rules they have set up either consciously or subconsciously to drive them toward a purchase decision?

❑ How much are they willing to spend to believe they got real value for their money?

❑ Are you going to hire an internal sales team, or are you going to hire a third party? How will you find and qualify a third-party sales group?

❑ What is your plan for compensating the sales staff, developing your sales team, and retaining your best people?

10. Accelerate Your Growth and Scale

❑ Have you taken recent inventory of your business? Has everything worked out as planned?

❑ Are you absolutely clear on the economic drivers of your business? Do the numbers in your financial forecasts match what is really occurring? If not, be sure to update them.

❑ Are you focused on the right opportunities for growth? Are you adding time and attention to areas of your business that are working, and killing off parts of your business that do not work or are not getting the kind of traction you thought they would with customers?

❏ Does your business have Monthly Recurring Revenue products or services? If not, could you convert your core products and services to MRR or add additional products or services? Can you turn one-time sales into auto-ship or box? Can you create memberships or associations and buyer's clubs for your industry? Can you add certifications to what you do?

❏ What expenses can you turn into profits? Can these expenses be converted into monthly recurring revenue? Who would pay for it?

❏ Have you created "bolt-on" businesses? If not, start by identifying your company's "superhero power." Look for businesses that attract your target customer with non-overlapping products and services. Determine which of these companies could use a superhero power like yours to grow their business. Then match your superhero power to their needs and bolt it on.

❏ Are you currently leveraging content to grow your brand, increase awareness, add reach, and build your credibility? Have you explored becoming a Brand Ambassador for a larger organization? Are you leveraging social media to build your influence? Have you started contributing content to a media organization that is well read and respected by your target customer?

Last But Not Least . . .

❏ Are you part of an entrepreneur group or organization that provides mentoring, support, feedback, education, and community?

acknowledgments

There are so many people I would like to thank for their contributions to this book. First, to David Meltzer and Bill Shaw, who got this whole process started. This book would have never happened without the unwavering support of Ryan Shea, Vanessa Campos, Jennifer Dorsey, and Rich Mintzer. Special thanks to Deepa Shah, Stephanie Belsky, Jason Feifer, and the rest of the amazing team at Entrepreneur Media. And of course, big thanks to Nena Madonia and the team at Dupree Miller.

On a personal note, I would like to thank David Meltzer, Greg Reid, Alan Taylor, Jason Reid, Steve Fielding, and Randy Garn. You have been there for me through it all—the good times and bad. You are the true definition of what a friend should be. I love you and thank you!

Alan Taylor, you taught me what it meant to have fun again and how to find a great burger! Thank you for all of your mentorship and support. I love ya, man!

I would like to thank my mother for being so incredibly supportive and for going on this ride with me for the past 30 years. You taught me the value of persistence, hard work, and always looking at the bright side of a situation, no matter how hard it may have seemed in the moment.

To Big D, thanks for being the rock in our family and having the patience to sit with me, on so many long nights, to talk about business. You were the greatest influence on my career when I was getting started.

To my sister Ashley and brother Shane, you have always been there for me. You have helped me in so many ways on more than one occasion. Thank you!

To my dad, I'll never forget all the football, baseball, and basketball memories growing up. What a great dad.

To Mike, Erin, Spencer, Charlie, and Christopher Sinclair. I miss you and love you!

Additional thanks to those who gave me a shot and were super supportive somewhere along the way: Gabriel Baldinucci, Richard Branson, Jerry Chen, Steve Chien, Jarvis Cho, Chris Cottle, Steve Fielding, Ron Garret, Dave Hutchison, Mike Hutchison, Russell Hyzen, Chris Kitze, Ross Levinsohn, Mike Levy, Gene Lim, Laurent Massa, Tom McCarthy, Mark Moses, Bill Peck, Jason Port, Dan Porter, Tony Robbins, Jed Savage, Nirmal Saverimuttu, Eric Schoenfeld, Jeff Tang, and Sita Thompson.

about the author

Scott Duffy is a television/online personality, keynote speaker, and business coach. He began his career working for bestselling author and speaker Tony Robbins, and went on to work at the early stage for several big media brands like CBS Sportsline, NBC Internet, and FOXSports.com. He founded Smart Charter, an online booking tool for private aviation, which was later acquired by Richard Branson's Virgin Group.

Today, Scott is a champion for entrepreneurship. He has been listed as a "Top 10 Keynote Speaker" by Entrepreneur. He has spoken at the NYSE and provided commentary for numerous media outlets including CNBC, FOX News, and CBS Radio. He is the co-host of *Business &*

Burgers and bestselling author of *Launch! The Critical 90 Days from Idea to Market.*

To learn more about Scott Duffy visit www.scottduffy.com.

index